A Light Too Bright

The Enlightenment Today

SUNY Series in
Religious Studies

Harold Coward, Editor

A Light Too Bright
The Enlightenment Today

An Assessment of the Values of the European Enlightenment and a Search for New Foundations

Paulos Mar Gregorios

STATE UNIVERSITY OF NEW YORK PRESS

Production by Ruth Fisher
Marketing by Theresa A. Swierzowski

Published by
State University of New York Press, Albany

Printed in the United States of America

For information, address the State University of New York Press, State University Plaza, Albany, NY 12246

Library of Congress Cataloging-in-Publication Data
Paulos Gregorios, 1922–
A light too bright : the enlightenment today : an assessment of the values of the European enlightenment and a search for new foundations / Paulos Mar Gregorios.
p. cm.
Includes index.
ISBN 0-7914-1133-8 (alk. paper). – ISBN 0-7914-1134-6 (pbk. : alk. paper)
1. Enlightenment. I. Title.
B802.P28 1992
001—dc20 91-30801
CIP

Contents

Preface

This is not an academic work. It fits into no discipline, according to western divisions of academic discipline. It does not seek to prove anything, or to add to the stock of human knowledge. It is a plea to consider the foundations of our existence in this world.

I wish to express my gratitude to many who have helped. To Mr. William Eastman, the director of the SUNY Press, who persuaded me to try, I owe the inspiration. And once I had signed a contract, it acted as an impetus to bring the work to some form of completion. I am most grateful to the Isthmus Institute in Dallas, Texas who gave me a three-month fellowship, where I did half my work. I must especially thank Mr. Devlin for his generous hospitality, and Dr. Ruth Tiffany Barnhouse for her kind assistance. Dr. Larry Dossey also helped with his counsel and kindness.

I owe a special debt of gratitude to the Indian Institute of Advanced Study, Shimla, where I completed the second half of this work, during a three-month fellowship.

And since it is not an academic study, may I be permitted also to express my deep gratitude to God. To Him I owe everything, my very existence, and any trace of wisdom in this work.

Shimla, The Himalayas — Paulos Mar Gregorios

Chapter One

GETTING ORIENTED

We live in a sea-change period of world history. As ancient values crumble, time-honored institutions of social living disintegrate, without new ones ready to take their place. Some social inequalities begin to disappear, only to give place to new, equally undesirable ones. As power shifts from one group to another, old categories and classifications for understanding the social process quickly become obsolete. Reality baffles us, and scholars disagree on the basics of what is happening, in physics as in biology, in sociology as in economics, in politics as in international relations.

Before the Gulf War of January–February 1991, most people would have agreed in their analysis of the power configuration system in the world. I offer below what I wrote in early 1990 in an attempt to capture what I then saw as the world political reality; I will follow this up with my present post-Gulf War version of how I see that same reality.

Pre-Gulf War

As I write, we are into the last decade of the second millennium of the Christian era. We can all observe three major systems of political economy vying with each other to gain dominance:

1. Temporarily triumphant worldwide Western liberal democracy with its creaking market-economy capitalism, already in the initial stages of a daunting recession
2. Defeated Marxist-Leninist socialism desperately striving to survive by making every possible compromise with its erstwhile sworn enemy, Capitalist Imperialism

3. Renascent Pan-Islamism, though now disunited, yet strong-willed and determined to bring about a worldwide Islamic commonwealth governed by Shariah, the Quranic law

In terms of sheer vitality and inner determination, the third now turns out to be a more powerful rival to the first and the second than these two to each other. Alas, Islam remains the one major world religion least understood, and even less sympathized with, by others. The West thinks it can be handled by military and economic power; the Marxists think that it is obscurantist and that "history" will dispose of it neatly. Meanwhile, Islamic fundamentalism continues on the warpath and regards both western liberalism and Marxist socialism as ungodly systems destined to disappear, sooner or later, before the "Sword of Islam."

Post-Gulf War (April 1991)

It is one of the great ironies of history that Soviet President Gorbachev's globalist "New Thinking" has ultimately resulted in consequences disastrously contrary to what he had intended. There is less security in the world than before; there is a new sense of helplessness on the part of the powerless; the prospect of a world without war has receded further; the victims of injustice no longer have a strong champion of their cause; the world has become more miserable than ever before since the Second World War. The Gulf War, alas, is as much a consequence of Soviet New Thinking as of anything else.

This asymmetric, short-duration, super-high-tech war has achieved more than the liberation of Kuwait from Iraqi aggression and occupation. It seems to have been even more effective in achieving six or seven of the covert goals of the US and the Western Alliance, as well as their temporary allies in the Middle East.

1. Israel, Saudi Arabia, Egypt, Iran, Kuwait, and Syria all wanted the rising power of Iraq to be curbed; this was also in the Allied interest, but it would have been counterproductive (because of the likely strong Arab reaction) if Israel had been allowed to do the job on her own as she wanted to. Now it has been done with minimum cost to Israel and with maximum winning over of the Arabs into the Allied camp. If the US and Iraq had really negotiated, such a war would have been impossible, because the Americans knew that Saddam Hussein was willing to withdraw his troops from Kuwait if he had been treated with the dignity due to the head of a people, offered some significant promises on settling the Palestinian question, and granted a financial contribution from Kuwait. Without a war, Iraq

could not have been crushed so brutally; but a negotiated settlement would have stood in the way of achieving the real purpose, namely, crushing a country that had dared to defy the power and supremacy of the western alliance in the world of today.

2. Ever since the collapse of the "Soviet threat" in 1988, there had been no justification for stationing American troops in Western Europe. The Gulf War gave the Allies a pretext for a new military outpost in the Middle East, so essential to Allied imperialist interests.

3. The US and its allies had been looking for an opportunity to field-test and demonstrate the prowess of their new post-SDI high-tech weapons; a successful sales pitch has been made for Western armaments, and the Soviet Union and others can no longer compete in the arms market without updating their technology. The important thing is that the human cost of the field test was borne by the people of Iraq and Kuwait.

4. The UN has been a major force resisting Allied hegemony in the world. It has now been captured and domesticated. The voice of the Second and Third World in that august body has at least been temporarily muted.

5. A real boost has been given to the waning Western rate of economic growth, and to the arms industry on which the market economy's health is now based. The big corporations, the "dealers in death," have now been rewarded enough so that they can continue to contribute quite liberally to the political process that sustains the market economy.

6. The US has been enabled to assert its uncontested global leadership, to test friends, and to severely warn any would-be challengers to that global authority.

7. The cost of the operation has been largely paid by Japan, Germany, Saudi Arabia, and others, and the new contracts for the reconstruction of Kuwait and possibly of Iraq, along with a few mammoth arms sales already effected, will more than compensate for the rest of the expenditure. Economically, the war has been a "good deal" for the West.

The short Gulf War has radically altered the power configuration in the world; categories of yesterday no longer fit. It is not profitable to keep on talking about superpowers in the plural or about a unipolar versus a multipolar or bipolar world. What we now have is a global market economy that includes almost all countries in the world, including the USSR, China, and Vietnam, and the US has emerged as the general manager of the New Global Order, assisted by her white allies and perhaps Japan as assistant managers. The latter do not always agree with everything the general manager does; but to disagree with him openly may have rather catastrophic consequences; so they can only go along, hoping some day the manager will make a major *faux pas*, at which point they can oust him from power and take his place.

For the powerless, especially for many Second and Third World countries, the question arises: Where would one look for some countervailing force to offset the power of the US? Economically, the two most powerful assistant managers are Germany (or the European Community, if you like, and if you believe in it) and Japan, but they have to play the general manager's game, at least for the time being, for their very survival. And there is a private power game played between the general manager and the two most powerful assistant managers. The general manager knows these two are rivals who have to be "fixed" before they manage to overthrow him and take his place. But he also knows that he has to keep them as allies until he later has strength enough to crush them.

The collapse of the Soviet economy and its policy of the defense of socialism has also led to the collapse of the effectiveness of any kind of nonaligned policy. Without Soviet military power willing to confront Western Allied power, can a powerless nation in the Two Third World sustain a foreign policy based on principles of international morality?

The other bastion of a principled global policy was the United Nations. It was, until the Gulf War a force to be reckoned with. It could in the past stand up to the high-handed actions of the US and its allies on many occasions (Vietnam, for example). But now the US has shown remarkable skill and finesse in capturing and castrating the UN. The UN Resolution gave *carte blanche* to member nations to "use all necessary means" to get Iraq out of Kuwait, while Israel was still occupying Arab lands for decades, Syria was occupying part of Lebanon, and Turkey part of Cyprus. This was a blatant betrayal of all that the UN stood for; it was a rape and violation of its own charter. The UN should have used a peacekeeping force under the UN flag and command, to implement its resolutions. Inviting the world's nations for a "free-for-all" is not in the UN Charter. It is common knowledge now that the UN Resolution was bought by bribe and cajolement. It is an unconstitutional resolution, fully *ultra vires*. But it has served the purposes of the Western Alliance.

Now it seems the US is interested in solving the Middle East problem under its own aegis, again bringing in the UN insofar as it suits American policy aims. It will take a lot of doing to bring back a semblance of real power to the UN. The UN system will also come under the control of the general manager, unless someone sees the danger and does something drastic about it, like breaking the power of the five permanent members of the Security Council by amending the charter itself.

Two-third World countries as well as the less powerful among the European powers may soon wake up, and see the new global power configuration picture with fresh eyes. Not much will be gained by hanging on to old and obsolete structures like the nonaligned movement or to largely ineffective instruments like the South Asian Association for Regional Cooperation or South-South Cooperation. The Two-Third World is far from united, and the general manager is interested in keeping it that way. It is unrealistic to suppose that even an India-China alliance could bring the Two-third World together on a common platform, but China is an important player in the new power game, and could some day, in cooperation with others, develop some kind of countervailing power.

The Two-third World will need to win or earn the friendship and support of all progressive elements both in the West as well as in the ex-socialist countries. A New International for Global Justice will need to be conceived and a platform formulated to counter the new power structure and to seek dignity, freedom, justice, peace, and a life-sustaining environment for all humanity.

It seems beyond doubt that the countervailing power we need is not military, but economic and social-cultural; the power of the people, the power of more than 4 billion dispossessed and marginalized people, but organized and mobilized. The sense of outrage at the presence and arrogant manifestation of nonresponsible technological-military power seems widespread, but still remains faltering in expression. To give unmistakable expression to that sense of deep moral outrage, and to demand a more responsible, more democratic, control of global power, seems a high priority for the people of the world today.

* * * *

Cutting across these struggles and conflicts, there are scores of other contentions and power battles. The feminist struggle is prominent in the industrialised Western societies, but the male mullah leadership in Islam regards feminism itself as somehow satanic, merely another aspect of Western and Marxist decadence. Too many Muslim women agree, though among them many inwardly identify themselves with an overthrown but still assertive modern Muslim woman like Benazir Bhutto of Pakistan. Generally speaking, however, feminism or any kind of gender conflict remains a taboo subject for Islamic fundamentalism.

At least five other power struggles accompany these foreboding struggles between the male and the female of the species, a struggle yet to reach its full maturity, now confined to some regions and classes. These other five seem to have little to do with the class struggle:

1. The conflict between ethnic identity and national loyalty, not only in the Soviet Union, but also in many other countries such as Yugoslavia (Croats, Serbians, Slovenians, Macedonians), China (Hans, Central Asian Muslims, Tibetan Buddhists), India (Hindus, Muslims, Sikhs), Czechoslovakia (Czechs and Slovaks), Romania (Romanians, Transylvanians, Hungarians), Belgium (French and Walloons), Canada (Anglophones, Quebecois, other minorities), the US (whites, blacks, hispanics, Native Americans, Asians), in many African countries with more than one tribe, and so on
2. The tension among nationalism, regionalism, and internationalism, as peoples and nations recognize their growing economic and social interdependence; as the transnational corporations develop their empires; as bodies for regional economic and scientific-technological cooperation (Organization of African Unity, Organization of American States, South Asian Association for Regional Cooperation) begin to develop
3. Conflict among the three contenders for leadership within the world market economy, namely Japan, US, and Europe
4. Tensions that arise from the resistance of particular local cultures to the road roller of a technological civilization that claims to be universal
5. Tensions between those who want to make a fast pile and others who want to conserve a healthy environment for life on this planet.

All these conflicts are interconnected. There are two other pervasive major conflicts that cut across these and which we can ignore only at grave peril.

First, there is the ominous conflict between the growing international middle class that has incorporated into itself some forty percent of the global population, and the remaining sixty percent who seem to be divided between those who want to climb into the middle class and be co-opted, and others who see global revolution as the only way to justice for all within and among nations. We can call the two positions *reformist* and *revolutionary,* respectively. There is little love lost between these two subgroups of the latter group, though sometimes they manage to cooperate on a particular issue of social change. Some in the middle classes also seek to identify themselves with one or the other of these two subgroups, though in general the reformist position is definitely less threatening to their own perceived interests. The dispossessed sixty per cent seem to have lost a stalwart champion of their cause with the capitulation of the Marxists to the market economy's allurements, and their consequent near abandonment of the international class struggle in the interests of survival and affluence.

A second major conflict seems as yet inchoate and undefined. Simply put, it is the conflict between the secular and the religious worldviews. The inchoateness comes from the fact that there are many people who do not even acknowledge such a conflict, though it is in their own experience and consciousness. A deeply religious person may also be a successful practicing scientist, and may not be fully aware that he or she subscribes to conflicting worldviews. Part of the lack of clarity results from misconceptions about what secularity and religion signify.

While science seldom states its worldview, modern science stands on the assumption that God or the Transcendent is an "unnecessary hypothesis" for science. It is a matter of faith for scientists that the universe can be explained and understood in terms of causality (strict or only statistical or operational) without reference to any reality that transcends the universe itself. Modern science is based on a qualified commonsense, on a naive realism that believes either that things are what they appear to be or that their true nature can be revealed by science. In quantum physics this view has come under question, with the experimental realization that the observer with his or her time-space measuring equipment is an integral part of reality as he or she observes it. Knowledgeable physicists tell us that we have no access to reality as it exists independent of our observation; what we know is not necessarily objective reality, but only our subjective perception of it. The only objectivity available is agreement among the observers in accordance with criteria mutually agreed upon in the scientific community.

Religious worldviews, on the other hand, are incredibly diverse and incompatible with each other. There is no interreligious global community that can lay down criteria for agreement among all religions. They agree mostly in rejecting the naive realism of a science that confuses reality with phenomena. Where science openly admits that scientific knowledge is only operational and that it has no access to the ultimate nature of reality, coexistence between religion and science can be peaceful, and sometimes even productive.

We are living, however, in a civilization where science has taken over from religion the seat of authority in society. The science establishment today occupies a place analogous to that occupied by the Roman Catholic clergy in medieval Europe. Many people still think that modern science has the last word on everything. Good scientists may not think so. Good philosophers and theologians should also recognize that their own pronouncements have no ultimate validity either. That applies to what is said in this book as well. Fortunately, the philosopher and the theologian have much less authority than the scientist in our society. When religious leaders do gain such authority, as for example in the case of Christian fundamentalism in the Moral Majority of the Reagan era, they wreak a lot of havoc.

The dialogue between science and religion has barely begun in our time. There are few religious thinkers whom scientists find worth listening to, mainly because neither side has developed the philosophical competence necessary for dialogue at a sufficiently profound level. So the tension between science and religion continues, despite much new thinking that seeks to bridge the gap and relax the tension. Modern science presupposes the secular framework, which religions cannot accept. True dialogue between then is not possible if its precondition is that the religions accept the secular frame of thought and understanding.

The point here is simply that there is a conflict between the secular and the religious that constitutes a major obstacle on our way to finding reliable foundations for a new civilization. The secular assumption remains the hallmark of post-Enlightenment European civilization, and to the origins of this assumption we should devote considerable space in this work. The secular assumption underlies both Western liberal ideology and Marxist ideology; religious fundamentalism avoids such an assumption, but that does not make the latter any more adequate a foundation for a new civilization.

The rise of the concept *secular* in its modern sense is itself an interesting story. Since this concept is so central to our problematic, we will need to turn briefly to that story. Before we do so, we must also have a quick look at transformations that have taken place historically in the meaning of the word *religion* in our societies.

Chapter Two

Religion, Culture, and the Secular: Concepts to be Clarified

Human thinking, increasingly dependent on words and concepts, goes dangerously wrong when there is confusion about what a word signifies in different contexts. We have three of these words in the title of this chapter, all of which need historical analysis before we can recognize the different ways in which we use them.[1] These three concepts are central to this book and to any efforts to find building blocks for new and more healthy foundations for new civilizations.

Religion: A Creation of the Secular

The word *religion* in the sense in which we use it today, did not exist in the Western tradition until the process of secularization advanced in the seventeenth century. When the Treaty of Westphalia in 1648 established the principle "*cuius regio, eius religio,*"[2] the drafter of that treaty gave the Latin word *religio* a meaning that it did not previously have. The drafter meant Protestantism and Roman Catholicism as two separate "religions," thus making the word *religion* a generic term for all organized religious communities.

It is interesting to observe that *religio* in medieval Latin meant precisely "a state of life bound by monastic vows; the condition of a member of a religious order," as the Oxford Latin Dictionary puts it. It was never used for a particular religion like Christianity or Islam. Not only in Latin but also in Medieval Old English the meaning was the same. In 1449, Pecock wrote:

> In oon maner religioun is . . . a binding vp or a bynding . . . of a mannys fre wil with certain ordinauncis . . . or with vowis or oothis.[3]

The medieval distinction was always between *religiosus* and *saecularis;* the first meant "one who has devoted himself to an ascetic order"; the second had many meanings, including: (a) secular or of this world, profane; (b) secular as opposed to "regular" or bound by monastic rules; and (c) secular as opposed to ecclesiastical.[4] Even today the Roman Catholic Church distinguishes between "regular" and "religious" priests (i.e., bound by the rules of a monastic order) and "secular" clergy, meaning nonmonastic (even if celibate) priests serving in the diocesan parishes.

By the sixteenth century a new meaning comes into being. In 1577, Vautrouiller's English translation of Martin Luther's *Commentary on the Epistle to the Galatians* gives one of the early examples of this use:

> They that trust in theyr owne righteousnes, thinke to pacifie the wrath of God by theyr . . . voluntarie religion.[5]

Here religion means devoutness or religious practices as we now speak of them. Richard Hooker (1554–1600), in his Ecclesiastical Polity[6] in an English more like ours says:

> The church of Rome, they say, . . . did almost out of all religions take whatsoever had any fair and gorgeous show.

It seems thus to be the case that the word *religion* came to have its present meaning after the Protestant Reformation of 1517. In 1625 Ben Johnson can say: "I wonder what religion he is of."[7]

The non-Latin languages do not seem to have an exact equivalent of "religion" in the sense of organized religions or commitment to a particular religion. The Hebrews, for example, can speak of faith (*emunah*), or fear of God (*yere'ath-yahweh* or *yere'ath-elohim* or *yere'ath-shamaim*) but have no word for religion in our sense. Neither has classical or New Testament Greek. In the Greek New Testament one finds *eusebeia, theosebeia, threskeia,* and *deisidaimonia,* but all these words refer to loyalty and fear of God or of gods and daemons, but not to religion in our sense. Nor does classical Sanskrit have a word for religion. In modern times people use *mata* (opinion or religious view), *sampradaya* (particular schools of religious practice within Hinduism), or *dharma* (literally that which sustains human life and society), but none of these words were originally equivalents of religion in the sense people use it today.

The concept of religion is the result of a long process. The European Renaissance, the Protestant Reformation, and finally the European Enlightenment, mark different stages in the development of both concepts—the religious and the secular. We need to take a quick look at this process, for it has shaped our civilization in ways of which we are not fully aware. The transformation in the concepts of religion and the secular affects all civilization, not just Europe. We are all under its influence if we have been exposed to modern education, modern medicine, and modern political and social institutions like the state system or the communications media. And there are very few in the world today who have not been so exposed. Hence the importance of our enquiry.

What is Religion?

Fr. Andrew Greeley, in his exploration for a satisfactory definition of religion, became so infuriated that he left it with the observation that religion is whatever religious people think it is. That may not be the case. Yet he went on to give a "secular" definition of religion. His thesis is that religion is congenital for all human beings, as "meaning-seeking behavior . . . incoded in 'unique' symbolic explanations, . . . rooted in experiences of grace which renew human hopefulness in a given individual biography."[8]

In the human sciences we get the philosophy of religion, the sociology of religion, the psychology of religion and the cultural anthropology of religion. Each one gives a different definition of religion.

Edward Tylor, an earnest Quaker and one of the pioneers in the anthropological study of the religions of "primitive" peoples, sought to give intellectualistic explanations for the peculiar and puzzling behavior of primitive peoples. For him religion meant belief structures and rituals of distant peoples, not his own Quaker religion. James Frazer, the celebrated author of *The Golden Bough*, (1890) was, like most nineteenth-century students of religion, an evolutionist. Auguste Comte, the father of modern Positivism, had stated the thesis most clearly. European thought has evolved in a three-stage line of progress from religion to metaphysics to science. Clearly, then, religion belongs to the most primitive of European man's attempt to deal with reality, while science is the most advanced. This was also Frazer's view, that is, that humanity progressed by evolution from primitive magic (the basic content of religion) to modern science. Emile Durkheim saw the evolution as from the sacred to the profane, religion functioning in the primitive sacred time as the integrating symbol-system of society.

These views of religion were heavily colored by the three prevailing views in nineteenth-century European thought—historicism, evolutionism, and positivism. In the latter half of the nineteenth century, German thought (Wilhelm Dilthey (1833–1911) had laid the foundations) sought to enthrone history as the sovereign science, while English empirical thought still regarded Newtonian physics as the model for all science. This is an interesting conflict that remains effective today. The Germans wanted to conceive the world as composed of events in time, within which things in space played their part. Non-German philosophers like Bergson and Whitehead follow this line. For the empiricists of the English-speaking world, the quest was to master things in space, and the physical sciences, which are basically ahistorical, provide the model for all understanding. Out of a finite number of historical experiences (*empirical* means based on experience), one inductively develops a timeless "natural law" that will work irrespective of time. But since English empiricist science could not escape the theory of evolution, in which time is central, French positivism gave it a nice alibi.

Auguste Comte, the patriarch of positivism, had put it plainly:

> Before explaining the nature and the character of Positive Philosophy, it is absolutely necessary to examine the totality (*l'ensemble*) of the progressive march of human thought (*l'esprit humain*). For a conception cannot be properly understood except through its history.
>
> In studying the development of the (human) intelligence since its most simple origins to our own day, I believe I have discovered a great law to which this development is subjected. Such a law can be established, it seems to me, whether by proofs furnished by the knowledge of our (social) organisation, or by historical verification resulting from an examination of the past. It consists in the three different states of theory through which each branch of our knowledge successively passes: the fictive or theological state, the metaphysical or abstract state, and the scientific or positive state (*l'etat theologique ou fictiv, l'etat metaphysique ou abstrait, l'etat scientifique ou positif*). In other words, the human spirit successively employs, in each of its enquiries, three methods of philosophizing, different and even opposed to each other: first the theological method, then the metaphysical method, and then finally the positive method. The first is the point of departure for the intelligence; the third its final, fixed and definite state; the second is uniquely destined to serve as the transition.[9]

This of course is the classical expression of the evolutionary-positivistic approach, which, despite the collapse of positivism as a philosophical position, remains the dominant view of our modern civilization. Religion, this view boldly affirms, belongs to the infancy of humanity and modern science alone is adequate for its adulthood. The very concept that in our time humanity has reached its adulthood (*mundigkeit*) is a hallmark of the European Enlightenment, as we shall soon see.

A brief look at the study of religion, especially by cultural anthropologists, will reveal how dominant this paternalistic, condescending attitude towards religion has been in the past. The evolutionary presupposition is there in all the great early students of religion: Edward Tylor, James Frazer, Emile Durkheim, Max Weber, Sigmund Freud, Malinowski, Radcliffe-Brown, and others. Even Levy-Bruhl spoke of the "prelogical mentality" of the primitives, it being implied that being logical in our way is a definite advance over the prelogicality of the primitive. Malinowski did oppose Levy-Bruhl's too-neat separation of the prelogical and the logical, holding that the primitive had both modes of dealing with reality, the mystical-magical and the empirical-pragmatic, and did not always confuse the two.

Emile Durkheim's view of religion was more functionalist—that religion was mainly an integrative tool for society. Even as late as 1952, Radcliffe-Brown held that the main function of religion was to celebrate and support the norms on which social integration depends.[10] Nowadays, functionalists and structuralists have become more modest. Instead of suggesting that the sole function of religion is social integration, they would hold that religion plays a role in social integration of individuals and in maintaining equilibrium among contending or conflicting groups in society.[11]

With Talcott Parsons and Robert Bellah, religion comes to be regarded as a symbolically controlled, symbolically organized action-communication behavior system of a biosocial organism, which helps regulate the energy generated by the organism's genetic endowment (an analogy with Freud's ego regulating the id), and which provides a cognitively adequate and motivationally meaningful identity system for the social organism and its individual members, useful in crises and situations that produce anxiety, fear, hope, or other peaks of feeling and emotion.[12]

The evolutionist preconception seems to be less operative in such a conception of religion. The main thrust is in terms of function. It is a social system of action and communication through agreed upon symbols. Its main purposes are: (a) to regulate social behavior; (b) to provide a basis for identity; and (c) to help face crises of feeling and experience.

Clifford Geertz would offer the following definition of religion:

> A religion is a system of symbols which acts to establish powerful, pervasive and long-lasting moods and motivations in men by formulating conceptions of a general order of existence and clothing these conceptions with such an aura of factuality that the moods and motivations seem uniquely realistic.[13]

Helpful as this definition seems, it raises several questions: the emphasis on "formulating" and "conceptions" betray an academic bias. Who does this formulating? Whose conceptions are they? How do these conceptions and formulations become assimilated and acknowledged by the people? It seems to avoid the questions about the origins of religion and its sustaining authority structures.

But our basic quarrel with these attempts to define religion is of a different kind. Before the European Enlightenment and the resultant process of secularization, religion was the all-pervasive basis of human existence. It now is reduced to something simply useful, functional, a utility for social integration, identity maintenance, and crisis confrontation. It becomes a "department" of life. As Bryan Wilson puts it in *The Encyclopedia of Religion:* "Religion in the West has generally become merely a department of the social order rather than the pervasive, or even determinant, influence it once was."[14]

Religion, in our modern societies, has recently been compartmentalized, privatized and marginalized. We act as if the whole world were secular. In fact, less than twenty percent of the world's population today profess no religion. Eighty percent of the world is religious in one degree or another. The organized religions of the world, with their myriad subsects, have great political and social clout, but we practically ignore them in our reflections about the future of our civilizations. Should the rest of us allow the twenty percent minority that claims to be secular decide the destiny of humanity? The religious people of the world cannot, of course, settle world-destiny questions without the full cooperation of the secular minority. But at the moment that minority seems to be in control, and is concerned about religion mostly in terms of votes for public office.

This, I submit, is, along with the justice conflict, the central conflict of our world. The justice conflict and the other conflicts that divide our humanity cannot be settled until religion is healed and restored to its proper place in society, not as a tool for secular politics, but as a transcendent power not subordinated to the political.

It is the process of secularization that has resulted in this marginalization-compartmentalization-privatization of religion. And behind the process of secularization and the discounting of religion lies the European Enlightenment. Both of these historical-spiritual processes deserve a closer look, to help us find our way to searching for new bases for new civilizations.

The very concept of religion in our modern usage and therefore our understanding of the function of religion in society need to be further studied. We should do this with particular reference to Hegel, for in Hegel we see a view of religion that is classical and represents the human tradition in a more adequate way than the later Enlightenment concept of religion as a private matter. Before we do so, it may be useful to take a brief look at the process of secularization and the ideology of secularism.

Secular, Secularism, and Secularization

The adjective *secular* in its medieval sense is a peculiarly Christian word, like *layman* (*laywoman* is a derivative of comparatively recent origin). The church made a distinction between *klerikos* (clerical) and *laikos* (lay) as early as the apostolic times. Clement of Rome (ca. 98 A.D.) uses this distinction in his *Epistle to the Corinthians* about the misbehavior of the laity in relation to the clergy.[15] Clement, direct disciple of the Apostles, seems to be the first to use the word *laikos* (lay) in this sense in Christian literature.

The second distinction seems to have originated in the fourth century or later, when the monastic movement developed in Africa and Asia. In the Syriac language (very close to the language that Christ and the Apostles spoke, a language that was probably created by the Christians of the first century using a new script for the *lingua franca* of that period of history, Aramaic) the contrast was made between *dairo* and *ólmo* (in western Syriac; the Eastern Syriac equivalent would be *daira* and *álma*); *dairo,* originally meaning just 'house', became a technical term for the monastery. *Ólmo,* the definite articled form of *ólam,* which, as also in the cognate Hebrew, means 'world' or 'age', has the same meaning as the Greek *aion* and the Latin *saeculum.* It is fascinating to observe that, in Syriac at least, the word for our 'layman' (Greek *laikos*) and for our 'secular' is exactly the same: *ólmoyo* (*álmaya* in Eastern Syriac), literally meaning 'worldly'. The medieval Latin meaning of the words *saecularis* and *regularis* or *religiosus* seems to have had its origin in the Syriac usage. Pre-Christian Latin used the word *saecularis,* largely to denote the celebration of the end of one century and the beginning of another, since *saeculum* meant also 'century'. The *ludi saeculares,* or the Century Games, with their *carmen saeculares,* or Century Hymn seem to have come into being in Rome as early as 348 B.C.[16] The use of the word *secular* as opposed to *monastic* or *ecclesiastical* seems thus a Christian creation. The present author is not competent to make a judgment whether a parallel or similar distinction occurs in the Buddhist tradition, which seems to be the font of coenobitic monasticism (*sangha*).

This somewhat obscure excursus into the linguistic origins of words and concepts has some significance for the main line of our thinking. Most of the time when we use the word *secular* in contemporary usage we are hardly aware of this history of the evolution of its meaning. While the adjective *secular* has a hoary antiquity, this is not the case with the two derivatives, *secularism* and *secularization*. These two are words generated by the European Enlightenment, as is the use of the adjective *secular* as qualifying the state.

Secularization comes into the English language only at the beginning of the eighteenth century. The *Oxford English Dictionary* (*OED*) gives the first instance as occurring in 1706 when the word meant conversion of an ecclesiastical or religious institution or its property to secular, that is, nonreligious or nonecclesiastical, possession and use; or the conversion of an ecclesiastical state to lay control. Before the European Enlightenment of the eighteenth and nineteenth centuries, its meaning is limited to this conversion of state authority, property, or institution from ecclesiastical to lay control. This process does not seem to have exact parallels in non-European cultures. Other religions do not seem to have had such a comprehensive, almost totalitarian organizational structure as the medieval Roman Catholic church in controlling state authority, institutions, property, and even ideas. The medieval European church seems a unique phenomenon in history.

Even the Byzantine church, which often imitated the medieval Western church, did not achieve that kind of monopoly of power over state, institutions, and property. Israel, Pakistan, and Saudi Arabia are modern religious states, yet no religious organization analogous to the Medieval European church holds monopoly power in these countries. In some modern Islamic states like Iran we begin to see something similar to medieval Christendom, but the intellectual domination of religion over society even in these states is mitigated by the copresence of European Enlightenment ideas of economy and government.

The uniqueness of the medieval European church in turn makes secularization, as reaction from monopoly control by the church, a uniquely European phenomenon, with worldwide consequences and attempts at emulation outside Europe. This uniqueness of the European phenomenon of secularization needs further examination, but since we have done that at some length in an earlier work, *Enlightenment: East and West,* we shall only allude to it later.

By 1863, when the European Enlightenment has fully blossomed, the word *secularization* took on a new meaning. The *OED* gives this definition for that date: the giving of a secular or nonsacred character or direction to (e.g., art, studies, etc.); the placing (of morality) on a secular basis; the restriction (of education) to secular subjects. This means that the process of secularization now extends beyond state, institutions, and property, to include the world of art, the university, and the school, as well as morality. It is this latter post-Enlightenment transition that deserves our particular attention here.

The first transition, that is, the transfer of state authority, large institutions, and their large properties from control by the church to public control, has been one of the most fruitful of historical developments. Democracy as we now know it could not have developed without that transition, and we should be grateful for the change. But can we say the same without qualifications about the latter transition, the secularization of the academy and of morality? These two needed to be liberated from ecclesiastical control; that need not of course be disputed. But in making the transition and shift to a secular basis, has not another assumption been made, namely that human beings can be better educated and lead their lives more ethically without rather than with any reference to the Transcendent? Many people would today ask: What is wrong with that assumption? It seems so natural for us post-Enlightenment humans to assume that secular education and secular morality are better than religious education and religious morality. We do not even stop to examine the logical validity of such an assumption.

Of course, the present author is not making the opposite assumption, namely that religious education and religious morality have been better than their secular counterparts. As we have already moved into a pluralistic world where people in each society follow either varying religions or no religion at all, it would certainly be unthinkable to impose one particular religious education or morality on the people by law. But what then is the justification for giving the "secular" assumption a special preference over religious assumptions and making secular education mandatory for all? Is this not a totalitarianism almost as bad as that of medieval Christendom?

Few people realize how great is the power of the Academy and the educational system to shape the basic value perceptions and life orientations of human beings. The very way we perceive material reality has been shaped by the training we all received in school. The state legislates compulsory education for all and imposes one particular form of secular education, whether in the socialist countries or in liberal democracies. We seem to have handed over the shaping of our minds and thoughts to the state.

It is time now to make a reference to secularism, which increasingly becomes the religion imposed upon the people, even against their will. Secularism is also a creation of the European Enlightenment; it came to birth around the middle of the nineteenth century. Its most articulate spokesman was G. J. Holyoake (1817–1906). Holyoake proposed this as the new religion for the modern period, reflecting the positivistic assumption that the kind of religions we had in the past all belong to the infancy of humanity, and that since we have now moved out of theology and metaphysics and into the self-assured domain of positive science, we need a new religion that does not require any dependence on a transcendent reality.

Even apart from Holyoake, whose name so few secular people know, secularism has become the religion of our civilization. The *OED* defines its meaning as "the doctrine that morality should be based solely on regard to the well-being of mankind in the present life, to the exclusion of all considerations drawn from belief in God or in a future state."[17]

That may or may not be a very precise definition of the religion of secularism. Secularism as a religious ideology has to do with much more than mere morality. The *OED* definition implies the characteristically English notion that religion is an adjunct to morality. Put very bluntly, this view says that it is morality that we really want, and that religion is relevant only if it is indispensable for sustaining morality. If morality can be sustained without religion, then why bother about religion, this view seems to ask. This perhaps is the greatest possible, though very common, distortion of religion; that is, to have chosen something like peace of mind, salvation, or crisis help as one's goal and then to seek to use God as an instrument or agency to achieve that goal.

Holyoake's secularism had the advantage that it did not seek to use God to achieve one's own goals. But it too was consciously proposed as a substitute for religion. While Holyoake's ideology did not become an organized religion in the strict sense, it now functions as a surrogate religion for so many people in our secular culture.

European thinkers, however, are far from unanimous about the content of secularization or secularism. For Romano Guardini it is the negation of traditional medieval theology. For Karl Loewith, secular thought is but a pseudotheology secretly but actively guided by ancient Christian dogmas. Some theologians like Gogarten and Altizer have tried to claim for secular thought and culture a direct descent from the Christian doctrine of Incarnation. Karl Schmitt derives modern political theories directly from Christian theological concepts. Hans Sedlmayr has argued that the key to modern art can be found in medieval religious symbolism.[18] Today, Western scholars generally agree that the process of secularization can be understood only within the context and horizon of medieval European Christendom. The present author has argued this at some length elsewhere.[19] The dispute is simply about whether the secular is more of a reaction against the constrictions of medieval Christendom or a continuation of it in another form. It is safe to say that both elements are present—reaction against and continuity with.

Louis Dupré has convincingly argued that the continuity is in the resuscitation of the premedieval quest for a nonsubjective objectivity—a quest essentially Greek in origin and suppressed by medieval Christendom. According to Dupré, the Greeks were the first in systematic thinking (this may be true for those who know only European thought) to study the real as it is. In that process the Greeks paid more attention to the external aspects of reality, though there were some who were concerned also about the internal reality of the soul. It was Christianity that once more opened up the internal dimension.[20]

Dupré thinks that Western culture was never fully Christianized; the two currents, the Greco-Roman and the Judeo-Christian coexisted, the former stressing objectivity and the latter internal piety. The end of the Middle Ages signified the weakening of the internal spiritual energy that kept the objectivity quest under control. As the dam broke the torrents of objectivity began to flow and flood the continent, but the other took refuge in the continuing mystical tradition. The transition was in scholasticism, which emphasized objectivity, while the Protestant Reformation, by stressing personal faith, held up the subjectivity aspect. As the *scientia* of scholasticism gave place to modern science, the mystical or the religious was marginalized, and as science and objectivity triumphed, the basic assumption was that precise knowledge would help overcome the "other" or the objective world and control it. Only control would emancipate humanity from the constraints of external reality and lead to the true emancipation of the human being. Control is power, and power is the perennial quest of the West.

In conclusion, we can observe the following significant elements in the process of secularization:

1. A general tendency to ignore the transcendent dimensions of reality, in order to keep it objective

2. A general confidence in the authority of reason and empirical observation
3. A general mistrust of the subjective element (aside from reason and observation but including religion) as erratic and unreliable, likely to lead astray
4. A negative reaction to the whole heritage of the Western church, including the rejection of its authority, tradition, and clericalism
5. A desire and an attempt to understand and explain all reality within the categories of historical, social, human finite entities; also to create institutions based on this understanding of reality
6. A general satisfaction and great pride about the achievements of the scientific-technological achievements of Western civilization, both in industry and in world and space conquest
7. Based on all this, an effort to impose this view and way of life on the world by claiming universality and objectivity to the knowledge and the approach.

Culture

The question of culture is so integrally related to religion and secularism that we need to gain some clarity about it. The meaning of the word is extremely polyvalent. Again, it is the European Enlightenment that gave it a meaning which it did not formerly have. Originally, culture was opposed to nature, the idea being that nature exists by itself while culture is created by humanity. Of course, there is no foundation to the idea that nature exists by itself; neither do we find much nature that has not been affected by humanity's presence and action in it.

We are here concerned with the sense which Edward Tylor gave the word in his 1871 work on primitive culture:

> Culture or Civilization, taken in its wide ethnographic sense, is that complex whole which includes knowledge, belief, art, morals, law, custom and any other capabilities and habits acquired by man as a member of society.[21]

With Talcott Parsons in 1958 "culture" in the ethnographic sense becomes more inclusive, comprehending "culture patterns" and "social structures." This was an improvement on the definition given by A. L. Kroeber and Clyde Kluckhorn in their comprehensive survey of several hundred definitions:

> Culture consists of patterns, explicit and implicit, of and for behavior acquired and transmitted by symbols, constituting the distinct achievement of human groups, including their embodiment in artefacts; the essential core of culture consists of traditional (i.e., historically derived and selected) ideas and especially their attached values; culture systems may, on the one hand, be considered as products of action, on the other, as conditioning elements of further action.[22]

As Parsons has shown, culture systems are also social systems, and the structure of a particular society, with its relational and organizational aspects, should be included in our vision of culture. The unity of a social system is both in its culture and in its relational structures. The problem, however, is that no contemporary society is so homogeneous as to have a single culture for the whole, though it is possible to have dreams of such an homogeneous culture. We saw that when European ministers of culture sat down with seventy intellectuals from twenty European countries on November 2–3, 1989 in Blois, France to work out ground rules for "a greater cultural continent of Europe."[23]

Swedish sociologists Jonas Frykman and Orvar Loefgren have studied the process of formation of a Swedish middle-class worldview and life-style in the nineteenth and early twentieth centuries, which then became the stereotype for the Swedish personality: "a rational, nature-loving, conflict-avoiding person, obsessed with self-discipline and punctuality."[24] The authors show how this stereotype of middle-class culture fails to fit the other classes in Swedish society, the industrial working class, the peasantry, and the "insincere and shallow" aristocratic class. Each of these other classes has its own culture and worldview.

There is another sense of the word *culture* that we cannot overlook: the sense of refinement in manners, skills, tastes in art and music, literary awareness, and so on. This is the sense in which an emeritus professor of the humanities deplores the steady decline of culture in America:

> There is widespread and justified concern over the steady decline of culture in America—and in the West generally. . . . Among the societal forces . . . largely responsible for this dis-

> quieting tendency I identify the loss of psychic and intellectual immunity to Bad Art (cultural AIDS); the century-long slide into vulgarity, tawdriness and sleaziness, which have helped turn America into the Land of Entertainment (or Disneyland of Culture); the loss of standards and criteria of taste and judgment in both the production of art and its critical evaluation; the loss—especially in America—of innocence brought on by the corrosion of human values; and finally, the rise of sentimentality and the consequent triumph of *kitsch*, which has come to be accepted as an illusory substitute for genuine seriousness and sentiment.[25]

Our concept of culture should be comprehensive enough to include this more restricted use of the word to denote tastes in art, music, literature, and so on. For these latter are, after all, artifacts and symbols, the coinage of culture. Too often, however, when people speak of a cultural heritage they fail to include the behavioral and relational standards and patterns in the concept. The custom of shaking hands would, in our view, be as much a part of culture as music and art, or political and economic systems.

For our purposes here, we need to note the integral relation of culture to religion, to ideology, and to secular assumptions in the state and the academy. If culture means more than mere individual refinement, if it shapes the basic value orientations of a society, then we have to take into account the fact that secularization and the consequent marginalization and personalization of religion have made all the difference in the world to culture. If new foundations are to be sought for new civilizations, we cannot proceed by defining some moral values that we want to inject into an existing civilization. We will need to become fully aware of the foundations of the present civilization, and how culture, religion, and secularization have already been built into it. That indeed is the main thrust of this present enterprise.

Religion and Philosophy: Hegel's View

In modern Western thought, Hegel's (1770–1831) view of religion and philosophy is unique. For him, each religion is a particular shaping in thought of the spirit becoming conscious of itself. This shape determines all higher ideas coming into its matrix. So is art, though it is a less developed form created by the spirit. Art produces, so to speak, the outer shape of the spirit, giving but a glimpse of the outward appearance of one form of the spirit. The statue, for example, wears the outer shape of the Incarnation of the Divine Being, but it lacks inwardness, the characteristic of consciousness, or the Self's true activity.[26] Religion is a superior form of the spirit than art, because in it this "inward" element is predominant.

> We know that in religion we withdraw ourselves from what is temporal, and religion is for our consciousness that region in which all the enigmas are solved, all the contradictions of deeper-reaching thought have their meaning unveiled, and where the voice of the heart's pain is silenced—the region of eternal rest, of eternal peace. . . and from man as Spirit proceed all the many developments of the sciences and arts, the interests of political life, and all those conditions which have reference to man's freedom and will. But all these manifold forms of human relations, activities and pleasures, and all the ways in which these are intertwined; all that has worth and dignity for man, all wherein he seeks his happiness, his glory and his pride, finds its ultimate centre in religion, in the thought, the consciousness, and the feeling of God. Thus God is the beginning of all things, and the end of all things. As all things proceed from this point, so all return back to it again. He is the centre which gives life and quickening to all things, and which animates and preserves in existence all the various forms of being. In religion man places himself in a relation to this centre, in which all other relations concentrate themselves, and in so doing he rises up to the highest level of consciousness.[27]

Here religion is certainly not one of the activities of life, a department or a matter of personal choice, but the highest level attained by the overall human consciousness. It is the basis, the hub and the center of all existence, of all life and of all awareness. Devoid of this awareness, man falls into the trap of "naive realism," the view that things are in fact what they appear to be, which is the basis of secularism.

God is not simply the First "cause" of something called *nature* as many Naturalist Deists still believe. Starting from that standpoint, modern science simply assumes that if God can be a self-existent Uncaused Cause, so can nature be; thus the God hypothesis has no function in the logic of science. Marxists used to prefer the term *matter* as the name of the self-existent, but now have shifted to "Matter-Energy in Dialectical Process of Development" as the name of the Absolute. From the Hegelian perspective all these different forms of secularism, materialism, deism, naturalism, and so on are all various religions rising out of naive realism. All these err and at the same point—namely that of seeking the explanation for the finite within the finite itself or regarding the finite itself as simply the infinite. Hegel castigates modern science and its famous category, the understanding, for doing this:

> Knowledge, science, in this manner places the manifold material in mutual relation, takes away from it the contingency which it has through its immediacy, and while contemplating the relations which belong to the wealth of finite phenomena, encloses the world of finiteness in itself so as to form a system of the universe, of such a kind that knowledge requires nothing for this system outside of the system itself. . . In this manner science forms a universe of knowledge, to which God is not necessary.[28]

But this is not a simple contest of faith against science. Faith itself has made the mistake of being so involved in a false notion of the transcendent as to forget the reality, though contingent, of this world and thus to banish God to the transcendent world. It is a dialectical development, in which the two poles of the one reality, the transcendent and the immanent, become alienated from each other. And as science takes over more and more areas of knowledge about the finite world, religion retreats into compartmentalization, privatization and spiritualization, unrelated to the social, political, economic, and cultural aspects of contemporary life.

For Hegel, the present conflict between science and religion is a normal stage in the dialectical development of the spirit, and the polarities of thesis and antithesis have to be resolved or reconciled at a higher level of synthesis. Both science and religion are revealing their defective development, science by losing the transcendent has become imprisoned within the finite and the immanent; religion, by becoming "devoid of knowledge," has shrivelled up into simple feeling, into the contentless or empty elevation of the spiritual to the Eternal. Science itself "can, however, affirm nothing regarding the Eternal, for all that could be regarded as knowledge would be a drawing down of the Eternal into the sphere of the finite, and of finite connections of things."[29]

Hegel perceived very clearly the nature of the conflict and mutual distrust between science and religion almost six generations ago. Religion distrusts finitude; science distrusts totality and the transcendent. Feeling and reason are alienated from each other. Hegel sought a reconciliation of the two, and there is no other way of understanding his philosophy, as we shall show in a later chapter. His perception of the problem remains accurate to this day, but it is his solution that has failed to carry conviction. His own philosophy was proposed as the ultimate reconciliation of science and faith; that, as Hegel saw it, was the true function of philosophy, to go beyond and behind faith and knowledge and to work out their contradiction into a higher synthesis:

> Now that the opposition has arrived at this stage of development, where the one side, whenever it is approached by the other, invariably thrusts it away from it as an enemy, the necessity for an adjustment comes in, of such a kind that the infinite shall appear in the finite, and the finite in the infinite, and each no longer form a separate realm. This would be the reconciliation of religious, genuine simple feeling (*die Versoehnung des religiosen, gediegenen Gefuhls*) with knowledge and intelligence (*Erkenntnis und Intelligenz*).[30]

We should not overlook the fact that for Hegel, religion and philosophy have both the same function and purpose:

> The object of religion as well as of philosophy is eternal truth in its objectivity, God and nothing but God, and the explication of God. Philosophy is not a wisdom of the world, but is knowledge of what is not of the world; it is not knowledge which concerns external mass, or empirical existence and life, but is knowledge of that which is eternal, of what God is, and of what flows out of his nature. . . Philosophy is itself, in fact, worship; it is religion, for in the same way it renounced subjective notions and opinions in order to occupy itself with God. Philosophy is thus identical with religion, but the distinction is that it is so in a peculiar manner, distinct from the manner of looking at things which is commonly called religion as such. What they (philosophy and religion) have in common is, that they are religion; what distinguishes them from each other is merely the kind and manner of religion we find in each.[28]

We shall look at Hegel's thought in a little more detail later on. Here we are only pointing out a different way of looking at science, philosophy, and religion than what we post-Enlightenment thinkers have become used to. It is the present writer's considered judgment that while Hegel's concept of religion may need to be revised in the light of further reflection, it offers a perspective we should not ignore. Neither is Hegel's understanding of philosophy as *Gottesdienst* or 'worship' to be sniffed at. This, it seems, is the way Heidegger, for example, went at it. Whether Heidegger succeeded in his project need not detain us here. We, too, need not be bound by the conventions with which post-Enlightenment thought has hamstrung philosophy. The human spirit is still free, and even the Enlightenment cannot bind it with chains of authority.

Hegel's conception of religion and philosophy sound strange to modern ears. Philosophy has long abdicated its vocation to seek all-comprehending truth. Today it seems afraid to relate philosophy even to the social good of the public, let alone any transcendent concern about God as the source and ground of all. It assumes a false modesty when it sets itself out to be merely a tool for solving technical problems in thought, or to preoccupy itself with endless discussions of method at the expense of content. Both philosophy and religion are concerned about the meaning of the whole. The difference lies, as Hegel said, in the method used. Hegel himself thought that philosophy supercedes religion. In my view, religion, philosophy, and science belong to a single group of activity, namely humanity's search for meaning and direction for life. It seems they can do so only in a three-cornered dialogue with each other; but before the dialogue begins religion itself will have to be rescued and redeemed from its present orientation, as a private choice for individuals to seek personal salvation. That kind of religion will continue to be marginalized; only a wider outlook on the part of religion that includes a concern for the whole of humanity and its destiny in this world as well as beyond can claim the attention of true philosophy or science.

Religion is the comprehensive foundation of a community's approach to the whole. In that sense secularism has all the attributes of a religion, for it makes an affirmation about the whole, that the world open to our senses, to our measuring instruments, and to our rational thought constitutes the whole of reality. But secularism has as much right to exist as the other religions have; only it must not monopolize the academy and the institutions of social existence. Secularism stands to gain when it opens itself to dialogue with the religions, as has begun to happen in the Soviet Union and other countries of Central and Eastern Europe. Secularism needs as much redemption from bigotry as the religions do.

Hegel's major mistake was in thinking that thought can do the business of religion better. Thought should be an essential part of all human activity, including religion. But Hegel's overconfidence in the capacity of thought to reveal the truth seems to be misplaced.

Thought cannot comprehend Truth, but can often illuminate it. Religion is more than thought or conviction or feeling or worship or moral rules. The attempt to reduce religion to one or more of these is bound to fail. The word that is difficult for post-Enlightenment thinkers is *ritual* or the symbolic act of a community in which the community gives expression to and informs itself in the transconceptual reality of human existence. Ritual expresses a hope that cannot be expressed in words, concepts, or even in symbols; it is a participatory act of a community that affirms the meaning of its own existence in actions that can be transmitted from generation to generation. But consciously fabricated rituals will fail to move or to take root. They should grow out of the community's experience, and continue to grow, taking modified forms in changing situations. In such communities religion, philosophy, and science have their part, but cannot usurp the whole.

The European Enlightenment has been a decisive factor in shaping the various cultures of our present time. The pervasiveness of this factor is often not taken into account: Too often people see the conflict as one between technology and culture. Such an analysis fails to get to the root of the problem. Religion and secularization are integral elements in the formation of cultures, whether in India or America, Australia or New Caledonia. What has recently happened to religion and philosophy, as well as the worldwide process of secularization can be understood only in the context of the European Enlightenment. To that subject we now turn.

Chapter Three

What is the European Enlightenment?

Briefly put, the European Enlightenment is a spiritual-intellectual fever that spread among the European peoples from about the middle of the eighteenth century. The fever has not yet subsided. In that sense the Enlightenment remains unfinished. It has only begun to manifest some of its secondary symptoms. It has affected the mental, moral, and aesthetic tastes of the people brought under its influence all over the world.

At least five aspects of the European Enlightenment need to be held together in order to provide an elementary understanding of this unique phenomenon that broke out in Europe in the eighteenth century and has managed to shape or misshape the entire world in two centuries. There is no way of understanding the various trends and struggles that we outlined in Chapter One of this book without some grasp of the nature of the European Enlightenment. We insist on calling it the European Enlightenment (sometimes *EE* for short) in order to distinguish it from the various other historical instances of enlightenment in other parts of the world (e.g., the great Buddhist Enlightenment in the sixth century B.C. in India).

Briefly stated, the five elements are:

1. Some special features of European identity that seem to endure through the centuries and shape the actions of European nations and peoples
2. The particular political and socioeconomic conditions of Europe in the eighteenth century and after
3. Religious-philosophical ideas that suddenly sprang up in Europe in the eighteenth century, following the collapse of the metaphysical systems that sought to replace religious philosophy

4. The new movements in the areas of the arts and literature in Europe
5. The development of modern science and the technology based on it.

We shall discuss some of these aspects that powered the European Enlightenment, after some preliminary remarks.

The Terminology

The Europeans have their special word for the Enlightenment in each European language: *Aufklaerung* in German, meaning 'clearing up'; *le siecle des lumieres* or the 'age of lights' in French; *Illuminismo* in Italian; *Laerdom* in Swedish, *Prosvezhenie* in Russian, *Osvichenske* in Czech, and so on. The one European Enlightenment took a different form in each European country depending upon its specific cultural and political-economic situation.

Interestingly enough, the French, who played such a decisive role in the Enlightenment, did not develop a word for it. They do not speak of an *Eclaircissement,* which would be the parallel word for the German *Aufklaerung,* both of which mean literally 'clearing up' rather than 'enlightenment'. The French prefer to speak of a *siecle des lumieres* meaning a century or age of lights.

The prophets of the Enlightenment are numerous. No list can be exhaustive. One could mention Voltaire and Montesquieu, Pierre Bayle and Isaac Newton, Bacon, Locke and Hume, Rousseau and Descartes, Diderot, Condorcet and D'Alembert, Hobbes and Paine, Hegel, Herder and Heine, Goethe and Goya, Kant and Mendelssohn, Reimarus and Robertson, Robespierre and De la Mettrie, Adam Smith and Charles Darwin, and an innumerable host of others. No one man or woman or country can take the whole credit for it. As we have stated, it spread like an epidemic. In the leadership were four countries: Germany, France, Britain (especially Scotland), and, as a place of refuge for intellectuals, the Netherlands. Whether one European country heard about what was happening in other European countries or not, it sprung up practically everywhere in Europe, more or less simultaneously. Of course, there were many cross-country contacts and influences, but each country developed its own Enlightenment suited to its social and economic conditions. It spread soon to America and other European colonies, where it developed radically new institutional structures that have also spread across the world. More slowly it went wherever there were people trained in European or American academic systems. Its ideas spread as if they were self-evident. Its institutions were copied worldwide wherever the leadership had been trained in the Enlightenment system of education.

It thus transformed the way people all over the world perceive and understand. "Understanding" was its special focus. Based on the new understanding, it created tremendous movements of social change, eventually in all countries of the world. Because of the uniform general orientation of the changes in all countries despite difference in pace and style, it soon developed a universal system of science, technology, communication, information, and institutions, which bid fair to unite the world into one single historical stream, marked by many struggles and conflicts, alliances and enmities, and influences and reactions, but inside one interconnected historical process. The European Enlightenment itself could not have happened without these global interconnections, which began developing long before the eighteenth century.

What marked the beginning of the European Enlightenment? If you were a Scot, you would say it began in 1739–40 with Hume's *Treatise on Human Nature* and Richardson's *Pamela*. Depending on your knowledge and experience you could also say it began in 1732–34 with Pope's *Essay on Man*, or in 1734 with Voltaire's *Lettres Philosophiques*. Or you could choose an earlier date, citing Montesquieu's *Lettres Persanes* (1721), or even go back to the seventeenth century, citing Thomas Hobbes (1588–1679), or the 1690 publication of John Locke's *Essay on Human Understanding*.

The present writer would regard Hobbes, Locke, Hume, and Descartes as forerunners rather than initiators of the European Enlightenment. The precise point in time and space is not important; the period of beginning for such a huge and powerful movement is never definite; it began generally in the eighteenth century, though much in the earlier centuries led to it. The space of its origin can be determined as the European continent. Hence we call it the European Enlightenment.

Many would prefer the publication date of *L'Encyclopedie* in France (1751–72) as the noticeable event in the inauguration of the Enlightenment. In Germany they may choose 1766 when Lessing's *Laocooen* was published, or 1781 when Kant's *Critique of Pure Reason* came out. Baron Christian von Wolff, son of Frederick William I (1688–1740), King of Prussia, seems to have coined the word *Aufklaerung* in the German language.[32]

Americans may prefer the dates of their own American Revolution (1775–83), or the date of the American Declaration of Independence (1776), to mark the beginning of the European Enlightenment in America. In any case, the French Revolution of 1789 must be regarded, not as the beginning of the European Enlightenment, but as its first major outburst. It is therefore reasonable to mark the beginning around the middle of the eighteenth century.

Has the European Enlightenment come to an end? Not at all. On the contrary, it is still very much on the upswing, spreading into all parts of the world with a dynamic strength that surprises its critics. One curious fact remains, however: while the phenomenon of the European Enlightenment has from the beginning been recognized, serious studies about the phenomenon as a whole, with attention to its meaning and significance, date largely from the end of the Second World War.[33] And in the last forty years or so, there have been a great proliferation of such studies.

Strangely enough, however, there is no agreement among these studies as to what specifically constitutes the European Enlightenment.

Ira O. Wade in his most perceptive and monumental (more than eleven-hundred pages) study of the French Enlightenment, *The Structure and Form of the French Enlightenment,* makes a helpful distinction between *l'esprit philosophique* and *l'esprit revolutionnaire* (i.e., between the conceptual elements and the activist elements).[34] But within what he calls *l'esprit philosophique* he includes more than the conceptual: art and aesthetics, religion and morality, science and laws, among others. We shall, for our own analysis stick to some of the five aspects of the European Enlightenment listed earlier, though we cannot be monumental or comprehensive in our quick brush-stroke depiction of that unique European phenomenon. Meanwhile, it may be useful to look at some self-understandings of the *Erklaerung* among some of its eighteenth-century progenitors and prophets. This can give us a working concept on which we can improve or develop later.

What is the European Enlightenment?

Perhaps it was easier for the eighteenth-century thinkers to define the Enlightenment when the process was only beginning to be clearly noticed. Around 1784, five years before the French Revolution, the discussion gets started in the *Berlinische Monatsschrift* on the question "*Was ist Aufklaerung?*" The great Jewish philosopher Moses Mendelssohn wrote in the September 1784 issue:

> The words Enlightenment, Culture and Education (*Aufklaerung, Kultur, Bildung*) are still newcomers in our language (i.e. in German). They belong at present to the language of the elite

> (*Baichersprache*). The common people understand nothing of all this. Should this be taken to mean that the substance of it is still quite new to us? I do not think so. . . Education, Culture and Enlightenment are modifications of social life, effects of the drives and desires of human beings to better their social existence.[35]

Mendelssohn makes the interesting distinction between Human Enlightenment (*Menschenaufklaerung*) and the Citizen's or Bourgeois Enlightenment (*Buergeraufklaerung*). He thinks the two can be in conflict, and was not quite ready to start out with the Enlightenment of the whole of humanity. In fact, he and many others thought that it would be disastrous to extend the Enlightenment to the common people; it would make people difficult to control and unavailable to do the dirty work they have to do in order to enable the bourgeoisie to enjoy life. The people would have to wait another sixty years before a Marx or an Engels would come along to demand an *Arbeiteraufklaerung* or 'Workers' Enlightenment'.

Immanuel Kant was a participant in that German debate of 1784. He was already an old man (born 1724) when he published in the same *Berlinische Monatsschrift* (December 1784) his brief piece: "Answer to the Question: What is the Enlightenment?" (*Beantwortung der Frage: Was ist Aufklaerung?*).[36] His opening words reflect the youth of Kant's spirit even in his advanced age:

> Enlightenment is the coming out of Man from his self-imposed immaturity. Immaturity is the lack of will to serve one's own understanding without direction (*Leitung*) from another. This is a self-imposed immaturity; if Reason languishes, it is not for lack of understanding, but only of resolve and courage to serve oneself without direction from another. *Sapere aude!* Dare to think! Think boldly! Wake up! Take courage, to serve your own understanding. This is the motto (*Wahlspruch*) of the Enlightenment.[36]

In other words, the Germans saw Enlightenment as the assertion of humanity's adulthood and its revolt against all external authority outside one's own understanding. This meant repudiation of the authority structure that had prevailed in medieval Europe, namely the authority of the Church, the tradition of the Christian Fathers of the Church, of Christian theology and the clergy, as well as a lot of superstitious folklore. For a Protestant like Kant, it meant much more. The authority of the Christian Scriptures had to be repudiated, as well as of all traditional wisdom, including the traditional Protestant understanding of what Christianity is all about. It was indeed a radical move for Kant, rejecting all external authority, and seeking to found a system of perceiving the world, as he thought, without presuppositions or external authority, with no reliance whatsoever on any kind of tradition.

It seems in fact that this repudiation of all external authority and of any debt to tradition, and the use of reason without presuppositions, seems to constitute the essence, not only of the European Enlightenment, but also of what we mean today by the adjective *modern* when applied to thought or philosophy. To be modern is to be able to think without presuppositions and to reject all authority of tradition. In fact, modernity implies hostility to tradition and authority. Modernity is another Enlightenment word, though it seems to have come into existence slightly earlier with the breakup of medieval European society.[37]

From Moses Mendelssohn and Immanuel Kant we get a general idea of what they understood by the European Enlightenment. It is an affirmation of human adulthood and autonomy, and a rejection of all heteronomy, including the authority of those who claim to represent God. The only reliable authority is one's own understanding, or reason, if you want to call it that. Mendelssohn helps us to see the elitist character of the European Enlightenment, that it was not originally meant for the whole of humanity, but was intended mainly for the rising middle class of Europe. Mendelssohn tells us plainly that there can actually be a collision between the Human Enlightenment and the Bourgeois Enlightenment, in the essential or nonessential, formal or nonformal decision-making structures of society.[38]

Immanuel Kant, though in many respects an ardent advocate of the principle of equality, did not think that all human beings were entitled to participation in the state. In principle he would say that no citizen can be placed under an obligation that is not also binding on others: All are equal before the law, as he would say in his *Reflexionen zur Moralphilosophie.*[39] While adhering to this principle with some vehemence, Kant would go on to say that equality is only in terms of equal opportunity for all. This has now become a favorite motto of capitalism. Only those who are truly free and independent and have property or some skill by which he or she can easily make an independent living, is entitled to citizenship; even a tutor who lives in someone else's house and shares his table would not be regarded as independent or worthy of the right to vote.

Only a burgher or citizen can be a colegislator. Every citizen must be his own master, *sui iuris,* a legislator laying down his own law. Only the free can legislate, for to submit to a law that he or she does not make would be forfeiting his or her own freedom.[40] Servants, journeymen, apprentices, peasants, handymen, and so on have no citizen's rights at all, until they become independent and have property or profession.

Lest people misunderstand my attribution of elitism to the European Enlightenment, it may be necessary to refer to another eighteenth-century debate in Germany, on the philosophical question: Is it useful to deceive the people? The debate was precisely about the advisability of taking the common people into confidence and letting them share in the benefits of the European Enlightenment. The 1780 debate in the *Academie des Sciences et de Belles-lettres de Berlin* has been edited for us by W. Krauss.[41] It is clear that the issue was more than merely academic. It roused great passions because the economic interests of the "educated classes" or *Gebildete Staende* would be imperiled if the common people shared in the benefits of the Enlightenment. Only the educated could be enlightened. Education and Enlightenment always go together.

Variations on a Theme

The European Enlightenment as we have stated earlier was certainly not uniform in all European countries. We need to note briefly here some special features of the Enlightenment in several specific European environments.

French Materialism

Materialism is not necessarily a French creation, nor is a materialist philosophy the only distinguishing feature of the French Enlightenment. But we need to put some emphasis on this aspect of the Enlightenment since it is one of the major intellectual aspects of civilization that needs reexamination and restatement before we can build new civilizations on new foundations.

In France, La Mettrie (1709–1751) is thought to be the originator of the materialist point of view in his two key works: *Histoire naturelle de l'ame* (*Natural History of the Soul*, 1745) and *L'Homme Machine* (*Man a Machine*), published in Leiden in 1748.[42] La Mettrie was trained as a physician and generally despised the philosophers. The theologians pounced upon his "heresies" and he was forced to flee France for refuge in the Netherlands, then a hospitable home to liberals and radicals. Even there the theologians harrassed him.

La Mettrie was influenced significantly both by René Descartes (1596–1650) and by the British Deists like Hobbes (1588–1679), John

Toland (1670–1721), and John Locke (1632–1704). It was Descartes's teaching that was the starting point of La Mettrie's thought, and he wrote a commentary on it, but the dualism of Descartes bothered him. Why did Descartes divide reality into two worlds, *res cogitans* and *res extensa,* the thinking thing and the extended thing? Could he not see that the thinking thing was also an extended thing, and that there was only one kind of reality, *the* thing? In thus reducing Descartes's dualism into a philosophically more respectable monism, La Mettrie was probably influenced also by the early Greek Monists like Thales and Anaximander, as well as by the Atomists like Democritus and Epicurus. La Mettrie was waging the same war against the theologians that Buddha in India and Epicurus and Lucretius in Greece were fighting. It was the fear of death, the fear of gods, and the fear of some unpleasant future life for the soul that were used by the religionists to hold the people down in thralldom.

This classical Greek materialism had been repressed by medieval Christendom, and was coming back into European thought through the Renaissance revival of the Greek classics. Just as Marx a century later, La Mettrie must have been gripped by Epicurus's developed system and by Lucretius's poetic outburst in *De rerum natura,* during his premedical studies of natural philosophy at the College de Harcourt.

As a physician he was attracted to empiricism and this is what drew him to the British Empiricists Hobbes, Toland, and Locke. La Mettrie took the God of the Deists (including Descartes) as a concession they made to appease the terrifying theologians, and found no difficulty in dismissing God as more or less irrelevant for the understanding of reality. Everything can be understood with matter as the only reality, provided you understand matter as capable not only of motion, but also of feeling. All knowledge comes through the senses, and sense-experience is a motion in matter.

The French Sensationalists; like the Abbe de Condillac (1715–1780) and Helvetius (1715–1771) seem to have also been influenced by La Mettrie, though they do not cite him by name. For Condillac and Helvetius the existence of God is a certainty; while for La Mettrie, God may exist, but it makes no difference.

But none of these had made any attempt to ground materialism on systematic philosophical grounds. That task fell to a German aristocrat living in Paris at that time, Baron Paul Heinrich Dietrich von Holbach (1723–1789). His work *Le systeme de la nature,* published anonymously in Amsterdam in 1776, soon became the bible of materialism, published throughout Europe in translations of practically every European language. He was in no hesitation about the question whether God existed or not; for him, belief in God was an obstacle to human progress and had therefore to be fought, not just left undetermined. His attack on Christianity was forthright. His *Ecce Homo* (*Behold the Man!*) subtitled: *A Critical Enquiry into the History of Jesus of Nazareth being a Rational Analysis of the Gospels,* demolished all the mythical and miraculous elements in the Gospels, and presented a Jesus who was essentially a moral reformer.[43]

But for modern people, morality had to be based on something more rational than the teachings of Jesus. His publication in 1776, also in Amsterdam, of *La morale Universelle ou les devoirs de l'homme fondes sur sa nature*[44] provided a natural basis for universal human morality based only on a study of human nature as a material entity. The emancipation of the human was now complete. Human beings were liberated from the fear of God or of the future, and were now free to develop themselves in freedom and autonomy.

Materialism was thus manufactured in France by a German baron, drawing on British thought of a century earlier, and published in the Netherlands. But it could not have found the success it did without the work of the Encyclopaedists, the *philosophes,* and the revolutionaries: Denis Diderot (1713–1784), Jean le Rond D'Alembert (ca. 1717–1783), Voltaire (Francois-Marie Arouet, 1694–1778), Jean Jacques Rousseau (1712–1778), Count Georges-Louis Buffon (1707–1788), the Marquis de Condorcet (1743–1794), and countless others.

By no means all revolutionaries or *philosophes* were materialists. Deism of one sort or other was still powerful. The coterie of Holbachists continued to battle the tribe of Rousseauists for a long time. The important consideration for us, however, is the motivating force behind this materialism-atheism-deism. Obviously, it was not a logical necessity imposed by reason. The German debate on materialism was just as intense as the one in France, but neither Kant nor Hegel were materialists or atheists.

There was a strong and pervasive perception among most of the *philosophes* and reformers that the old order drew its strength from the churches, both Roman Catholic and Protestant, and unless the power of organized religion was undermined the new order could not come into being. Heinrich Heine (1797–1856), the popular German poet and a father of the German Enlightenment, made the point explicit when he wrote, addressing a French reading public:

> It is important at the moment to neutralize the power of religion. You see, we Germans are in the same situation as you were before the revolution, when Christianity and the old regime formed an absolutely inseparable alliance. This could not be

destroyed as long as Christianity still exerted its influence on the masses. Voltaire had to start up his cutting laughter before Samson [the executioner in Paris during the French Revolution] could let his axe fall.[45]

In Heine's case it was a conscious perception, but for many others it was latent at less than conscious levels in their mind. And for many traditional Christian clergymen it was difficult to distinguish between the political and the religious as it is today. Eric Hobsbawm cites the Vatican's official journal on civic affairs, *La Civilta Cattolica,* expressing this connection from the perspective of established religion:

> Give me a people where boiling passions and worldly greed are calmed by faith, hope and charity; a people which sees this earth as a pilgrimage and the other life as its true fatherland; a people taught to admire and revere in Christian heroism its very poverty and its very sufferings; a people that loves and adores in Jesus Christ the first-born of all the oppressed, and in his cross the instrument of universal salvation. Give me, I say, a people formed in his mould and socialism will not merely be easily defeated, but impossible to be thought of . . . [46]

It seems that for the writer of that passage the final goal is to defeat socialism, and religion is simply an instrument to be used to that end. Peter Gay, the most prolific American writer on the Enlightenment, concludes that its essence is *The Rise of Modern Paganism,*[47] as a rival to the religion of the Christian establishment, as well as the quest for freedom from the trammels of constricting authority that keeps humanity in bondage. The *Civilta Cattolica* writer wants to reinstate traditional individual-pietistic otherworldly religion as the massive bulwark against the encroachment of socialism. Both confirm the integral relation between the *ancien regime* and traditional religion. And it also helps us understand the vehement opposition of Marx and Engels to any form of religion.

In fact, there were no two independent entities called religion and society. That very distinction is a creation of the European Enlightenment. Pre-Enlightenment religion was not a disparate element distinct from the total life of society. It was all-embracing and all life was under the sway of religion. Even a leftist writer like Eric Hobsbawm recognized this:

> For most of history and for most of the world (China being perhaps the main exception) the terms in which all but a handful

> of educated and emancipated men thought about the world were those of traditional religion, . . . At some stage before 1848 this ceased to be so in parts of Europe, though not yet outside the area transformed by the two revolutions. Religion, from being something like the sky, from which no man can escape and which contains all that is above the earth, became something like a bank of clouds, a large but limited and changing feature of the human firmament. Of all the ideological changes this is by far the most profound, though its practical consequences were more ambiguous and undetermined than was then supposed. At all events, it is the most unprecedented.[48]

The hold of religion was so enormous over the minds of the people that it took some very strong measures to break even some people loose from that hold. Atheistic materialism was one such strong tool. It was far from philosophically worked out; it was enough to give a simple naive-realist-naturalistic framework as an alternative to the equally simplistic theist-creationist framework that prevailed. Everything could be explained in terms of "nature," of which "matter in motion" was the only content.

Others used softer tools, like a mild deism which would be socially respectable in that it gave its homage to God in the first sentence and then promptly forgot all about His relevance to reality. But the effect was the same. Darwin's theory of evolution came in very handy for Deists and Atheists alike, for it was supposed to explain how life came out of matter and how every separate species evolved out of that single blob of life. Darwin's *Origin of the Species* in fact explained nothing of the kind. It did not even explain how the species originated, but something like Darwin's theory of evolution by "natural selection" and "survival of the fittest" was the crying need of the time, and it was thought quite unwise to be so nit-picking about its theoretical difficulties, which only now find some recognition among scientists.

Philosophically speaking, today neither deism nor theism, neither atheism nor materialism, can be acknowledged to have a sound theoretical basis. Academic philosophy prefers the Ostrich Approach and fights shy of the question itself. This may be another indication that the accepted ideas of science and philosophy at any time owe much more than we recognize to needs of the hour strongly enough felt. We need to take a quick look at the German development that took this materialism a step further before it collapsed in our own century with the advent of quantum physics and relativity.

A German Voltaire

Voltaire (1694–1778) in France was an iconoclast, but his counterpart in Germany two generations later, David Friedrich Strauss (1808–1874), was more devastating in the damage he did to religion, particularly to the Protestant religion. In France, the Roman Catholic church regarded the *philosophes* and the reformers as enemies of God, and gave battle to them with all the power at its disposal. In German Protestantism, this was an attack from inside. Unlike his contemporary Ludwig Feuerbach (1804–1872) who claimed no allegiance to Christianity, Strauss was writing as a faithful Hegelian and a Christian. Hegelianism was the ideology of monarchianism, and monarchs were regarded by Hegelians as the upholders of religion. Heine was an antimonarchian, and therefore wanted to attack religion, the fortress of monarchianism.

When Strauss's *The Life of Jesus* appeared in Tuebingen in 1835, shock waves spread through post-Hegelian (Hegel had died in 1831) German society, where intellectuals were divided into three camps: right-wing Hegelians, left-wing Hegelians, and anti-Hegelians. Strauss's book took the miraculous and supernatural out of the biblical narratives and presented a credible, human Jesus of Nazareth. The way for this had already been prepared by Hegel's contemporary Friedrich Schleiermacher (1768–1834) who, by making religious feeling or experience the foundation of Christianity, had dispensed with the need for Christian orthodoxy and revelation, and had thus laid the foundations of modern Liberal Protestantism. Hegel, on the other hand, had sought to establish the "absoluteness of Christianity" on a strictly philosophical basis. The issue between the Hegelian right and the Hegelian left (to which Feuerbach belonged) centered around the question of religion and the need of a monarchical state. The two issues were of course interconnected, and the right-wing defenders of religion were also the defenders of the monarchical state.

Within the Hegelian framework of regarding religion as a particular expression of the absolute truth of philosophy, Strauss raised the issue whether the miracle stories and the supernatural elements were integral parts of the absolute universal truth. Obviously they were not, and therefore there was no need to keep them in the religious part either. In fact, insofar as faith was absolute knowledge, the nonessential miraculous and supernatural could not be held by the intelligent Christian.

Both Schleiermacher and Strauss were trying to "save" religion by divesting it of those elements that the rationalistic critics in France and elsewhere were laughing at or attacking. In this sense they were different from Voltaire or the other French *philosophes*, who along with Heine, wanted to destroy or neutralize the power of religion, in order to bring about freedom and emancipation. They were more on the positivist road, which the German Hegelians did not want to follow. Strauss used, at least at this early stage of the attack (he was only twenty-six), no laughter or mockery like Voltaire. His attack was from inside—inside both Hegelianism and Protestant Christianity, and a philosophically respectable attack, especially within the Hegelian framework that so few critical New Testament scholars of the twentieth century fully comprehend. The later Strauss, both in his reply to his right-wing Hegelian critics (*In Defense of my Life of Jesus Against the Hegelians*[49]) and in his more systematic work on *The Old and The New Faith*,[50] had already mastered the Voltairian technique of mockery and laughter as a major instrument of criticism.

Very subtly, and perhaps unintentionally, Strauss, remaining a Hegelian and a Protestant Christian, made the basic transition from Hegelian idealism to a sophisticated theological materialism which became the father of much of modern secular and liberal theological thought. But since he retained his claim to be a Christian, the Hegelian left to which Feuerbach belonged and out of which Marx and Engels came refused to accept Strauss into their ranks, though he very much belonged there. As he wails in the concluding words of his *In Defense:*

> . . . the truth of the gospel history is not to be liberated by philosophy, either as a whole or in part, but only by the investigation of the same by historical critique. Thus I would have passed over to the Left Wing of the Hegelian School, if this school had not advanced to exclude me completely from its ranks and to throw me into other intellectual camps—of course, only to catch me when, just like a ball, I bounced back again.[51]

Kant and The Critical Philosophy

In nineteenth-century Germany, to leave the Hegelian camp was to join the Kantian camp of critical philosophy. That philosophy remains powerful to this day, even if systematic and fundamental philosophical reflection has today become such a rarity. Critical philosophy is the foundation of modern liberalism, though not of Marxism, which prefers the Hegelian platform to the Kantian. The rise of critical philosophy is itself a saga that needs lengthy exposition. We can mark the stages of that process by looking at the midcentury transformations of European thought in the last four centuries, as D'Alembert pointed out in his *Elements of Philosophy*.[52]

The Second European Renaissance (the first is, of course, the Carolingian Renaissance in the ninth century) began around the middle of the fifteenth century; at the middle of the sixteenth, the Protestant Reformation is triumphant; by the middle of the seventeenth, Cartesian dualism takes over, rocking the foundations of traditional European thought; the middle of the eighteenth saw the burgeoning of the European Enlightenment; and that is as far as D'Alembert could go since he lived in the middle of the eighteenth century. The characteristic of the eighteenth century was stated by D'Alembert in the following words:

> Our century is called, accordingly, the century of philosophy par excellence. . . The true system of the world has been recognised, developed and perfected. . . everything has been discussed and analysed.[53]

Citing D'Alembert, Ernst Cassirer, the brilliant twentieth-century Neo-Kantian student of the eighteenth-century Enlightenment, goes on to make that point more explicit:

> When the eighteenth century wants to characterise this power in a single word, it calls it 'reason.' 'Reason' becomes the unifying and central power of this century, expressing all that it longs and strives for, and all that it achieves. . . The eighteenth century is imbued with a belief in the unity and immutability of reason. Reason is the same for all thinking subjects, all nations, all epochs, and all cultures.[54]

Cassirer admits that today the concepts of reason and rationalism are no longer so simple to comprehend, especially since the middle of the nineteenth century saw history as a conditioning factor on reason. Reason itself is part of the evolutionary process and cannot be understood apart from it, in itself. Fichte certainly thought that there was only one philosophy, the one objectively given by reason. The Germans particularly set out boldly to build the system, with laborious and painstaking care, like a modern surgeon working on the inside of a human body. Kant's and Hegel's are the two systems that have had most impact on European thought, though neither Fichte and Schelling, nor Spinoza and Leibniz earlier, are to be excluded.

The Sensationalism of the French *philosophes* reiterating the ancient Greek claim that the senses are the source of all knowledge was called in question by the Scot David Hume (1711–1776), who had spent considerable time in France with the *philosophes*. Sensations are physical events experienced by the human body through the senses, but the memory of a sense-experience is not the same kind of event. When experience moves from sensation to knowledge, a transition has already taken place, and one cannot be as immediately certain of that knowledge as one could be of the sense-experience when one is actually experiencing it. Hume argued that the farther you go away from the immediate experience, the less the certainty of your knowledge. For Hume, the sense-experience and knowing are two stages in the process of perception; the transition from the first to the second stage takes away the immediacy and therefore reduces certainty. All mental concepts, according to Hume, thus lack certainty.

It was this situation that Immanuel Kant (1724–1804) found intolerable, for it deprives all knowledge of validity, if sense-experience is the only certainty we can have. Kant merged the two stages of perception into one. There is no pure sense-experience without the impact of the mind. Sense-experience and mental form-giving are woven together like warp and woof to form the concept. Every concept bears the imprint of the structure of the mind, for it is only in that mould that concepts can be formed at all. Kant then goes on to describe the universal category structure of a universal human mind, whose proper application would yield unerring knowledge. To test the validity of any knowledge it is only necessary to trace the process by which that knowledge was acquired, making sure that there were no errors in the application of "pure reason."

Hegel raised the critical question as to whether Kant's knowledge of the category structure of the mind came from the same process of pure reason that Kant prescribes for all knowledge. This is of course a perennial question: If the way we know (epistemology) can be known, would it be known by any way other than itself? What could be the norm for epistemology other than epistemology itself? Alas, norms for knowledge cannot be verified by those same norms.

Despite this perennial problem, Kant set out valiantly to divide the human faculties into three distinct compartments: pure reason (cognitive intellect), practical reason (moral volition) and aesthetic judgment (assessment of taste). Kant, unlike the naturalists, Sensationalists, and Materialists, boldly admits that there are limits to reason. The thing-in-itself cannot be known; knowledge without the imprint of our mental structure is a priori impossible. Pure reason which can know objects cannot make ethical or aesthetic judgments; there are special departments in the mind for these. In these two latter departments the rules are different, but the kind of certainty for which many were groping was just not possible. It is not by Pure Reason that one can get at the validity of the categorical (i.e. unconditioned) imperative, but it is a decision of practical reason to so act that your action can also be willed as a universal law for all human beings. This was probably the new philosophical form of Rousseau's 'Social Contract', the fictitious idea (a modern myth like the Christian myth of the Fall of Man) that society has as its base a contract among its individual members.

The Romantic Reaction against the Rationalism of the Enlightenment

Kant himself was a product of the dialectic between Enlightenment rationalism and the Romantic movement's stress on feeling. No poet can be a pure rationalist: Kant, then, was not much of a poet. Poetry demands a different kind of imagination and creativity, both taboos in strict rationalism, and culture is more a creation of imagination and creativity than of pure reason, which can only know, but not create. The conflict between dry reason on the one hand and fertile, imaginative, creative, feeling on the other, was already present among the *philosophes,* but they were unable to resolve the contradiction between them. Diderot, for example, could reach dry, rational conclusions in his *La physiologie* and *L'entretien,* that the world is a machine, that man is an accident, that vice and virtue were mere words without meaning. But he did have doubts about his own conclusions which he expressed in his literary masterpiece, *Le neveu de Rameau;* there the conflict between the mind and the heart is faithfully posed, but left without an answer.

Romanticism found Kant's rational morality dry, as uninspiring as it is impractical. Humanity is essentially good, and only reason's extremely rational, calculating and unfeeling attitude towards reality makes human beings so alienated and unhappy. The Romantic reaction was in a sense a revolt against the coldness of extreme rationalism and a call to exercise the human power of imagination and intuition, not only in the appreciation of beauty, but also in experiencing one's basic oneness with the nature that reason seeks to objectify. It is a revolt that continues to this day in the counterculture syndrome, in rock and other modern forms of gut music, in the anti-intellectualism of the Right, but also in the writings of thoughtful people like Rudolf Steiner and Theodore Roszak, and before them Soren Kierkegaard and Feodor Dostoievsky, not to mention Jean-Jacques Rousseau, William James, and Franz Kafka.

Italian Illuminismo in a Class by Itself

The specificity of the Italian Enlightenment (*Illuminismo*) comes from the fact that the main carriers of the Enlightenment were Roman

Catholic priests, as the more educated among the people. Naples led the way, with the young priest Antonio Genovesi fighting for academic freedom and the unification of Italy mainly in order that it could be economically strong. Gianbattista Vico's *La Scienza Nuova* had been published in 1725, though hardly noticed by contemporaries. A much greater impact was made by Filangieri's *La Scienza della Legislazione* (ca. 1785). Even Benjamin Franklin in America took notice of it.

Italian *illuminismo* was rational, but not necessarily antireligious, hard-nosed about the realities of this world, but still mystical in its basic attitude. Filangieri's book, written two centuries ago, opens with a passage which to us is strikingly contemporary:

> What are the only aims of European governments these days? Armaments, artillery, well-trained troops. Every single discussion in the cabinets is directed to one problem alone: What is the best means of killing most men in the shortest possible time?[55]

As Owen Chadwick says in his illuminating article on the Italian Enlightenment, compassion for the suffering of the people was more evident in Italy than elsewhere in Europe. One reason could be the large number of priests and ex-priests involved in the Enlightenment. The other reason may be that it was not the isolated academic professor who gave leadership, but ordinary people meeting, as in Scotland, in cafes and bistros to discuss ideas. *Il Caffe* (*The Cafe*) played a major role in the spread of *Illuminismo,* and in Milan, then under Austrian rule, the Verri brothers started a somewhat subversive journal by the name *Il Caffe.* It did not last beyond a couple of years, but while it did it became a major vehicle for the spread of Enlightenment ideas among the common people. Cesari Beccaria wrote a compassionate work on the ill-treatment of inmates in Italian prisons—*Dei Delitti e delle Pena or On Crime and Punishment.* The book became a bestseller and a popular pamphlet for social reform. Voltaire in France and Jeremy Bentham in Britain took up this work and popularized it in their own countries. Did Dostoievsky get his novel title from this source?

The Italians had for centuries a religious tradition of Enlightenment, called precisely *Illuminismo.* It had its origins in the Spanish movement of *Alumbrado* (in Spanish, *The Enlightened*). This was an anticlerical, antiauthority movement of Spanish Christians, claiming direct illumination from the Holy Spirit. It was a positive response to the new knowledge spreading in Europe, Averroist in tone, owing much to Islamic mysticism. It affected all classes of people, and was particularly strong in the dioceses of Cadiz and Seville. The new movement taught that it was not necessary to attend mass or obey the traditional clergy. It taught a new mysticism of the recollection of God's presence in mental prayer, without the use of images and rosaries which characterised Spanish official piety at that time. There seems to have also been some influence from the Mt. Athos tradition of Hesychasm, which the official Western church was fighting as heretical.

The *Alumbrado* movement was brutally suppressed by the Spanish Inquisition. That condemnation in 1623 gives us the best sources for the study of the movement. It had affinities with the Zen Buddhism and Chan Buddhism already prevailing in Japan and China, though we do not know of any direct contacts. By simply recollecting in mental prayer the presence of God, without discursive reflection or any mental images, the soul was to rise in the ecstasy of nonthought to behold the Divine Essence as Light.

The Spanish movement spread wherever there was protest and resentment against the apalling abuses of papal power and the corruption prevailing amongst the official Roman Catholic clergy. In the Italian states the *Alumbrado* movement took new forms with the name *Illuminismo.* It became associated with Freemasonry as well, which was the rising parachurch movement in Europe. Many of the Italian clergy became followers, either openly or in secret, of this vital movement. In Latin countries, the movement of *illuminismo* and the eighteenth-century spread of European Enlightenment were sometimes indistinguishable from each other since *Illuminismo* was also the word for Enlightenment. The movement took care not to break away from the official church, which in Italy with its poor church organization was easier than in Spain.

Ferdinando Galiani was a leading Illuminist, well versed in the new thought of the European Enlightenment. He remained a pious Catholic priest, a monsignore and a mitred abbot to the end. Karl Marx studied his writings with respect and interest. In fact, it seems Galiani was the only Italian author that Marx studied seriously.[57]

The Italian movement of *Illuminismo* deserves further study as an attempt on the part of European spirituality to keep the 'mystical' and the social together. Though as a movement it died out, it has left some permanent marks on the Italian soul even to this day.

Elsewhere in Europe

In Britain, the Scots led the movement of Enlightenment. Some would even claim that they were the pioneers. In Scotland, too, the pub or the coffeehouse was the agent to spread the ideas of the

Enlightenment, which was closely connected with the idea of Scotland's independence from England. Adam Smith and David Hume already were in debt to these coffeehouse conversations for many of their ideas. Voltaire lived in England from 1726 to 1729, and Montesquieu visited that country from 1729 to 1731. The English took in many of the ideas of the Enlightenment and expressed them through the Methodist and other reform movements in the Anglican Church. The growth of Congregationalism and Presbyterianism can also be related to Enlightenment ideas. Unlike in France, there was no direct confrontation between the growing scientific temperament and the established church. Many of Britain's eminent scientists were also loyal members of the churches.

For our modest purposes here, it is necessary only to emphasize the wide variety that existed in the various regions and countries in Europe in developing the ideas and energy of the one European Enlightenment.

The American Enlightenment

Henry F. May, in his *The Enlightenment in America,* claims that his book is "not about the Enlightenment and Religion, but about the Enlightenment *as* religion."[58] For him "the Enlightenment consists of all those who believe two propositions: first, that the present age is more enlightened than the past; and second, that we understand nature and man best through the use of our natural faculties."[59] He attaches some importance to developments in Protestant Christianity—the grace of the "New Light" of Wesleyan Revivalism, for example. There was rivalry, of course, between the two contending giants, Protestantism and the Enlightenment, but many Protestant thinkers had imbibed the first of the two propositions, as well as a qualified acceptance of the latter, as compatible with their religious convictions. May distinguishes among four different kinds of Enlightenment: the Moderate Enlightenment of a George Washington, a Rev. William Smith, or a James Madison; the Skeptical Enlightenment of Benjamin Franklin, Thomas Paine, and Thomas Jefferson; the Revolutionary Enlightenment "with its sweeping prophecies of a Secular Millennium," to which group Jefferson and Paine also belonged; and finally the Didactic Enlightenment of the colleges and universities.

Thomas Jefferson ascribed the origin of his principles to Bacon, Newton, and Locke. He accepted Diderot's dictum that "Beauty is founded on the eternal, original, sovereign and essential rules of order, proportion, relation and harmony." Thomas Paine, the English polemicist, who went to America for thirteen years from 1774 to 1787, published his *Rights of Man* in 1791. During his stay in America, where he helped his friend Thomas Jefferson draft the American Declaration of Independence in July 1776, he served as the secretary of the Congressional Committee on Foreign Affairs. His pamphlet entitled *Common Sense* (1776) had a great influence on Jefferson and on American history. It was a defense of republicanism as opposed to monarchy. His later *The Rights of Man* was a scathing response to Edmund Burke's denunciatory *Reflections on the Revolution in France* (1790).

Paine was as uncritical in his eulogising of the Declaration of the Rights of Man, made by the National Assembly of the New Republic of France in 1789, as Burke was uncritical in denouncing the French Revolution. If Burke was an undiscerning advocate of the status quo in Britain, Paine was unduly relying on a document with noble ideas that were soon to be belied by the historical reality of the Jacobin tyranny of the French Committee on Public Safety, and even more by the reign of Napoleon Bonaparte. It is one thing to put noble ideas into a declaration; it seems more difficult to embody these ideas in a political economy. This is a principle we should always keep in mind when we discuss questions like human rights.

The French Declaration on the Rights of Man had twenty-seven articles. According to Paine, the first three were of the essence:

1. Men (*sic*) are born, and always continue, free and equal in respect of their rights. Civil distinction, therefore, can be founded only on public utility.
2. The end of all political associations is the preservation of the natural and imprescriptible rights of man; and these rights are Liberty, Property, Security, and Resistance of Oppression.
3. The Nation is essentially the source of all sovereignty; nor can any individual, or any body of men, be entitled to any authority which is not expressly derived from it.

In Paine's view,

> the first three articles are the basis of Liberty, as well individual as national; nor can any country be called free whose Government does not take its beginning from the principles they contain, and continue to preserve them pure; and the whole of the Declaration of Rights is of more value to the world, and will do more good, than all the laws and statutes that have yet been promulgated.[60]

The European Enlightenment could not, in the forms and institutions developed in Europe, be embodied in America. It was antitraditional and antiauthoritarian even before the European Enlightenment. What Europe lacked and America supplied were democracy and pragmatism. May's four different aspects of the Enlightenment were all fundamentally transformed in the melting pot of America's peculiar cultural development.

* * * *

We will examine the phenomenon in more detail in the following chapters, but here we need to make one more important observation.

That observation has to do with the astounding similarity this central conception of the European Enlightenment (except for the bourgeois-human distinction) shares with the teaching of the Buddha in India some two-thousand-three-hundred years earlier. Buddha taught his disciples to refuse to accept anything because someone else told you so. Buddha was reacting against the constricting authority of the Hindu scriptures, of the Brahmins, and of any kind of *guru* whatsoever. He wanted the seeker to find out things for oneself and not to depend on authority. And yet it needs to be observed that the two repudiations of authority have had vastly different historical consequences, and have behind them two diametrically opposed conceptions of what is meant by *Enlightenment* which is a classical Buddhist word, after all. We shall deal with the substance of the Buddhist Enlightenment later on. Here we need to point out only that *Buddha* literally means the 'Enlightened One' in Sanskrit, and is not a proper name. Gautama Buddha means Gautama the Enlightened One, just as Jesus Christ means Jesus the Messiah. Buddhism, as we shall see later, is all about Enlightenment, though of a different kind from the one developed in Europe two-thousand-three-hundred years later. The similarity in principle, namely that of repudiation of the authority of prevailing or traditional religions, is however quite striking.

Neither shall we attempt here to give some reasons for the wide divergence in consequences between the two great historical repudiations of authority, the European and the Indian. We shall reserve that also to a later chapter, after we have dealt with the ideas and aspects of the European Enlightenment.

Chapter Four

EUROPE: ADVENTURE AND EXPANSION

Europe "from the Urals to the Atlantic" may be a geographical entity, though the mountain ranges of the Soviet Union are no longer the decisive dividing line they once may have been. Certainly such a Europe never existed in the past as a political entity. Even as a cultural entity, her claims to a separate identity can be questioned. Europe remains largely an idea in the minds of people. Europe as such has no common history, any more than Asia or Africa or the world as a whole has. Europe has in fact no long-term economic interests that unite her, apart from the interests of the whole of humanity, though many present-day Europeans seem to act under the illusion or delusion that she has a separate common identity and common interests.

Since the European Enlightenment seems, in origin at least, a basically European phenomenon, we need to understand that European identity, if such exists. Europe has colonized the Americas and Australasia as well as South Africa and other regions of the world, including Siberia and the Far Eastern republic of the Soviet Union. When we speak of Europe we cannot legitimately exclude these European colonies of the last half millennium. In fact, that expansion into the world seems part of Europe's personality. And when we say Europe we include the Slavs, though many Europeans are still reluctant to do so.

Europe: Myth and History

One thing the process of secularization has managed to obliterate from our minds is the fact that myth is an essential part of the less conscious levels of our awareness. The most secularized people do not escape the effects of myth in their deeper consciousness, because myth is the collective history of a community's collective soul, held in symbols, narratives and archetypes. For "modern" humanity, critical rationality may operate at the top levels of our consciousness, but underneath are mythical operators which deflect that critical rationality, and even shape it.

Europe has many myths that give expression to her collective consciousness, like the *Illiad* of Homer in which Ulysses symbolizes Europe and becomes a hero in his war against the Trojans. Troy, in the Near East, represents the non-European peoples. Helen, symbol of virtue and beauty, has to be captured to save the honor of the West from the Asian barbarians who have abducted her. The job is done, but instead of settling down to celebrate the victory in peace and happiness with Penelope at home in Ithaca, Ulysses prefers to continue on the path of adventure and expansion, preferring the voyage to the destination; piloting the ship of life between the twin perils of Scylla and Charybdis yields what Europe most wants, not peace and happiness, but the excitement of adventure. The Swiss professor Denis de Rougemont, a very self-consciously European savant, gives us this quite plausible interpretation of the Ulysses myth and Europe's Odyssey into "adventure and expansion" in his *The Meaning of Europe*,[61] the text of four lectures given at the University of Geneva in 1962.

Equally important is the myth of Europa from which Europe seems to take her name. The mythical Europa was the daughter of Agenor, King of Tyre (modern Syria). The Greek god Zeus, abducts the Syrian princess, who is to become the mother of Europe. Agenor sends his sons in search of his daughter. These sons founded cities on the north and south coasts of the Mediterranean, as well as in the Greek islands and in the interior of present-day Greece. But they could not find their sister. Cadmus, the most famous of the brothers, went to Delphi to question Pythia, the Oracle there.

> Cadmus: Where is Europa?
>
> Pythia: You will not find her. Your task is to follow a cow, driving her on before you without respite, until she falls down exhausted. On that spot build a city.

So Cadmus did, according to the myth, follow the cow, traveling to Thebes in Upper Egypt, where the cow collapsed and there Cadmus founded another city.[62]

Whatever else the myths may signify, they refer to the deep awareness of the Greek people that their civilization came from Asia, something modern scholars of Europe and of Greece in particular often deny with great vehemence. The whole Mediterranean civilization, including that of Egypt, is here seen to have been of West Asian origin rather than autochthonous. We do not, however, need to draw conclusions about history from what are, after all, "mere"(!) myths.

Euripides, in *The Bacchae,* makes the god Dionysus (son of Zeus) come from Asia to bring justice to the Greeks. Michael Cacoyannis, in his introduction to his new translation of the classical Greek play, suggests that Euripides' message was "about the arrival of new religions from the East to sweep away the old."[63] The myths of Europe always hark back to Asia as the source of wisdom, though many Greeks regarded the Asians as "Barbarians."

The "adventure and expansion" image of Europe is, however, confirmed by history. We can think of four great historical expansions, all of them impressively adventurous, that have characterized European civilization throughout the history of the last two-thousand-three-hundred years:

1. Alexander's conquest of the Persian Empire in the 4th century B.C.
2. The Crusades of 1095–1270 A.D.
3. The trade expeditions of the Venetians and other Europeans who followed in their wake
4. The plundering, trading, and later empire-building advances of Spain, Portugal, the Netherlands, Britain, and France into the whole world, an expansion continuing to this day in the form of neocolonialism and Transnational Corporations.

Yes, Europe was adventurously expanding all through its history and Prof. de Rougemont is right in characterizing Europe's personality as one of "adventure and expansion." Europe's is an outgoing personality, not afraid of the strange, not visibly afraid of the unknown, with a slightly exaggerated self-confidence that manages successfully to repress most subconscious fears. Europe has already fulfilled a historic mission—that of developing not only modern science and the technology based on it, but also a secular liberal-humanistic civilization with the aid of which science and technology has managed to put every nation into effective contact with all others.

De Rougemont reveals the limits of his knowledge when he claims that Europe is the "creator of the world" and that it was in Europe that the idea of the human race was born. Yet there are some of his dicta that deserve our attention. He says, for example, that while Europeans have held sway in all other continents, no non-

European power has ever ruled Europe. Can any other continent make such a claim? (Never mind the fact that Asian and African Muslims ruled Spain and the Balkans for a long time!). He is also correct in claiming that Europe has produced a civilization that is now being imitated by the whole world, while the converse has never happened (it is quibbling to say that Europe is now imitating America in so many respects). In that sense, he is right in saying that the phenomenon of Europe is without precedent or parallel in history:

> . . . it is Europe which made the world, in the sense that she discovered it, explored it, awakened it and set it on the road to unity by creating first of all its network of exchanges and centres of production and then the first world-wide institutions.[64]

It is possible of course to take issue with that judgment. We wish only to state the converse of the theorem: it is just as true to say that the world created Europe. De Rougemont himself admits that the Mediterranean peoples came from West or Central Asia. An impartial observer would also have to agree that the two great forces that made Europe what it is came from Asia: Europe's wealth and Europe's religion. The second seems more obvious than the first. We should say a word about both, to illustrate rather than describe, what has been a centuries-long process.

Wealth Flow into Europe

Take Alexander's conquest of Persia. Alexander seized from Babylon, Susa, and Persepolis as conqueror's booty the neat sum of 180,000 talents, in the fourth century B.C. One can see how enormous this wealth was by the standards of that time, when we are told that at that time the total annual revenue of Alexander's Macedonia was one-thousand talents! Athens then had an annual revenue of four-hundred talents.[65] In one shot Europe had taken from Asia one-hundred-eighty times the annual revenue of Macedonia or four-hundred-fifty times the annual revenue of Athens!

In each of the four stages of Europe's expansion into the world the process has continued. Even the crusades, supposedly religious in motivation, were largely raiding parties for the plunder of the wealth of Byzantium and West Asia, as well as of Egypt.

Plunder and piracy were the source of fifteenth-century Europe's wealth, robbing ships on the high seas or plundering gold and silver from the "New World." Vasco da Gama came to India for the first time in 1498, and went back to Lisbon with ten large ships laden with enormous wealth, gained not as much by trade as by pure plunder. On his third expedition to India in 1504, he brought with him thirteen of the largest ships ever built by Portugal, and went back in 1506 to load his ships with spices and rubies, pearls and embroidery of the finest kind that Europe had ever seen. Every year scores of such ships carried the wealth of Asia into Europe. Albuquerque, the leader of the fourth Portuguese expedition to the East, carried back with him wealth beyond description:

> castles of woodwork, ornamented with brocades, . . . very rich palanquins for his personal use, all plated with gold and large quantities of jewellery and precious stones . . . a table with its feet all overlaid with plates of gold.[66]

We need not belabor this point. It is too embarrassing. I shall satisfy myself at this point by citing two recent Western writers on this subject:

> From the time of classical antiquity, Europe had been enriched spiritually and materially by Asia. Under Darius, the Persians had created the first world empire. The migration of Jews from their main areas of settlement in Palestine, Asia Minor, Babylonia, and Egypt had an enormous impact on European life. In Europe's commercial revolution their contribution was incalculable. The Arab civilization was at full bloom when Europe was in its Dark Ages. Even as late as the fifteenth century, western and eastern cartographers, while they were unaware of each other's maps, were agreed that the center of the earth and human activity was either in Palestine or China. All the sixteenth-century empires were Asian. At that time the Ottoman Turks held much of south-west Asia, the north African plains, and part of the Balkans. In Persia the Muslim Safavid Empire (1501–1722) ruled. In northern India the stage was set for the Mogul conquest. In China the Ming Dynasty (1368–1644) had driven out the Mongols (1260–1368) and had itself expanded into Outer Mongolia and south-east Asia. Mongol, Arab and Turk had all been feared by the West. Any one of these empires, whether measured in terms of area, numbers, or organisation, was superior to western Christendom. The population of Ming China in the 1400s (about 100 million) was equal to that of the whole of Europe. In the sixteenth century Europe had few cities to compare with the size of Kyoto in Japan or

Canton in China. As for wealth, all riches flowed from the East.[67]

A highly competent modern economist, Prof. Joan Robinson, put it this way:

> Few would deny that the extension of capitalism into new territories was the mainspring of . . . the "vast secular boom" of the last two hundred years.[68]

The fact of the matter is deeper than what even Joan Robinson states. There would be no such Europe as we have today without the inflow of the vast wealth of Asia and Africa and the New World. Hence our insistence that if it is true that Europe created the world, it is even more true that the world created Europe.

Europe's Cultural Debt

Europe's personality is one of adventure and expansion serving the interests of greed and domination, one could say without malice. It is not just wealth that Europe has taken from the rest of the world. In culture and ideas too she owes a large debt, a debt that need not be repaid, but would make things easier (and more honest) if openly acknowledged. Again we can only illustrate, not catalogue.

What Greece and Rome learned from West Asia in the pre-Christian centuries is seldom acknowledged in the history textbooks. Sumeria and Accadia, Babylon and Egypt had generously shared their engineering, mathematics, astronomy, and agriculture with Europe. The diaspora Jews as well as the conquered Jews of the three centuries before Christ were a great civilizing influence on the Europeans.

Alexander[69] learned the art of empire-building from the Persians. A comprehensive study has yet to be made of what the Greek and Macedonian colonies that Alexander established wherever he went contributed to the culture of Europe. Callisthenes, who accompanied Alexander on his Babylonian campaign, picked up Chaldean-Babylonian astronomy and brought it back to Europe in the fourth century B.C. Callisthenes became the source-spring of a great astronomical and mathematical tradition that reached Ptolemy, the Egyptian astronomer (100–178 A.D.) through Hipparchus (ca. 130 B.C.). Ptolemy became the foundation for all European mathematics and astronomy, until Copernicus and Kepler came along.[70]

In fact, one of Alexander's great (though unintended) contributions to Europe was the tearing down of the "Persian Curtain" that isolated Europe from the rest of the world. One result was a widespread Greek presence in parts of Central Asia and North India, and the generation in these colonies of a cosmopolitan culture. The ancient University of Taxila or Takshasila became a center of learning from which Asians and Europeans drank freely of the wisdom of India and Greece, Babylon and Persia. Menander, the Greek invader, became a Buddhist, and ruled a vast empire in India from 166 to 145 B.C. with his capital at Sialkot. During his time, Buddhist spirituality spread in Europe.

Long before that, in the time of Aśōka, the Emperor of India (295–232 B.C.), Buddhist monks began spreading the message of the Buddha (the Enlightened One) to all parts of the world including Europe, since the road had been opened up by Alexander and his successors. Again, the comprehensive study of the impact of this Buddhist expansion on European and Middle Eastern cultures needs to be undertaken, but it is not too wild a conjecture to think that the Jewish monastic communities of Qumran in the first century B.C. came under their influence. Brahmins and Buddhists were in Alexandria at least by the first century A.D., and the links if any between Christian and Jewish monasticism on the one hand and Buddhist monasticism as a pioneer movement on the other, need to be further explored. It is quite clear from the Rock Edicts of Aśōka that in the third century B.C. another kind of expansion had consciously begun, from India, to send medicinal herbs and treatment for both humans and animals to all parts of the known world, including the Greek countries (Rock Edict II).[71]

Aśōka's triumph was not in his political empire-building, but in *Dharmavijaya,* the triumph of virtue; he transmitted this concept to lands three-thousand miles away, and specifically mentions the five kings with whom he was in contact: Antiochus II of Syria (261–246 B.C.), Ptolemy Philadelphos of Egypt (285–247 B.C.), Antigonos Gonatas of Macedonia (278–239 B.C.), Magas of Cyrene or Libya (300–258 B.C.), and Alexander of Epirus (ca. 272–258 B.C.). In his Rock Edict XIII he says that he has communicated the Dharma to these five kings and their peoples, naming the kings as Antiyoka, Turamaya, Antikini, Maka, and Alikasudara.

It is quite unnecessary to point out the obvious fact that the major civilizing agent in European cultural history has been Christianity, an Asian religion. It is true that Europe managed to give it forms and shapes radically different from the original. But without the Christian Bible and the writings of the Asian Christian Fathers (very few of the Eastern Fathers were Greek, though they wrote in Greek, just as the present writer writes in English but is not English) the culture of Europe could not have taken the shape it did. Much of Milan and southern Europe were Christianized by Asian missionaries like John Cassian and Ireneus of Lyons. Ireland and parts of Switzerland were probably Christianized by Egyptian (Coptic) monks.

Enough has been said to show that civilization in Europe was a gift of the world, as most other civilizations were. Europe is adventure and expansion. Europe also means great and deliberate unwillingness to acknowledge her cultural debts in order to conserve the snobbish illusion of her being entirely self-made. We have not mentioned here the debts in the field of philosophy with which we shall deal briefly in a later chapter.

These personality traits of Europe played a significant role in the European Enlightenment. Hence the relevance of these remarks.

It is not inconceivable that Europe may change her personality and become modest once again. That calls for greater self-confidence in her own true identity, which has so many noble elements in it. But so long as Europe's self-identity remains bloated and untrue, it will have to continue to be a pest for the rest of the world. If, on the other hand, it rises out if its parochialism and greed for possession and domination, it has the resources to make a decisive contribution to the emergence of new civilizations, both on its own continent and elsewhere in the world.

Unfortunately, however, Europe seems still preoccupied with regaining her ancient glory vis-à-vis competitors like America and Japan, and with unity for the sake of economic power. That could very well change, particularly if something happens to the world economic system that forces people to rethink their priorities.

The characterization of Europe as "Adventure and Expansion" comes from the Swiss professor Denis de Rougemont. He may be wrong on several points, but in this characterization of Europe's personality, he has opened up many new vistas.

Eighteenth Century and After

How can we characterize the Europe of the eighteenth and nineteenth centuries that gave birth to the European Enlightenment? What interests were dominant, in order to lead up to this kind of Enlightenment? What forces were at play, both in the European psyche and in European societies?

The eighteenth is of course the century of the French Revolution (1789). Not long ago we celebrated its bicentennial, with much less fanfare than most people anticipated. There lurks somewhere a sneaking suspicion that the revolution which proclaimed "*liberté, égalité, fraternité*" (freedom, equality and brotherhood) two centuries ago turned out to be not quite what it was trumped up to be.

In the same year, on the fourth of March, George Washington was inaugurated the first President of the United States of America, bringing to fruition the Declaration of Independence approved by the American Congress on the fourth of July 1776. It was more than a declaration of independence from the British colonial masters: it was the first official ideological statement justifying modern democracy. George III of England (not Britain as a nation) was depicted as the tyrant against whom the people of the British colonies in America revolted. Sovereignty was in the people, and the government, chosen by the people, was meant to secure for the people the exercise of certain rights. For the first time a major state based wholly on a contractual theory and the theory of people's sovereignty arose—a theory that was to serve as a model for many nations around the globe.

There is no doubt that something momentous had happened, not only to Europe and America, but to the whole world. A contemporary Western writer puts it thus:

> Somewhere between 1775 and 1847, the fate of the world was settled by the West. India passed almost completely under British rule. The door to China was kicked open and her long march into revolution began. A new nation and a future super-power came into existence which spread across the North American continent and established its first footholds on the Pacific coast. Meanwhile, in the European heartland of Western civilization there was a great political revolution and the first experience of what industrial society might be, two changes which in the next age, when the world domination of Western civilization was completed, would transform the lives of most of the inhabitants of the globe.[72]

It would be foolish to try to explain the French and the American Revolutions of the last part of the eighteenth century in terms of some strictly definable causes. Causality does not function in history that way. But some features of eighteenth-century Europe will help us understand the phenomenon of the Enlightenment, closely connected with these two epoch-making revolutions in the West.

Population

Europe at the beginning of the eighteenth century was still rather sparsely populated. Since the Black Death had taken its toll on one third of the population of Europe in the fourteenth century, the growth rate was rather meagre, largely due to wars, poverty, ignorance, and ill health, large-scale starvation, and frequent epidemics. Most experts estimate the growth rate as less than one-half of one percent per annum.[73] Exact figures are hard to come by, since the institution of a census of individual persons did not then exist. The very large number of celibate priests partly accounted for the low growth rate. There was also the factor that marriage for the male was delayed till he could earn a living and feed his family.

As money came in from outside of Europe and jobs increased, people could marry earlier. As knowledge spread, people were able to cope better with disease. Affluence actually brought about an increase in population rather than a decrease as modern theories demand. In Britain, Prussia, and the Scandinavian countries there was a spurt in population growth as the standard of living began going up. But in southern Europe malaria and smallpox were still taking their toll and left large chunks of territory unpeopled.

London, the largest city of Europe, had about one million people. Paris had about half a million. The whole of Europe, by 1800, had about 187 million, more than ninety per cent rural; while there were only a score of cities with more than twenty-thousand, small towns were growing, the bourgeoisie or city-dwellers becoming more ubiquitous.

Of course, affluence was not the only factor controlling population growth. Around the 1700s, northern Europe's climate underwent a welcome change, average temperatures rising, as the "little ice age" (1300–1700) receded. Epidemics became less frequent in the north, after the huge smallpox wave in 1725–29 in Britain; while in Spain malaria was epidemic as late as 1784–87 and 1790–92. The bubonic plague had quit Europe around 1721. More favorable weather conditions meant better harvests; but equally important was the fact that there was more money with which to buy food. Expanding foreign trade and improving agriculture were not of course totally unconnected. Even new items of food that came in from the outside, Indian maize or corn, rice, and so on, helped the population growth. Europe was less and less hungry.

Trade

An increase in foreign trade and the greater influx of foreign goods also meant a spurt in internal European trade. Both European trade and trade with the Americas and Asia-Africa centered around the Atlantic seaports; the Baltic seaports specialized in timber and food, as well as in iron that was plentiful in Sweden and Russia.[74]

The trade from China and India, mainly cotton goods, silks, spices, sugar, rice, tea, and precious and semiprecious stones, came to Britain, France, and the Netherlands, as well as to Prussia and the small German states. There was sudden economic growth in these areas, and the Enlightenment took root. Between the rich nobility and the poor agricultural peasantry, the city-dwelling middle class grew, benefitting from the new wealth that trade and mercantile capitalism was bringing in. Without that urban middle class, there would probably have been no European Enlightenment.

Industry

James Watt invented the steam engine in 1775. Steam power soon began running not only railways, but also ships and factories, mines and mills. The new industry soon linked up with the old trade, and mercantile capitalism was beginning to give place to industrial capitalism. When the possibilities of increasing production by existing methods were exhausted, attention was concentrated on devising new methods. The textile industry was one of the first to be mechanized, and even the French weavers protested against the unfair competition of the British machines. China and India, which for centuries led textile manufacture in the world, began feeling the pinch as machine-made cloth became cheaper, and textile exports to the West diminished.

The interplay between trade and industry in the context of political colonialism over the rest of the world was the matrix for the Enlightenment and not simply the ideas of philosophers in isolation. Until the end of the eighteenth century, the better goods came from China and India, and Europe's exports to these countries were in low demand there. The balance of trade was in favor of Asia, and Europe had to pay in bullion and silver, even if that gold and silver came from plunder and piracy on the new continent and on the high seas. Industrial technology gave the muscle and nerve to mercantile capitalism by which it grew to industrial capitalism, without which Europe could not have held its dominion over the world, or developed its science and technology to serve as the instrument of its power. The European Enlightenment took shape in the course of that transition.

Eric Hobsbawm puts it this way:

> Some time in the 1780s, and for the first time in human history, the shackles were taken off the productive power of human

> societies, which henceforth became capable of the constant, rapid, and up to the present limitless multiplication of men, goods, and services. This is now technically known to the economists as the "take-off into self-sustained growth." No previous society had been able to break through the ceiling which a pre-industrial social structure, defective science and technology, and consequently periodic breakdown, famine, and death, imposed on production.[75]

World Conquest

Britain, of course, takes pride of place among the world conquerors. Ruled by that indomitable woman, Queen Victoria (1819–1901), who must have provided a historical model for Margaret Thatcher, it was only in 1876 that the British Empire was consolidated; but Britannia began "ruling the waves" much earlier. The end of the Seven Years' War (1756–63) marks the turning point. For that war, fought simultaneously in Europe, America, and India, settled the question as to which European power was to be paramount. The French were defeated by the British in India as well as in America. The power of Germany and Spain was broken. The oceans and the world trade were from now on to be under largely British control. As John Richards Green saw it:

> The Seven Years' War is a turning point in the history of the world. Till now the relative weight of the European states had been drawn from their possessions within Europe itself. But from the close of the war it mattered little whether England counted for less or more with the nations around her. She was no longer a mere European power, no longer a mere rival of Germany or Russia or France. Mistress of Northern America, the future mistress of India, claiming as her own the empire of the seas, Britain suddenly towered high above the nations whose position in a single continent doomed them to comparative insignificance in the after history of the world. The war indeed was hardly ended when a consciousness of the destinies that lay before the English people showed itself in the restlessness with which our seamen penetrated into far-off seas. The Atlantic was dwindling into a mere strait within the British Empire; but beyond it to the westward lay a reach of waters (the Pacific Ocean) where the British flag was almost unknown. In the year which followed the Peace of Paris (1763) two English ships were sent on a cruise of discovery to the Straits of Magellan; three years later Captain Wallis reached the coral reefs of Tahiti; and in 1768 Cap-

> tain Cook traversed the Pacific from end to end, and wherever he touched, in New Zealand, in Australia, he claimed the soil for the English Crown, and opened a new world for the expansion of the English race.
>
> Statesmen and people alike felt the change in their country's attitude. In the words of Burke, the Parliament of Britain claimed "an imperial character in which as from the throne of heaven she superintends all the several inferior legislatures, and guides and controls them all, without annihilating any."[76]

There in that proud outburst of a British historian at the beginning of our century one hears all the overtones of Europe as "adventure and expansion," bent on world dominion and exploitation as if it were a God-given mission of Europe. What Britain achieved, her white colonies and ex-colonies like the US, Canada, Australia, New Zealand, and South Africa came to share. Though grudgingly, and not without some struggle, other white European nations were also allowed to have a share in the spoils of Empire.

The important point, however, is the change in the spirit and attitude of Europe. It was a fairly quick jump from misery to grandeur. Pride and arrogance are not always easy to distinguish from each other. When I read Edmund Burke or Immanuel Kant, Thomas Jefferson or Winston Churchill, it is this smugly high self-exaltation of Europe or the West as guide, mistress, and protector of the world that comes through to me from the historians and politicians of the white nations of Europe and her white colonies and ex-colonies. It is in the spirit of that smug self-exaltation that the European Enlightenment boasts of the autonomy of human reason, and of humanity recognizing no higher authority; and spreads that secular tempo that regards humanity as sovereign and self-sufficient, free to lord it over the world as her legal and legitimate property, with absolutely no obligations to anyone else.

The New Imperialism

If Europe had not developed the muscle and the mind to dominate the world,[77] and had not experienced that great triumph of a new imperialism, the European Enlightenment could hardly have taken place. In the earlier imperialisms of the world (for example, that of Darius or Alexander), the goals were rather limited: exaction of tribute, establishment of colonies, plunder and extraction of wealth, capture of slaves, and general glory and power. Former empires had by and large left the economies of the conquered territories exploited but still basically intact. European mercantile capitalism grew by controlling the trade routes, and taking over a substantial portion of the internal trade within the colonies through the elimination of traditional merchants and replacing them with new ones more subservient to the interests of the colonial masters.

With the transition from mercantile to industrial capitalism, the goals changed. It was now necessary to

a. change the economic base of the colonies in such a way that they serve mainly as suppliers of cheap raw materials, cheap labour and guaranteed markets for the production machinery of the metropolitan country; and

b. assure political, cultural and military hegemony in order to prevent the "natives" or competitors from outside taking over or interfering with the system of exploitation that would be set up.

The new imperialism demanded the setting up of a vast array of different systems: international banking and finance, shipping and transport, research and development of new consumer needs, new products, new investment opportunities and new industries, new credit and distribution systems, new markets and consumers, and new technologies. The transition from mercantile to industrial capitalism was thus the key to economic progress. Countries of southern Europe that were slow in deploying their large mercantile capital to industrial purposes lost the game and soon became back numbers. It was in those countries where the transition was fast that the European Enlightenment took root first.

The New Imperialism had to make sure that the whole value system of the world would be changed in order to fit the needs of the new system. Existing land and property relations, be they feudal or prefeudal, had to be revolutionized through the introduction of private property as a new human right and as the basis of individual liberty. Work had to be sanctified as a noble endeavor (dignity of labor), for the system could not be sustained without a constant supply of cheap labor. The doctrine of the racial superiority of the white people had to be inculcated in order to justify control of the world economy by the white minority. Small middle classes had to be created in the colonies, who, whether brown or black-skinned, would still be white in mentality and would serve as agents for the colonial powers.

The main instrument for inculcating these value systems was to be education. Education was the means by which imperialism was to be kept going, both in Europe and in the colonies. The Enlightenment could not have spread as it did in the world without the new education system for the elite in the colonies.

The eighteenth century only saw the beginning of this worldwide system: it was the nineteenth century that marked the most dramatic changes and the abolition of slavery was perhaps the most impressive of these. Credit has to be given to the European Enlightenment for this exceptionally enlightened advance in human relations, on the surface a major plus among the positive aspects of imperialism. The economic aspects of this abolition of slavery in the beginning of the nineteenth century should not, however, be overlooked.

Legally, slavery was abolished in Britain in 1807 and in 1808 in the United States. In the 1820s, Holland, France, and Sweden followed suit. On August 31, 1833, the British Parliament passed a law abolishing slavery in the colonies. The names of William Wilberforce and Abraham Lincoln should be remembered with gratitude by humanity for having led the movement for the abolition of slavery.

By the beginning of the nineteenth century, economic conditions in the imperial system were ripe for abolition. Sugar and cotton were among the major products of the slaves, but machines took over in cotton production and the sugar markets were glutted. By the beginning of the nineteenth century, slave demand was low and the slave trade soon became unprofitable. One way to increase demand in the market for sugar was to cut down sugar production; for without slave labor sugar production was bound to go down, as it did in fact. The European sugar planters in the colonies were going bankrupt, and the twenty million pounds that the British government paid to the planters not only bailed them out, but also rescued the British bankers who had loaned out enormous sums to the planters. The abolition of slavery thus fitted with the needs of the system. But, of course, slavery and the slave trade went on for quite some time after it was legally abolished.

The African slave trade constituted an integral part of mercantile (trade and commerce) capitalism, but it was no longer an essential element in the new industrial capitalism where the machine and wage labor more than compensated for slave labor and made the latter redundant.

Imperialism entered a new stage by 1875, as Britain and the US became the superpowers of the world. At the beginning of the century European whites claimed title to fifty-five percent of the land surface of the earth. By 1878 they had acquired an additional 6.5 million square miles, raising their share to sixty-seven percent of the total. By 1914 that share was eighty-five percent.

But ownership had changed substantially during that period. By 1825 Spain had no colonies in South America, and only Cuba and Puerto Rico in Central America. The British liberally supported the independence movements in South America. Britain financed the radical Francisco de Miranda (early 1800s), the republican Simon de Bolivar (1783–1830), and the monarchist José de San Martin (1778–1850) in their insurrections against Spanish rule. The seven-vessel Chilean Navy was commanded by Lord Cochrane, formerly of the British Royal Navy. It was not the working class that supported the liberation movements of South America in the first quarter of the nineteenth century, but the merchants and financiers who planned to capture the South American markets from Spain. The British navy protected the shipments of supplies for the insurrectionaries, and also defended the British trade with South America that ensued. Even the North Americans were helpless, though the US tried to counter with the Monroe Doctrine of 1823; but the American Navy was powerless to enforce that doctrine on the British. In the first half of the nineteenth century, the largest single market for British textile exports was not India, but Latin America. Thus emerged the neocolonialist pattern. Political colonialism was no longer necessary to control the markets in the colonies. Economic control without administrative headaches was politically much more sensible. The new pattern became universally (almost) adopted only after 1945, but foundations were laid, models were tried, and patterns established almost a century earlier. Formally, South American nations were free, but informally Britain held empire over trade, investment, markets, and finance on that continent. The Americans were envious of the British, but could do little. The puny American Navy was no match against the majestic British Royal Navy, which ruled the seas everywhere. Neocolonialism may not need administrative control, but it cannot do without military power.

The Americans, however, were not idly standing by. The US empire was fast expanding in the nineteenth century. In 1803 she purchased Louisiana from the French. In 1819, Spain ceded the Floridas to the US, and the latter's Atlantic coast was clear. In 1829, Russia gave up claims to Oregon. In 1836 US settlers wrested Texas from Mexico, and in 1846–48 the US attacked Mexico and annexed the whole south-west between New Mexico and Utah, right up to the Pacific. Now the Pacific coast was also clear, and America was free to look for new frontiers. She began to flex her muscles even at the British, though without openly defying her former colonial masters.

If in the beginning of the nineteenth century the leading powers were Spain, Portugal, Britain, France and the Low Countries, by 1875 a new set of colonial masters had come on the scene: the US, Germany, Italy, Japan, and Belgium. During the first seventy-five years of the nineteenth century, when the European Enlightenment became the Euro-American Enlightenment, there was a very substantial acceleration of colonialism, which powered that Enlightenment. The average of acquisition of new colonies during those seventy-five years was about 210,000 square kilometers of territory a year. From 1848, America also launched out on a campaign of adventure and expansion, true to her European spirit.

The first struggle in America was to wrest away the South American markets and raw materials from British domination. The Monroe Doctrine (1822–23) was primarily a warning to Spain and Portugal to keep their hands off their former colonies, and to leave things in the hands of Britain and the US. Now that the US was confident of its own capacity to go it alone without the help of Britain, a new courting of the *caudillos* or semifeudal tyrant rulers of Latin America began. Everywhere, except in Chile, the *caudillos* ruled, and were glad to use North American power both to defend themselves from outside forces as well as from democratic or revolutionary movements inside. Gradually, American companies were able to establish themselves in South and Central America, with the *caudillos* as cobeneficiaries.

Denied the markets and raw materials of Latin America, the European powers turned their attention to further conquests in Asia and Africa. From 1875 to 1914, the annual average acquisition of territory rose by nearly two-hundred percent—620,000 square kilometers a year compared to the previous average of 210,000. The French, defeated in India, turned to Indochina. Vietnam had been taken over in 1858; in 1887 Cambodia and Vietnam were merged to form French Indochina; in 1893 Laos became a French "protectorate." In China, the Opium War had been fought by the British in 1839–42, since opium, banned and prohibited by the Chinese since 1729, had become a substantial element of British trade.

China had now to be "opened" to European trade by force, and the Nanking Treaty of 1842 saw to that, as well as legalizing the British occupation of Hong Kong. Chinese opium, tea, and silks were not the only items of trade. By the 1860s a hundred thousand Chinese "coolies" had been shipped to Peru and a hundred and fifty-thousand to Cuba as virtual slave labor. As China was "opened" by the British, others also claimed trading and residence privileges and got them: the US, France, Belgium, Sweden, Norway, and even Russia. In 1860, British and French troops occupied Beijing, to protect their interests. Two years earlier, Russia extracted her present Far Eastern province north of the river Amur by forcing on China the Treaty of Aigun in

1858. China gradually lost her empire to Western powers. Democratic revolts like the Indian Mutiny of 1857, the Chinese Taiping Rebellion (1851–64), and the Boxer Rebellion of 1900 were put down by the Western powers with incredibly barbarian brutality. Twenty-five million Chinese had been killed in the Taiping Rebellion and many more in the intermittently succeeding popular revolts, which were all conveniently labelled by the West as "rebellions" rather than human uprisings. This, remember, was during the period when the European Enlightenment was at its peak. Most students of the European Enlightenment conveniently ignore this side of the West's antihuman, barbarian, bestial activities around the world while the Bourgeois Enlightenment was going on in all the countries of the West, including Russia.

Japan had managed to ward off the whites from the West by an equally barbarian, bestial, policy which matched or surpassed that of the West. But with the arrival of Commodore Perry's American expedition in 1853, Japan began to give in and was forced to give trade concessions to the Americans in 1858; other Western nations now claimed the same privileges and got them. By 1868 the Meiji Era of modernization had begun in Japan, and if Japan has subsequently proved herself to be a match for the West, it was because she was able to successfully imitate the West in technology and militarism as well as in bestiality. There are few countries outside of the white countries to beat Japan in the spirit of "adventure and expansion."

By imitating the West, Japan managed to get power over Korea and Formosa (now Taiwan), the Pescadores Islands, the Liaotung Peninsula, and southern Manchuria. It received an "indemnity" of $180 million from China, and trading privileges in China almost on par with the westerners. Japan even managed, though with the aid of Britain, to inflict a crushing defeat on Russia in 1905. For the first time in history an Asian power had defeated a mighty European power, and this gave the Japanese status in the eyes of the other Western powers. They elevated the Japanese consulates in their countries to the rank of embassies. The Euro-American Enlightenment had already spread to Japan, beginning with the establishment of Tokyo University in 1877, renamed Imperial University in 1886. Many Japanese students went abroad to study and master the techniques and technologies of the West. Industrial capitalism soon became the foundation of the Japanese economy, and also developed the naval and military power needed to defend it. The Meiji restoration of 1868 had intelligently chosen the motto: "Rich Country, Strong Arms," capturing in a nutshell the wisdom of the West.

The Russians did not want to be left behind in the acquisition of empire. That was in those days a necessary qualification for being accepted as a European nation. Two provinces of Georgia, then in the Persian Empire, were annexed by Russia, leading to the Russo-Persian War of 1804–13. Persia lost the war and ceded Daghestan and Samarkhand to Russia. In another war fifteen years later Russia wrenched from Persia the rest of Georgia and other Persian territory, gradually leading up to a conquest of almost all the Islamic states of Central Asia, as well as the Christian states of Armenia and Georgia. This empire, perhaps the last to be decolonialized, included the vast Siberian wilderness and the Far East province, the Central Asian republics of the present Soviet Union, Turkey and Asia Minor to the south, Syria, Iraq, Palestine, and Egypt as well as Cyprus in the middle east, and also Greece, Crete, parts of Hungary and Austria to the west. Only since 1989 are we seeing the beginning of the dismantling of that great Russian Empire, laboriously built up by the czars of the Russian Enlightenment, and inherited by the Soviets in 1917.

Russia too had her Enlightenment powered and financed by the newly acquired empire of the eighteenth and nineteenth centuries. Catherine the Great of Russia was already in correspondence with Voltaire.[78] The Russian "intelligentsia" is a product of the European Enlightenment. So was Lomonosov, Lenin, and the Marxist ideology itself.

To conclude this chapter, we submit that no understanding of the European Enlightenment would be adequate if it does not take into account the imperialist context in which that Enlightenment came to be. Europe's sense of triumph at its domination of the world played a key role in generating the basic idea of the Enlightenment. That idea is that humanity is sovereign over the world, a sovereignty to be exercised through bold self-assertion and the use of human ingenuity (reason) to overcome all obstacles. The ultimate end is to conquer truth itself, using critical rationality as the handmaid and instrument of humanity's project to dominate and rule reality. In that basic hubris of the human race lies also the root of the human tragedy of the European Enlightenment.

Some Western feminists like Rosemary Reuther would attribute the domination tendency in modern science and technology to the fact that it is a Western male creation. It is interesting to speculate on what would have been the shape of that sci-tech civilization if Western women had their full say in it. But it would be rather idle speculation. The European women created by that civilization as yet seem no less dominant than their men. Rosemary Reuther's thesis is fascinating, but fails to carry conviction to non-Europeans who are aware of male chauvinism in their own culture, but who cannot attribute all the faults of their civilization to just male domination.

Neither are they willing to accept without debate the thesis that women in power would be less dominating than men in power have been. The problem of domination is more linked to power than to sex. The answer to male domination is certainly not female domination. What is even more important from the perspective of this book is that no alibi on the part of the European female in relation to Europe's past can be so easily accepted, by non-Europeans at least. European women were oppressed by males, perhaps in about the same degree as in other cultures. But European male action for dominating and exploiting the peoples of the world was certainly supported and benefited from by European females. The attempt of European women to pose as only the oppressed and not as oppressors as well, makes that pose inauthentic.

It is clear that the ruling classes of Europe as a whole share the responsibility for Europe's history in adventure and expansion. No doubt males and their ideas and initiatives played a leading role in developing the European personality, but many women also helped to shape that personality structure. Not only Victoria of Britain, Catherine of Russia, and Marie Antoinette of France, but also a host of other distinguished women played a leading role in shaping the history of Europe. Whether the peasants and serfs of Europe had a leading role in that development can be debated.

To the ideas of one of the men who shaped both Western liberal thought and Marxist thought, namely Hegel, we now turn.

Chapter Five

IDEAS: HEGEL

The culture of Europe has three main sources:

1. The fundamental human heritage that Europe shares with all cultures and all humanity
2. The Greco-Roman heritage
3. The Judeo-Christian tradition.

There are other elements that have from time to time contributed substantially to the European heritage, such as the Nordic or Scandinavian, Celtic and Teutonic traditions. But the three we have mentioned above constitute the foundation, and these local traditions of Europe are but variations within the first. Of these, Athens and Jerusalem are more consciously remembered; sometimes careful philosophers like Brand Blanshard have said that Athens and Jerusalem are the two main sources of the Western tradition.[79] This is only because of an unwillingness to recognize the presence in the Western psyche, not only of what it has borrowed from China and India, from Akkadia and Sumeria, from Babylon and Persia, from Syria and Egypt, but also of the "Primal Vision" that the West shares with all cultures, and which the modern West once regarded as "primitive" in a pejorative sense. The environmental crisis has reawakened that vision in the Western consciousness; its central element is the awareness that humanity and the universe are not two distinct entities, but two related elements in an integral whole, that the human being is not such an autonomous, independent, self-sufficient individual as some people thought and taught, and that the skin of the individual is not the boundary of his or her existence. The Native Americans as well as others in Europe still hold on to aspects of this Primal Vision.

A perpetual tension among the three elements seems to persist in the Western psyche; sometimes the temptation is to repudiate all three and to claim that one does not depend on any external tradition at all. This is characteristic of the psyche of the European Enlightenment; its most blatant instance is the American tradition, where for many only the new is true and the old is generally regarded as useless. This has been and perhaps still is part of America's strength, this seemingly total contempt for history and therefore presumed freedom from the shackles of the past. In Europe, tradition is still of some value; hence Europe cannot innovate as freely as America. And Europe is not always as self-consciously individualist as America can sometimes be; though it was the European Enlightenment that firmly established the intellectual foundations of that individualism for the West.

But when a crisis looms large, the West usually goes back and reconstructs one of these three traditions; right now both the Greco-Roman and the Judeo-Christian have gone sour and are out of fashion; only the primitive-integral or the Romantic-naturalistic counts as à la mode. Each reconstruction is of course never a simple copy of the past. It incorporates elements from the other two, as well as from elsewhere. Hegel (1770–1831) in Germany, critic as well as child of the Enlightenment, provides a good example.

A Bold Look at the Whole

No attempt to chart the whole course of Western philosophy can be free from error. Hegel tried, in his *History of Philosophy,* as also in the *Phenomenology of the Spirit, Lectures on the Philosophy of Religion,* and other works, to provide a comprehensive picture, not just of European philosophy, but of the whole world development of philosophy, religion, and thought in general. It was a monumental effort that has made such a decisive impact, whether positive or negative, on the whole body of Western thought and institutions, that the most astute criticism has not rendered his thought fruitless to this day. Twentieth-century philosophy tried to dismiss him as irrelevant, but often without taking the trouble of reading him carefully. G. R. G. Mure of Oxford, one of the more balanced British students of Hegel, expressed the hope that the "shamelessly ill-informed criticism" of Hegel had reached "its expiring splutter" in Sir Karl Popper's chapter on Hegel in his *The Open Society and Its Enemies.*[80] Fred G. Weiss had this to say about Anglo-American analytical philosophy's approach to Hegel:

> I think there is little question that the anti-Hegelian (or a-Hegelian) aspect of the recently dominant empiricist-positivist philosophies in Britain and America has gone hand-in-hand with its a-historical character.[81]

J. N. Findlay has a more positive assessment to give in his *Hegel: A Re-examination.*[82] He concludes his masterly work with the judgment that Hegel is "without doubt, the Aristotle of our post-Renaissance world, our synoptic thinker without peer." The word "synoptic" is the key. Hegel is not a piecemeal thinker, but seeks to comprehend the whole of reality as a historical process of development, at the center of which he sees what we call "hominisation" or "humanization."

Humanization

This term was popularized by the French Jesuit Teilhard de Chardin, within a holistic vision of the universe moving towards its fulfillment and integration. Many modern writers trivialize the concept of humanization by thinking of it mainly in terms of a more humane approach to social engineering. The original German word *Menschwerdung* has a deeper and richer content, basically grasped by Teilhard, but little understood by most others. It means literally becoming human or human becoming. In Hegel, however, it means much more. *Menschwerdung* is the German equivalent of the Greek word *enanthropesis,* usually translated as 'incarnation' in Christian theology. It refers to the central affirmation of the Christian faith that God became a human being in Jesus Christ. Why did Hegel choose this as his central theme? Thereby hangs a tale, which is the key to understanding Hegel.

Hegel's Basic Quest: A Religion for Humanity

Whether it is relevant or not, the fact is that Hegel started out as a theological student. Scholars have spilled a great deal of ink seeking to settle the question whether the juvenalia of Hegel have anything to do with his mature thought. Most of them seem to think that there is no connection at all; that at a certain stage in his youth, Hegel simply abandoned his Lutheran faith and decided to think in a secular framework. To the present writer this position seems contrary to the facts, and comes in the way of understanding Hegel.

A Jewish rabbi and noted contemporary philosopher, Emil Fackenheim, who disagrees with the mature Hegel in his affirmation of the Christian religion as the absolute, saw this clearly in his *The Re-*

ligious Dimension in Hegel's Thought.[83] But even Fackenheim does not make clear the connection between Hegel's early writings on theology (called the juvenalia, somewhat derisively, I believe) on the one hand, and his later, mature writings. Of course, Hegel himself did not publish his theological writings, not so much because he was dissatisfied with them but because he thought they would stand in the way of his philosophical writings being received by the academic community, which had already learned to look down on theology of any kind.

We base our considered judgment on Hegel's mature thought in the three volumes of his *System der Philosophie,* and on his *Lectures on the Philosophy of Religion,* rather than on his first published work, *The Phenomenology of Spirit,* (1807). But we must take into account the thought of Hegel as a young man, deeply concerned about the fact that Germany was sadly disunited and therefore unable to compete with the French and the British in Europe's "adventure and expansion." He felt he needed a religion to awaken and unite the people, but Christianity (Roman Catholic and Protestant) was helping only to divide. For some time he played with the idea that a reconstruction of classical Greek religion would help revive the spirit of the German peoples, but later gave up that idea as unfeasible. He then decided to reinterpret Christianity itself in a universal, naturalistic, secular framework. But it certainly was not the superficial secularism of our times. Most present-day secularists would find Hegel's secular framework way beyond their comprehension.

Hegel was, at the foundation of his personality, a German Christian theologian, graduate of the Theological Stift or Seminary of the University of Tuebingen, along with his two equally well known classmates, Schelling the philosopher and Hoelderlin the poet. The three were close friends at the seminary, and together constituted a team of radical students identified with both the French Revolution and the rising Kantianism, which they regarded as the political and philosophical charters of liberty and human reason.

All three were trained to be pastors in the Lutheran church of Wuerttemberg. All three rejected the content of their teachers' theology as philosophically unworthy and politically ineffective. But all three in their various ways sought to fulfill their pastoral vocation by changing society through philosophy, and in the case of Hoelderlin, by poetry.[84]

The basic distinction in those days was between "positivity" and "subjectivity" (*postitivitaet* und *subjectivitaet*). German pietism of the eighteenth century was too subjective, with no visible or positive impact on society and hence unable to emancipate humanity. On the other hand, most religion was too positive, with authority structures and legal obligations that stifled the human spirit. Even Kant's "religion within the limits of reason alone" appeared to Hegel a confining concept, insofar as it rested on a sense of duty or moral obligation, something outside oneself controlling a human being's free spirit. Hegel wanted a reconciliation between the positive and the subjective, a spontaneous world of humanity in which the Absolute Spirit could express itself through the human consciousness.

Hegel reacted against traditional Western Christianity, both Roman Catholic and Lutheran. But he did not reject the Christian religion itself, which he and his colleagues regarded as the final and absolute religion. He wanted, however, to divest Christianity of all its particularistic and authoritarian elements and to transform it into a genuinely civil, universal religion, but not in the superficial fashion some secular humanists attempt.

For Hegel, Hoelderlin, and Schelling, the ancient Greek religion of Socrates, Plato, and Aristotle was a more universal religion than traditional Christianity. Christianity in itself was, however, the absolute religion, for Hegel as well as for his colleagues. But traditional Christianity was too exclusive and not sufficiently oriented to the needs of civic society. It had to be transformed into a non-authoritarian, universal, civic religion, and that was the task of philosophy as Hegel saw it. It is that task that Hegel set out to perform in his monumental philosophical endeavor.

It is rather superficial to say that the ideology of the Enlightenment is a bastard of the illegal marriage between Jerusalem and Athens, or between Christianity and classical paganism. At least in the case of Hegel, there is evidence to show that he sought to transform the basic insights of the Christian faith into a secular and non-authoritarian mold in order to provide the foundations of a universal civic religion, at least for the cultivated people (*gebildete Leute*) of his day. Religion, whether positive (i.e., based on external authority) or natural (intrinsic to human nature) was for Hegel something to be transcended and comprehended (*aufhebt*) by something higher, namely, true philosophy. It was that higher philosophy which Hegel set out to create, and it was not a bastard, but something of a higher level of dialectical development, where the new synthesis comprehends and absorbs both the previous thesis and its antithesis.

It is equally superficial to decry such a transformation as illegitimate; for Hegel, what he was doing was a natural consequence of the force of history. He was the agent through whom human consciousness was being led to a higher level of development; he could do no other. One can dispute whether or not Hegel had illusions of grandeur not justified by subsequent history. Hegel did go out of fashion after the neo-Hegelians and the Marxians and Kierkegaardians had a bash at him. But wherever he is understood, he still makes a decisive impact on people's thinking. As Benedetto Croce, the perceptive Italian student of Hegel would ask us to do:

> Read his [i.e., Hegel's] books. . . ; put an end to the spectacle, half comical and half disgusting, of the accusation and the abuse of a philosopher by critics who do not know him, and who wage a foolish war with a ridiculous puppet created by their own imaginations, under the ignoble sway of traditional prejudice and intellectual laziness.[85]

Hegel's vision is a perennial that comes back in European thought from time to time, whenever it shows signs of vitality—whether in Husserl or Heidegger, Marx or Merleau-Ponty, Bergson or Whitehead, Sartre or Croce, Teilhard or Dilthey, Gadamer or Habermas.

It certainly yielded positive results through the Enlightenment and the civilization it has created. More than any other thinker, including Immanuel Kant, Hegel provided the vision that is at the root of modernity. The legitimacy of modernity has been ably defended by Hans Blumenberg in his *Legitimitaet der Neuzeit*[86] a seminal work still little known in English-speaking circles. Hans Blumenberg was obviously responding to Karl Loewith's classical work, *From Hegel to Nietzsche*[87] where Loewith argues that the post-Hegelian philosophy of history depends for its essential character on the assumption of the absolute truth of the Christian religion. Our submission here is that not only the philosophy of history, but the whole of Hegel's thought goes back to the theology he learned in the Tuebingen Stift, and to his life passion to convert that theology into a universal secular ideology which could be accepted by reasonable people without accepting the dogmatic premises of Christianity.

The question about the legitimacy of Hegel's project need not detain us here. What matters is that it has worked. Not that the whole world has accepted Hegel's thought; but it gave to the European Enlightenment a comprehensive ideology; it has provoked strong reactions such as those of Marx and Kierkegaard; it has been a molding factor in all subsequent European thought except perhaps in ahistorical and hence pseudological deviations like Logical or Linguistic Analysis. What is even more important is that it lies at the root of the two prevailing ideologies of the civilization of the West—democratic liberalism and Marxism. Take for an example the elite of India. If either of the two ideologies of the West had been presented to them by Christian missionaries in theological form, it would have been immediately rejected. But because both came in a secular form they found ready reception, though perhaps not always with deep perception of their roots in the Judeo-Christian tradition.

The philosophy of the Enlightenment comes basically from the secularization of Western Christianity, and its remodelling after the pattern of Greek civil religion. It is indeed a hybrid, but a very creative one. It has fulfilled a major role in history; it has brought the world together. As the author of that hybrid, Friedrich Hegel is more the father of the Enlightenment than René Descartes or Immanuel Kant. If we go on to examine the connections between Hegel's Christianity and the European Enlightenment, it is only to clarify, not to condemn, either Christianity or the Enlightenment. Something need not be regarded as wrong just because it is rooted in the Christian or any other religious tradition. In fact, most of the better ideas we cherish today have come from a religious matrix. As Carl Schmitt says: "All significant concepts of modern political theory are secularized theological concepts."[88] More specifically, Mircea Eliade puts it thus: "Hegel takes over the Judaeo-Christian ideology and applies it to history in its totality."[89] Rudolf Bultmann called it a "historization of eschatology."[90]

A Secular Theology

Pope Gregory I (Pope of Rome 590–604 A.D.) made it normative for the western church to evolve around the central themes of sin and grace, damnation and salvation, and the idea of the church as the manager and dispenser of truth and grace, as well as the builder and master of the City of God. Medieval Christendom was built on these ideas. These concepts are in the authentic Christian tradition, but the fundamental notions of that tradition are not these but a set of three: (a) the Triune God who creates, sustains, refines and brings the creation to fulfilment; (b) the historical incarnation of the second Person of the Trinity in order to redeem and perfect the alienated creation; and (c) the continuing work of the third Person of the Trinity to give form, unity, wisdom, power, goodness, and creativity in freedom to that created order. Without this larger framework, the first set of notions becomes confining, narrow, exclusivistic, and generally misleading; but then so would the reaction against these confining notions such as has taken shape in secular humanism, when it ignores the fundamental framework of reality by focusing on the human as basic. Hegel's "religionless Christianity" has far more depth than later versions of it like Dietrich Bonhoeffer's, or the "Death of God" theologians of yesteryear.

It is to Hegel's great credit as a trained theologian that he had a better grasp of the fundamental framework of the Christian tradition than say, Augustine or Thomas Aquinas, Martin Luther or John Calvin. I would dare to assert that even Hegel's friend, the theologian-poet Hoelderlin, shared that insight, which accounts for the depth of his poetry and inspired philosophers like Martin Heidegger, who always acknowledged his great debt to Hoelderlin. This may be the reason why even Karl Barth, no admirer of philosophy and no advocate of liberalism, could state that Hegel sought to do for the modern Protestant world what St. Thomas Aquinas had done for the Catholic Middle Ages.[91] One does not of course have to be a Hegelian to praise Hegel.

Religion and Philosophy in Hegel

For Hegel, unlike many moderns, religion and philosophy have the same intent. For him, philosophy is a more advanced form of religion—an idea that prompted Auguste Comte's formulation of positivism as the progression from religion to metaphysics to science. Hegel would certainly have disapproved the positivistic scheme; for him, philosophy was the highest stage, and he would put it this way:

> It is a false idea that these two, faith and free philosophical investigation, can subsist quietly side by side. There is no foundation for maintaining that faith in the content or essential element of positive religion can continue to exist, if reason has convinced itself of the opposite . . . If discord has arisen between intellectual insight and religion, and is not overcome in knowledge, it leads to despair, which comes in the place of reconciliation. This despair is reconciliation carried out in a one-sided manner. The one side is cast away, the other alone held fast; but a man cannot win true peace in this way. The one alternative is for the divided spirit to reject the demands of the intellect and try to return to simple religious feeling. To this, however, the spirit can only attain by doing violence to itself; for the independence of consciousness demands satisfaction, and will not be thrust aside by force; and to renounce independent thought, is not within the power of the healthy mind.[92]

In this passage one hears the agony of a young theological student's soul, expressed after decades of mature thought. Particular religions always come into conflict with the imperative demands of the intellect. Ignoring those demands and going back to the simple beliefs of particular religion is no solution, because consciousness is a power that will not brook such ignoring or defiance. There is an inner necessity, built into nature itself, that consciousness will not surrender itself to external authority. Reality pushes on for a reconciliation.

The Hegelian Trinity

"The absolute, eternal Idea is, in its essential existence, in and for itself, God in His eternity before the creation of the world, and outside of the world."[93] These opening words of part three of Hegel's *Lectures on the Philosophy of Religion* give us a succinct account of how Hegel has universalized the Christian notion of the Triune God.

This is an idea of thought alone—this God in Himself without the created order, without the Other, "the untroubled light, self-identity, an element which is as yet unaffected by the presence of Being other than itself."[94] The roots of this idea are to be sought more in the Neoplatonic notion of the One than in Christian teaching. God is here an object of thought, an idea that Plotinus would simply not have accepted. Of course, Hegel is here talking from the standpoint of religion, not philosophy. The reflective consciousness of human beings cannot conceive God in His eternal and absolute essentiality, Hegel admits. The God of religion exists only for thought, as a determined Being who is the object of thought. God is Spirit or *Geist,* but then so is the human consciousness. It is Spirit making Spirit an object. When humans conceive God, however, they make Him other than the Universe. They thus differentiate between God and the Universe, but they also conceive the universe as His Other, inseparable from Himself. In holding them together "these differences are done away with, in so far as this differentiation just means that the difference is actually shown to be no difference, and thus the One is at home with itself in the Other."[95]

Hegel interprets the Christian statement that God is love in this sense, that God is always at home in the Other:

> For love implies a distinguishing between two, and yet these two are, as a matter of fact, not distinguished from one another. Love, this sense of being outside of myself, is the feeling and consciousness of this identity. My self-consciousness is not in myself, but in another; but this other in whom alone I can find satisfaction and am at peace with myself—. . . this Other, just because it is outside of me, has its self-consciousness only in me. . . . this perception, this feeling, this knowledge of the unity, is love. . . God is love; i.e. He represents the distinction referred to, and the nullity of this distinction, the sort of play of

> this act of distinction which is not to be taken seriously . . . This eternal Idea, accordingly finds expression in the Christian Religion under the name of the Holy Trinity, and this is God Himself, the eternal Triune God.[96]

In simpler words, God as Spirit is the One who differentiates Himself from Himself in the Other and yet abolishes that differentiation in the identity of love. This is the key to Hegel's thought. And it is a universalization of the Christian doctrine of the Trinity. It is from this notion that even the idea of the dialectic arises. The thesis creates its Other, which is the antithesis, but then the two are subsumed in a higher synthesis where identity abolishes the difference and reconciles the contradictions.

Hegel's Notion of Incarnation

God is the Absolute Idea, thus He is Spirit.[97] The unmanifest God considered in His aseity, is Spirit, but so is the God who manifests Himself to His Other. In manifestation there has to be differentiation. One must manifest to someone else. The manifest is also Spirit, as is the Other to whom this manifestation takes place. The human nature to which the divine manifests itself is Spirit, but since the Spirit is by necessity one, the unity of the divine and human natures constitutes the Idea of the Spirit in its fullness.

The Absolute Idea remains only a notion until it manifests itself in reality. But with the manifestation there occurs duality and difference, and these must be resolved in identity. The whole world process is this seeking of the Identity and Oneness between the notion and reality of the Absolute Idea:

> The absolute Notion and the Idea as the absolute unity of their reality, are different the one from the other. Spirit is accordingly the living process by which the implicit unity of the divine and human natures becomes actual and comes to have a definite existence.[98]

Or,

> Eternal Being, in-and-for-itself, is something which unfolds itself, determines itself, differentiates itself, posits itself as its own difference, but the difference, again, is at the same time done away with and absorbed; what has essential Being, Being in-and-for-itself, eternally returns to itself in this, and only in so far as it does this, is it Spirit.[99]

Or again,

> The question as to the truth of the Christian religion directly divided itself into two questions: I. Is it really true that God does not exist apart from the Son, and that He has sent Him into the world? and II. Was this particular individual, Jesus of Nazareth, the carpenter's son, the son of God, the Christ?[100]

Hegel goes on to answer both questions in the affirmative. But then we have to make the transition from faith to knowledge. For that we must go beyond the particularity of the Christian religion to grasp its universal meaning, which is Absolute Knowledge, the stage of philosophy beyond particular religions.

Hegel thus reinterprets the Christian doctrine of the Incarnation of Jesus Christ as a universal process rather than as a particular event in Palestine in the first century of our era. The Christian doctrine of the Incarnation is thus taken to mean the whole process of the universe itself. It is no longer an event at a particular point of historical time and geographical space, but the whole cosmic process, including all of history itself. And it is specifically the Christian doctrine, because Hegel goes on to examine rudimentary doctrines of incarnation in other religions (such as the Hindu concept of *Avatara*) and dismisses them as "inadequately developed":[101]

> e.g., the incarnation of God which occurs in oriental religion has no truth, because the actual spirit of that religion is without this reconciliation.[102]

Hegel's Holy Spirit and Church

The Church or spiritual community is for Hegel the Kingdom of The Spirit par excellence, the realm where multiplicity is brought into unity, contradictions into reconciliation, for the *Geist* or Spirit is always a multiplicity of consciousnesses uniting themselves into a single self-consciousness.

The Father is Spirit, the Son is Spirit, and the Holy Spirit is also Spirit, as is obvious. Spirit does not, however, mean the exclusion of the material and the sensuous, but their reconciliation to the Spirit, in the Spirit. The Spirit does not stand apart from the material and the sensuous; "the true element in the determination of the nature of the Spirit, the union of the two sides of the infinite antithesis—God and the world, I, this particular *homuncio*—is what constitutes the content of the Christian religion, and makes it into a religion of Spirit."[103]

Hegel's premises are thus basically Christian: Trinitarian, Incarnational, Pneumatological. He affirms what the Christian tradition actually believes; he then goes on to make a transition from faith to knowledge that is free from all trammels of authority and particularity. It is this transition that remains questionable. The important point for us, however, is to note how these universalized ideas of Christianity, in a very much watered-down form, were appropriated by the secular tradition of the West and became the foundation of the European Enlightenment and its civilization, which is now spreading in the world. Few people suspect that Hegel's *Geist* has anything to do with the Christian belief in the *Heilige Geist* or Holy Ghost.

Hegel and the European Enlightenment

What indeed is Hegel's relation to the European Enlightenment? Certainly it far antedates Hegel. Hegel was an enthusiastic supporter of the French Revolution and of the French *philosophes* who molded its ideas. Hegel would thus appear to be more of a child than one of the fathers of the Enlightenment. But inside the German Enlightenment he plays more the role of a critic, as well as the generator of the transcendentalist point of view in modern thought. His fundamental departure from the naturalism and materialism of the French, from the empiricism of the British, and from the moralism of the Kantians is indeed worth examining, in order to find some foundations for new civilizations.

Hegel's basic criticism of the philosophy of the Enlightenment is that it tries to understand Nature as a self-existent, self-regulating, and all-comprehending reality that can be understood without any reference to anything that transcends it. He felt that the philosophy of the Enlightenment remained within the basic Cartesian dualism of Being and Thinking, of ego and world, though it paid practically no attention to the ego itself as a reality other than objective Nature. Its failure to take the ego or the subjective seriously means understanding everything in terms of "natural law," function, and mechanical causality. So much so that when they get around to the ego or the subjective, they still try to understand consciousness in terms of mechanical laws of causation, function, behavior, and laws.

For Hegel *Geist* (Spirit) and *Natur,* or Thinking and Being, Consciousness and World, are not two realities, but the dialectical poles of a single reality, poles that have become alienated from each other and need fundamental reconciliation. And in the logic that regulates consciousness as well as in the world process itself, the same dialectic of thesis, antithesis, and synthesis is operating. When both consciousness and world have fully developed, the poles will be reconciled; consciousness will become aware that it is the same Absolute Idea as Spirit that is operating in consciousness as well as in the world process. And with that vision not only will our own (ego's) feeling of the otherness of Nature disappear, but the Absolute Idea that has willed the Other or the Universe will have become reconciled to itself in the Other.

That is indeed Christian eschatology domesticated within history and consciousness. It is an attempt that has as such not stood the test of time; but through the ideas and institutions it has generated either by providing inspiration or by provoking a creative reaction, Hegelian thought is without parallel in the history of the human race. We will take a brief look at some of the reactions to Hegel in the next chapter.

Chapter Six

THE DIALECTICS OF THE ENLIGHTENMENT: KNOWLEDGE—ITS FUNCTION AND FOUNDATION

There was no realm of human, personal, social, cultural, economic, and political existence in Europe that the Enlightenment left unchanged. It was a total revolution with consequences for art and poetry, drama, and literature, music and painting, sculpture and architecture, education and medicine, banking and commerce, economics and politics, as well as science and technology, trade and industry, transport and communication, religion and philosophy, public health and sanitation, and a whole host of other aspects of human life. This modest work does not presume to give anything like a comprehensive account of the European Enlightenment; neither has the present writer the competence to do so.

We would like to focus attention on one question here—the nature, function, and foundation of knowledge. What we have today is a crisis of knowledge, with institutional consequences, and it is to that question that this book seeks to draw attention. Modern science is the prevailing system of knowledge; Western natural science is a child of Western natural philosophy, but it has managed to eclipse philosophy and the art of asking fundamental questions. Our world has become a place where those sorts of questions have gone out of fashion. This itself is a symptom of our malaise. Our universities continue to have faculties of philosophy, but somehow they manage to skirt the basic questions—on the meaning of existence, action and thought, or about Truth, Beauty and Goodness.

The great philosophers of the West in the eighteenth century were all ardently concerned about these questions, especially Schelling, Kant, and Hegel. Schelling, for example, expressed deep concern in his Jena lectures of 1802 about the rush from the theoretical to the practical, the impatience with theory and the fear of speculation.[104] If Schelling in his time sought to build a system of thought, his intention was not that such a system should be an end in itself. He wanted it to provide a framework for life and action. Today, our scientific preoccupation with facts and our academic indifference to meaning has brought us to a sad aridity in knowledge itself. We act without wisdom when we act out of unexamined knowledge, or out of what we regard as value-free facts.

Kant's intention was also surely noble, namely to draw strict limits for the exercise of pure reason, in order that we may become truly free from pure reason's constrictions in the significant realms of ethical or moral conduct (practical reason) and aesthetic appreciation (critique of judgment). And he has helped many to see that the criteria of validation used in the physical sciences cannot be applied to the social sciences or to judgments about Beauty and the Good.

But the hiatus between fact and value has only widened as a result of the Kantian critique. The three distinct departments into which Kant divided human knowledge are no longer able in the critical system itself, of coming together again. Intellect, Will, and Feeling cannot find their integrating principle. The Soul, the ancient integrative principle, has now been reduced to Ego or Reason. One seldom asks the question whether something called Reason or Mind really exists any more than the Soul. Even worse is the status of the Ego, which is so hard to locate objectively. So many attempts have been made in post-Kantian thought to achieve that unity, either in the knowing subjective consciousness or in the objectively known world. Kant had torn asunder the then existing unity of theory and practice, science and metaphysics, logic and ethics, the empirical and the transcendental.

The philosophical radicals in Britain like Bentham, Ricardo, Malthus, and James Stuart Mill tried to make up a rational social science. They held that all social phenomena are reducible to laws, and that all the laws of the social world are in their turn explicable by the "laws of human nature." There were two kinds of such laws, physical laws like in physics, chemistry, and biology, and "psychological laws"—that is, individual interest, public interest, and so on. It was the legislator's job to bring the conflict of interests into some harmony, based on an exact knowledge of human nature.[105]

History seems to have, at least for the time being, vindicated the next generation of English liberals who contended with Marx and the Marxists about the basic laws of a social program. John Stuart Mill (son of James Stuart Mill, 1806–1873) struggled hard to develop a social science based on precise laws of social development, but eventually gave up the effort, as Lewis S. Feuer has shown us in his introduction to Mill's *On Socialism.*[106] Already in 1849, while the European revolutions were going on in full swing, Mill questioned the authenticity of the "interest" of the Marxian revolutionaries. He felt that they were somehow really interested only in revolution for revolution's sake, or rather in revolution for the sake of venting the violence, aggression, and hatred pent up in themselves. Mill, working in the London headquarters of the East India Company, had acquired some experience in administering actual human societies, and could not pontificate as easily as Marx and Comte could about how human beings in fact behave. No wonder Sigmund Freud could psychoanalyze John Stuart Mill "as perhaps the man of the century who best managed to free himself from the domination of customary prejudices."[107]

Mill was a staunch supporter of the French Revolution, but could not see eye to eye with Marx and the revolutionaries. He suspected them of a lack of fairness, and questioned their uncontrolled impulsiveness and their free espousal of violence in the interest of justice. He had no qualms about calling himself a socialist, but he disagreed with the three fundamental aspects of Marxian socialism:

(1) The management of the whole productive resources of the country by one central authority

(2) That the working classes, or somebody in their behalf, should take possession of all the property of the country, and administer it for the general benefit

(3) The aim to substitute the new rule for the old at a single stroke, and to exchange the amount of good realized under the present system, and its large possibilities of improvement, for a plunge without any preparation into the most extreme form. [see note 106]

Acknowledging the fact that the Marxian revolutionary program had "great elements of popularity," which was not the case with "the more cautious and reasonable form of Socialism," Mill suspected the revolutionaries of being driven more by hatred and aggression than by the hunger and thirst for justice. The revolutionaries on the other hand would accuse people like Mill of being too comfortable in their middle-class affluence and of being afraid to rock the boat. They would regard him as a defender of the status quo, because his own needs were well taken care of by the system. He may have compassion for the poor, but he is not identified with them in their suffering. No wonder then that Marx himself broke out in a tirade against Mill in the closing days of the Communist International in April 1872.

This raises for us the crucial issue of the relation between knowledge and human interests. Can knowledge be entirely free from bias and interest? This is one of the obvious presuppositions of much of modern science, though in high energy physics it is no longer possible to conceive of objective knowledge as free from subjective interests. There is no knowledge that is validated beyond question by logic. Critical rationality, the principle of modern liberalism, finds itself in this dilemma, that the quest for foundations of knowledge is infinitely regressive; that all certainties of knowledge are self-fabricated; the acceptance of any method, including that of critical rationality, is a moral decision, and cannot be validated by the method itself. Juergen Habermas has clarified the problem for us in his *Knowledge and Human Interests*[108], following in the footsteps of his mentors Max Horkheimer and Theodor Adorno of the Frankfort School of Social Research. Horkheimer is probably the originator of the notion of "Critical Theory," based on a doctrine of "ideology" very similar to the Hindu doctrine of Maya. The whole of reality is pervaded by a totally deceptive illusoriness, and the job of critical theory is to break the spell of this illusion. All myths have to be dispelled, including the myth of a proletarian class able to do the correct kind of reflection, or the myth of a professional class of intellectuals called scientists who will by their method dispel every myth for us. We must question everything again and again, not only prevailing ideas, but also existing conditions of life.[109] This also explains his colleague Adorno's tirade, *Against Epistemology,*[110] for the quest for a foolproof epistemology makes the fatefully wrong assumption that the correct epistemology will yield unerring and indubitably certain knowledge.

Horkheimer was countering the Platonic understanding of theory, that theory can be a basis for reflective-mimetic knowledge that can then become the basis for action. Edmund Husserl was trying to reinstate traditional theory, but he was basing his arguments on three mistaken assumptions: that there is an objectivism in the physical sciences, a lawlike structure connecting objective facts to each other, which Husserl tried to formulate in his *Phenomenology;* that the phenomenological method could transcend all subjective interest to yield a universal entity called consciousness, free from all interest and particularity which seem to be the sources of error; and that an Absolute Universal-Ego-with-Consciousness-of-the-World can be contemplated as the absolute truth.

Horkheimer's major contribution is in the distinction he makes between "technical reason" and "ontological reason." Marx put all his emphasis on the first, swinging to the opposite extreme from the theorists of pure contemplation. For Marx all theory was not only for practice, but all theory arose only in practice. Practice is thus primary as well as final. Theory is only an interlude. He was right only insofar as he was thinking of technical reason with its practical or activist interest. But there is another side to reason—the ontological aspect, which is concerned not so much about technical activity to interact with nature and produce commodities, as with its own emancipation; Reason finds itself confined and constricted by nonknowledge and the presence of the Other as a threat; it seeks emancipation, not for the sake of technological practice, but for the sake of emancipation itself, which is an internal need of Reason.

Habermas picks up the argument at this point and carries on the battle against both positivism and historicism, the two quests for certainty, the first dominating the Anglo-American world, and the second the German-speaking world. In reacting to Hegel's speculative method, Habermas would build his general system of Universal Pragmatics, based on experience and critical rationality, as the Zeitgeist demands.

Dilthey in Germany tried another track of positing a separate realm called *Lebenswelt*, or life-world, which obeyed laws different from those of nature; only a *Lebensphilosophie* or philosophy of life could provide a basis for the *Geisteswissenschaften* or social sciences. Following Herder, Goethe, Schelling, Schliermacher, and Humboldt, Dilthey made *Verstehen* or understanding a different category from causal explanation, which could work only in the physical sciences. Understanding demanded the experience of living inside the actors of history (*Einleben*) and reconstructing their experience from the inside. This is possible, for the mind is universal, and the individual mind, participating in the universal mind, has access to the mind of others through reflection. Dilthey, with other German sociologist-philosophers like Windelband, Rickert, and Simmel, made a clear distinction between "nature" and "culture" with different methodologies appropriate for them. It was this distinction that Max Weber (1864–1920) used with such effect in sociology. Society is not to be studied in terms of "laws of development" as in the physical sciences, but through *deutend Verstehen,* or the art of understanding on the level of meaning and not merely of causal explanation.

Until recently the Anglo-American world entertained dreams of making science so pervasive that it could do away with both philosophy and religion and become the sole source of truth and true knowledge. The hope was that only scientific affirmations would be regarded as truth; obviously, religion, poetry, and art would in this view be relegated to the realm of untruth. The Germans once thought philosophy could be stated in its final and permanent form; Fichte, for example, held that there was only one philosophy possible, but in general the German tradition was averse to making Newtonian physics the model for all knowledge.

Edmund Husserl tried to discover the essence of pure consciousness, temporarily bracketing out the world of experience, so that the mind can be known in itself, independent of the material world. After acknowledging that consciousness and thinghood form one interconnected whole, he still believed that in thought at least consciousness can be understood in itself. He also saw that consciousness is linked with the material world in a twofold way: it is attached to and dependent on a body that is part of the material world; it is also always consciousness-of; consciousness cannot function without an object. Consciousness thus exists always between two poles, the subject and the object; one of these, namely the subject, has to be part of the material world. Husserl persisted, by making another "epoche," or suspension of the individual ego with all its particularities, to find a pure, universal world of "phenomena in consciousness,"—an "eidetic world," a realm of objects not in the material world, but in the mind, and not available to the empirical sciences for study by their methods of investigation.

Kant and Husserl saw the same problem, namely that the rising empirical sciences are not capable of doing what classical philosophy did, providing foundations for thought and knowledge. Both were inspired by the classically modern effort of Descartes (1596–1650) to provide such foundations without presuppositions. Descartes started out with the three realities of God, World, and Self. God was certainly not self-evident. The real objective existence of the world, apart from consciousness, is also doubtful. So Descartes starts out with the indubitable single fact, that he was thinking, and therefore the thinker must exist. Of course he was inspired by Augustine's effort in the fifth century of a similar kind, confronted with the havoc that the philosophy of Skepticism had done to the educated of his own time. The Skeptics and the Sophists had demonstrated that anything can be proved by logic and that any logical proof can be disproved by the same logic. In this situation, for Augustine, nothing was certain, everything was doubtful. In Augustine's fertile mind arose the idea that only one thing was certain, namely that everything was uncertain. So he latched on to that as his starting point, namely that he was doubting everything, except the fact that he was doubting. That, he thought, was not to be doubted: the indubitable existence of the doubting and the doubter. I, the doubter, exist—that much was self-evident to Augustine. Descrates, who had studied with the Jesuits and knew his Augustine, made a slight change and got to his *cogito, ergo sum:* I think, therefore I exist. Husserl takes the same starting point, but the thinking ego itself was difficult to locate; he therefore shifted attention from the *cogito* (I think) to the *cogita* (the things thought).

Husserl was trying to do the same thing that Kant did, to write a new critique of pure consciousness, that would not make the separation Kant made among the three departments of consciousness. He conceived the task of philosophy as something that science itself cannot do, that is, provide a theoretical science which would be the foundation of all the empirical sciences. Here he could not follow the scientific method, but chose rather the method opened up by Hegel's *Phenomenology of the Spirit,* namely a careful description of the way things work, which one can check with one's own experience.[111]

Husserl's was the last heroic effort of German thought to save both science and philosophy (which Kant had separated) in one blow. Martin Heidegger used the method of phenomenology to save philosophy, but of science he thought rather poorly. Husserl's problem was that ever since Fichte, Schelling, and Hegel tried to fly high in speculative thought and ended up by crash landing, the West had become allergic to speculation. Meanwhile, science had already become so powerful and productive in the nineteenth century that only a philosophy related to science could survive at all. Empiricism, of which Newton or Descartes knew next to nothing, had come to reign. *Zu den Sachen selbst:* 'To the Things themselves' was the warcry of the New Reich in knowledge.

The ancient Greeks put large stock by *theoria* or theory, the systematic purification and illumination of the mind in order that the soul may rise from the mundane to the cosmic, from matter to spirit, from the temporal-imperfect to the eternal-perfect, from the changing to the unchanging. Such knowledge was the true religion of the cultivated classes. Hegel effected on the Platonic line a gigantic *tour de force* on the basis of the Christian faith: he boldly speculated that the eternal was constantly manifesting itself through the temporal, that the two are not essentially different from or opposed to each other as perfect and imperfect, that one need not look for the Absolute outside the contingent, that all that is and all that happens is the Absolute working itself out from potentiality to actuality through the dialectical process of development in history.

Hegel's was a magnificent vision in the lecture room, but when one came out the reality one saw did not fit the vision. So Kierkegaard reacted, revolting against the grandeur of the cosmic vision and retreating into the more proximate area of subjective experience and fulfillment. Existentialism found in him a true prophet, but that noble philosophy has failed to endure. Marx and Engels revolted in the opposite direction, denying any absolute other than matter in motion, and seeking fulfilment in the classless society to be brought about by a victorious working class. That hope, too, fades from the horizon as we enter the last decade of the twentieth century.

Both Kierkegaard and Marx have taught us important lessons. Kierkegaard's emphasis on individual subjectivity as truth was gladly revived and welcomed where objective certainties were hard to come by in postwar Europe of the nineteen-fifties. It also fitted in with the prevailing individualist tempo of capitalism. Today, existentialist philosophy itself has moved out of focus, but in the second half of our century we have latched on in a strong way to individual-based convictions: the idea of the dignity of the human person and the inviolability of personal human rights.

Marx, too, has left us a legacy of social rights, of immense value to the poor and underprivileged of the world. The oppressed and exploited have also a right to seek their own emancipation, and not to be left where Kant left them, to wait till they come by *Bildung* and property and become middle class or bourgeois. What if Marxism-Leninism of the 1917 variety goes out of fashion in 1989, like existentialism did two decades earlier? History is still open, and we have not yet heard the last word about the struggle of the oppressed, though many East and Central Europeans as well as many westerners seem to think so. Did not Marx open the way for the oppressed and the exploited to hope and to seek emancipation through organized effort? The battlegrounds of history are strewn with the relics of those who fought and lost, but the battle goes on. Hegel's thought came in handy for Marx, though largely in reacting against it. Without Hegel, there would be no Marxism or Western liberal thought.

Marxism as an Integral System

Karl Marx (1818–1883) did not set out as a system philosopher. Well trained in European philosophy, an ardent student of Hegel (who died five years before Marx was born) in his late teens, he took his doctorate of philosophy from Jena University at the age of twenty-three. His doctoral dissertation was on the difference between the Natural Philosophies of Democritus and Epicurus. He had been baptized as a Lutheran at the age of six, when his whole family seems to have joined the Christian church, whether out of conviction or to paternal ancestors were all Jews, as was also his mother. The young Marx belonged to the Hegelian Left, and his doctoral dissertation was a final repudiation of religion and an embracing of atheism.[112]

Distrustful not only of systems, but of philosophers in general, Marx was convinced that the world of history and nature, of consciousness and world, was a single dynamic system. Philosophers have explained the world, but the point is to change it, as he said in the opening words of his *Poverty of Philosophy,* which in turn was a response to the French Anarchist Proudhon's (1809–1865) *Philosophy of Poverty* (actually, *Philosophie de Propriete*). Marx was no Kantian and he would not accept any separation between theory and practice, or between pure reason and practical reason. Neither would he accept the Platonic position that the function of theory was first to shape reality in the mind and then to shape external reality accordingly. Theory questions arise in the context of practice and are ancillary to practice. Truth is not to be sought in theory but in transformed social reality like the classless society, where all would be free and spontaneously good, and where there would be no need for a coercive state.

But Marx had a consistent theory of reality. He sought to set it forth in his *Grundrisse,* but he was obviously unsatisfied with the effort and refused to publish it in his lifetime. Between Marx and his more philosophically inclined colleague Engels, they did have a highly sophisticated and integrated theory of the whole, though they did encounter some insoluble problems in their quest for theoretical unity. Engels, for example, worked it out in his *Dialectics of Nature,* but when it came to the question whether the final end of the historical process of social formation would be a static final entity and whether the dialectics of nature would stop there, he could only have recourse to the Indian Tradition of *Pralaya* and *Vilaya,* or periodic expansion and contraction. He suggested that contradictions within the classless society would lead to its dissolution, and that the whole process of dialectical development would have to start all over again.

Nature and consciousness were, for Marx and Engels, of one piece, both temporally and spatially. It was out of material reality that life and consciousness rose and they do not exist apart from that material base. In fact, both nature and humanity are not only continuous in time, but symbiotic in space. They are nurtured by each other, in a mutual metabolism or *Stoffwechsel;* nature is both humanized by humanity's presence and action in it, and sustains humanity by providing not only food and air, light and heat, but also by nature's being the material reality through the handling of which a human infant becomes a human being and a society becomes human and sustains itself through organized labour.

It is a highly integrated system of theory, with three interacting levels quite different from Kant's three departments. At the first level are the forces of production, including human brain and muscle power and the technology that enhances that power through the creation of more sophisticated tools both founded upon and being perpetually advanced by the knowledge of science. We can take the liberty of labelling Marx's first level as *Forces of Production: Science and Technology.* At the second level one can find the patterns of organization of social labor, which we can now label: *Relations of Production: Political Economy.* The two are constantly interactive, not two separate departments. When science and technology progresses and the forces of production are consequently enhanced, changes are called for in political economy or the organization of social labor, in order to make social production efficient and effective. At the third level, constantly and in many ways affected by the levels below, we find what we commonly call *Culture and Ideology,* which in turn affects the other two levels. To this third level belongs not only art and music and all that we commonly call culture, but also ideology, which can in fact be either false or true theory.

Marx did not undervalue thought. Thought leads astray only when it becomes purely cerebral without any material or manual correlation or content. Marx accuses Feuerbach of having thus gone astray into a thought that is purely cerebral or pectoral, though Marx himself learned something from him, as his *Theses on Feuerbach* show. Thought, for Marx, is an integral aspect of both perception and action. It has to be critical, penetrative beyond appearances, and feedback interpretative. Truth is not a relationship in mere theory or contemplation, but in theory and practice as well, especially in the theory and practice of relationships, as Ernst Bloch would say. Practice is proof of theory, Marx would admit; but he would insist that practice is not ancillary to theory; when practice confirms theory, both theory and practice are simultaneously affirmed.

Hegel, too, was anxious to hold theory and practice together; for him theory gets worked out in practice, as the Spirit works itself out in history. There is a dialectical relation between theory and practice in Hegel. The transition is from the theoretical mind (perception, imagination, thought), to its antithesis, the practical mind (will, feeling, drive, happiness, social relationships, and work relationships). But the final synthesis is the concrete "rational State" that wills what it knows and knows what it wills.[113] The difference between Hegel and Marx is this: For Hegel, ultimately everything leads back to *Theoria,* the science of transcendent knowing of the Manifest, and knowing of the Transcendent through the Manifest. It is in *Theoria* that alienation occurs, and that is where the reconciliation has to take place. For Marx, on the other hand, it is theory-for-the-sake-of-practice and not practice in order to check theory and then to go back to theory in blissful contemplation. In this eleventh thesis on Feuerbach, Marx does not say that it is useless that "philosophers have interpreted the world"; he does not dispense with the need to interpret reality, but only so long as the point of the exercise is to change reality.

It is a pity that the Marxian system of holding theory and practice together is now (since 1989) losing its adherents by the millions. It is indeed a noble creed, a hope-generating set of beliefs leading to qualitatively high human action. Its atheistic premise, like the God-hypothesis for early Deist science, seems something extraneous that can be dispensed with. One form of establishment Marxism, the Marxist-Leninist model of 1917–1989, while it may have failed, has taught us many lessons in its seventy-two years of existence. But the basic vision of Marx-Engels, with due modifications of course, will continue to inspire generations to come with fresh insights and noble motivations for action. It was indeed an integral system of practice-theory, the first experimental model of which has failed. But that is the way history advances, stochastically aiming several times before hitting the target. The first arrow seems to have gone wide of the mark; history usually learns from its mistakes and tries again.

The problem of knowledge and its certainty, the validation of method and the justification of conditions of life, cannot appeal to any single objective authority. The dialectics of the Enlightenment have shown us how impossible it is to put our full trust either in critical reason or in Marxist ideology, because it is our fear of other methods that leads us to make a moral decision to embrace the methodology of critical reason, as one that is free from presuppositions, or the Marxist ideology as an illusion-free approach to reality. Both have their own hidden presuppositions, and our choice of one of these two or any other way forward, would not be based on any kind of indubitable authority; it will be only an act of humanity in freedom, undergirded by wisdom or unwisdom. It is always an act of faith more than anything else. There is no *prima philosophia* to be used as an indubitable or self-evident starting point. For every first premise is already a concept, not a self-evident reality. Whether it is the certainty of the ego that cogitates, or the indubitability of the doubter that doubts, these are but constructions of the mind, concepts that are not the same as self-evident realities. No one can be easily exculpated from this "original sin" of philosophy, whether it is Hegel with his "absolute knowledge" arrived at through philosophy, or Heidegger with his vaunted "destruction" of all previous Western Philosophy.

We shall later look at the question how some non-Western traditions went about dealing with this problem. It is an illusion of the European Enlightenment that there exists some presuppositionless, indubitable knowledge, which can be arrived at without reference to tradition or external authority, by the free exercise of adult human rationality, critical or otherwise. It seems that only a full realization of what this means can lead European civilization to firmer ground and create foundations for a new civilization. As it is, the ground is both shaky and crumbling.

Chapter Seven

THEORY FOR PRACTICE, OR THE OTHER WAY AROUND?

Theory and Practice: Which is the End?

It is important for us to grasp this problem of the relation between theory and practice, if we want to seek new foundations for new civilizations. The point has been worked out in some detail by Juergen Habermas, formerly of the Frankfort School of Social Research and the last of the disciples of Horkheimer and Adorno, in his *Theorie und Praxis,* as well as in his important 1965 Inaugural Lecture at Frankfort on *Erkenntnis und Interesse* or *Knowledge and Human Interests.*[114]

It was Max Horkheimer of the Frankfort School who first made clear the distinction between traditional theory and the new critical theory initiated by Immanuel Kant and furiously attacked by Marx in his *Holy Family.* Horkheimer was opposed to traditional theory; his epistemology was one of basic doubt, since there is in the world a "universal system of delusion" out to set traps for the seeker after knowledge, and so every bit of knowledge has first to be doubted and critically assessed before being accepted.[115]

Horkheimer felt the need to move from traditional theory to critical theory, but not just for the abstract pleasure of theoretical contemplation of truth: "a critical and oppositional theory" must manifest itself "in the activity of permanent and fundamental contestation and opposition to the existing conditions of life." Of course, he ends up by admitting that the claim of any theory to be absolute and final has to be taken with a grain of salt.

Classical theory, which follows Plato's notion of *theoria,* sought after an ontology of the whole as the true, the good, and the beautiful; but in order to find that ontology, the contemplative mind has to move away from surface appearances, from matter and the empirical, from the manifold and the imperfect, from those things that have to do with time and space. What lies behind and beyond the phenomena is the goal of the classical quest. They did it through myths and legends, gods and daemons, but above all with the thesis about a *kosmos noētos,* a world of mental objects, peopled by eternal and perfect noumena held together by the single-manifold unity of the *nous* or *logos* that held everything together in an interconnected system. It was this classical ontology that Marx rejected and which Husserl recreated without myth or legend, as he thought.

Classical theory had also a very elaborate technology for thus rising from the temporal and the eternal. These techniques are what you learn first in Plato's academy or Aristotle's peripatetic school. Hence their name: *mathēmata,* or the things that are taught in the academy or lyceum. If Pythagoras, the spiritual ancestor of Socrates, Plato, and in some sense all classical philosophers including Aristotle, taught geometry or arithmetic to his disciples (*mathētēs*), it was not for use in land survey or engineering, but to teach the technique of abstraction. While things are material, numbers are not. Rhythm, order, number, and relations like proportion, angle, or as Gregory Bateson was to say in our time, difference—these are not material realities, and by contemplating them the mind rises above the material, temporal and imperfect. The *mathēmata* or *mathēmatika* are not material or temporal. Mathematics, for the ancients, was training for the spiritual ascent, for cleansing the mind from its attachment to the sensual and the material, not for commercial calculations or banking, not for engineering, civil, mechanical, or electronic.

In the transition from the medieval to the modern period, it was Johannes Kepler (1571–1630), disciple and successor of Tycho Brahe as court astronomer for Emperor Rudolph II, who grasped this mathematical harmony of the universe as the foundation of truth. Science, the study of natural laws and mathematics, *is* truth, not a *way* to rise to the truth. This New Pythagoreanism, so radically different from the Pythagoreanism of Pythagoras himself, has provided the foundation for modern science. Kepler's neo-Pythagoreanism was strictly empirical: a mathematical harmony which can be checked through the way things are and behave. What Kepler and most prophets of mathematical logic do not often know is what Adorno pointed out (and long before him Plotinus)—that numbers themselves are concepts and not empirical reality. Five fingers, five books, five pens: these may be empirical, but not the number five as such. Mathematics belongs to the realm of the conceptual, not to that of real existents; in fact, number as abstraction depends on the old dualism of the objective and the subjective. In Plotinus' comprehensive polemic against Aristotle's categories, he insists that numbers are not empirical objects or substances, but abstract entities belonging only to the intelligible and not the sensible world.[116]

Classical Theory and Practice

But mathematics was only propaedeutic for the celestial ascent, as far as the classics are concerned. Mathematics will not take you up there: it is only initiatory training. The real ascent is achieved only through *katharsis* and *ellampsis,* or purification and illumination. Actually, illumination takes place only as an act of grace on the part of the gods, when the purification process is completed. This *illuminatio* or inner Enlightenment is something the seeker cannot control or generate. It is an ascent to the Logos who holds everything together in the manifold, but it has nothing to do with any sort of logic or system. It is our academic misunderstanding of Socrates or Plato that makes us think they taught that the dialogical method would by itself lead to the truth. It is only the seeker who has undergone *katharsis* who can benefit from the dialogical process, not the dry academic intellectual or strict logician who has not undergone the necessary process of purification. This is so in Socrates or Plato, Plotinus or Pythagoras.

Here is the fundamental cleavage between the classical tradition and the modern tradition—this understanding of the nature of the practice that leads to theory, and this decision about which is the final aim to attain, the theory or the practice. The classical tradition values practice only for the sake of theory. Theory is without doubt the final end. At this point Hegel belongs more to the classical tradition than to the modern. For him, too, "absolute knowledge," which is an end in itself, is theory, something that happens in consciousness and which makes a human being human.

We can see this by comparing Kant and Hegel. Kant does not overcome the dichotomy between knowing subject and known object. He simply takes Descartes' *cogito* as given. The ego that cogitates, however, remains elusive, also for Kant. When I begin to reflect on my own reflective ego, that latter ego is an object of thought and not subject. There has to be another ego which is subject that has to reflect on the ego as object, and the two cannot be the same. The ego as subject is always transcendent, and cannot be made an object, for when made an object the ego loses its basic characteristic, which is to be subject.

This was Hegel's fundamental criticism of Kant's critical philosophy, that it takes the ego, the subjective consciousness as self-evident or transparent to itself, and then goes on to delineate the categories that govern its rational activity. When ego-consciousness is integrated into the world of objects it is negated, and is no longer there as subject, to be self-evident. The real subjective ego cannot be an object; and is not given to itself in the primary act of knowing. It finds its place in the reflective ego, but not in the world that is the object of thought. Hegel takes Kant to task for knowing the ego only in its objective existence, and therefore not as ego. If ego and consciousness are that slippery, then knowledge based on a questionable description of the ego as pure reason, practical reason, aesthetic judgment, and so on cannot be truly reliable. When I look at the objective world, it has being for me, *pour-moi, fuer-mich,* but I do not know its being in-itself, *en-soi, in-sich.* When I make consciousness an object, I know its being for-me but not in itself. It do not know the *en-soi* of consciousness or ego.

The classical tradition does not have the high view moderns have of language or reason, which they sometimes regard as that which distinguishes the human from the animal, and therefore in some sense constitutive of the very essence of man. Plotinus, of the third century A.D., the study of whose writings was revived in Europe in the fifteenth century by the Byzantine student of Plato, Giorgios Gemistos Pletho (ca. 1355–1450), thought that the kind of rationality and language associated with the lower soul are but temporary and passing, for they are devices by which the soul that has fallen into body and therefore into time and space, can find its way about in this bewildering manifold world. Once the soul has by inner illumination risen to a higher level, our kind of language and our present kind of reason are perfectly superfluous.

What Kant and modern critical philosophy makes much of, Plotinus and the mystical tradition in the West takes lightly. The latter would assess the huge, tremendous, painstaking effort of modern critical reason to gain precision and accuracy in knowledge about the physical universe as a ludicrously misplaced effort, unless it were a propaedeutic or preparation for the transintellectual spiritual ascent that leads to true enlightenment. The task of philosophy, for Plotinus, is to make possible the *epistrophe* or conversion or reversion of the lower soul to the higher soul, and the adhesion of both to the One and the *Nous,* thereby overcoming all manifoldness and duality.[117]

And this cannot take place through discursive reasoning. The sixth tractate of the first Ennead waxes eloquent on virtue (*areté*) as the beauty (*kalon*) of the soul (*psuche*) and this manifold (*ekeina*) world as participation in the One and the *Nous.* Outside the Divine Logos (*exo theiou logou*), there is only the ugly (*aischron*), for what is not ruled by form and logos is the essence of ugliness. The beauties of the realm of sense are due to the invasion of form from the Logos. But there is another beauty or goodness (*kalon*) that is not attached to sense-objects. These can only be perceived by the soul, but not through sense perception. This is a higher perception of the soul because of its own affinity to the Good. This higher vision of the "face of righteousness and wisdom" (*to tes dikaiosunes kai sophrosunes prosopon*) gives higher delight, but

> such vision is for those only who see with the Soul's sight—and at the vision they will rejoice, and awe will fall on them and a trouble deeper than all the rest could ever stir, for now they are moving in the realm of truth.[118]

This, however, is part of the experience of the soul while still in the body, this "Dionysiac exultation that thrills through your being, this straining upwards of all your soul, this longing to break away from the body and live sunken within the veritable self," as Stephen McKenna's translation of Plotinus puts it. They are the "true lovers" (*oi ontos erotikoi*). In other words, even this level of moral beauty of the good, of justice and wisdom, can be seen, while still in the body, by the soul. But it is only part of the ascent towards something still higher.

Plotinus holds that the soul becomes ugly, not because of any distortion in it, but simply because of the accretion of the mud and filth of lusts and passions.

> So, we may justly say, a Soul becomes ugly—by something foisted upon it, by sinking itself into the alien, by a fall, by a descent into body, into Matter. The dishonour of the Soul is in its ceasing to be clean and apart. Gold is degraded when it is mixed with earthly particles; if these be worked out, the gold is left and is beautiful, gold with gold alone. And so the Soul; let it be but cleared of the desires that come by its too intimate converse with the body, emancipated from all the passions, purged of all that embodiment has thrust upon it, withdrawn, a solitary, to itself again—in that moment the ugliness that came only from the alien is stripped away.[119]

This is what Plotinus means by *katharsis* or purification leading to Enlightenment. As Plotinus puts it in the opening sentence of 1.6.6 (in my own translation, which seeks not to take liberties with the text, which a consummate scholar like Stephen MacKenna can afford to take): "It is so, as the ancient word has it, that wise discipline (*hé sophrosune*), and courage or manliness (*hé andria*) and all virtue (*pasa areté*), and even wisdom (*phronēsis*) itself, *is* purification (*katharsis*)."

It is only *katharsis* that leads to pure *theoria* for the ancients. This *katharsis* is moral purification, a self-discipline that makes one free from the passions that war against the soul, a moving away from the craving for material objects and for the satisfactions they yield. According to Plotinus, this demands "the sternest and uttermost combat" of the soul (*agon megistos kai eschatos psuchais prokeitai*); all effort and endeavor should be for this (*huper hou kai ho pas ponos*).[120]

Mystics who have attained the Great Vision usually do not speak much either about its content or about the way to it. For Plotinus, this vision takes us back to the soul's original homeland, from which we have wandered (*Patris de hemin, hothen parelthomen*—1.6.8), where the Father is (*pater ekei*).

For the Mystics at least, this is *theoria*, the final purpose of all human effort. Augustine learned it from Plotinus and handed it down to the Western Christian tradition as the essence of Christianity. Eastern Christianity sometimes followed the same road, though it had a different, and I think, nobler tradition, long before Augustine's time. We should have a look at this "Other Enlightenment" in its historical development. Then perhaps we can go on to look at this understanding of the final goal of all knowledge in Eastern Christianity and in some non-European religions.

The issue is indeed central to our enquiry. Is theory ancillary to practice, or is practice a means to theory, the final fulfilment for human beings? The whole "mystical tradition," as the West has come to call it, is a series of practices leading to the final *theoria* of the beatific vision or mystical union. So, too, other great traditions of the world see true enlightenment as the *theoria* that finally transforms all reality, and beyond which there is no further goal to be pursued, except, as in Buddhism, the similar enlightenment of others.

In the modern European Enlightenment, however, theory is always ancillary to practice: you know in order to act; this is so for liberals and Marxists. Occasionally someone says, like Habermas and the Frankfort School, that knowledge has an interest in itself as emancipatory and not instrumental. But Habermas seeks that emancipation in and through the European Enlightenment, not in the other enlightenment. Generally speaking, for most moderns, "knowledge is power" power to manipulate, control, and dominate. That fact becomes most dominantly clear in the new inseparability of science and technology. There was a time when scientists talked about pure science; but today the scientific enterprise is indistinguishable from the gigantic industry-communication-cybernetics-technology complex in which it is enmeshed and without which it cannot advance or continue to function.

Is the situation, then, one of hopeless opposition between the two approaches to theory and practice? Do we always have to counterpose "mysticism" on the one hand and "science and technology" on the other? Is there no other option? This is indeed a question to which we must give serious attention in this modest work. Before we do so, however, we need to examine some practical issues like the concept of justice and the nature of science and technology in the context of the European Enlightenment.

Chapter Eight

Justice, Human Rights, and the State in European Civilization

Among the ideas generated or distorted by the European Enlightenment, transformations undergone by a perennial idea like justice merit our attention. The new notion of human rights created by the Enlightenment has now become the foundation of this traditional concept of justice. The analysis will exemplify again the spirit of the Enlightenment and the problems of a rationalistic ethics falsely purporting to be without metaphysical presuppositions.

Just What is Justice?

The English word "justice" and the original latin *justitia,* with its cognates in various European languages, all have the underlying notion of *jus* = law. It so happens that in the German language, the word for law is *Recht,* which can also mean justice or right. This odd happenstance has made possible many equivocations. In German there is no need to say that *Recht* (justice) is based on *Recht* (right). But in English it has only been recently discovered (by John Rawls) that the notion of justice as well as the notion of law are based on the prior notion of right in modern European thought from the time of Immanuel Kant.

For the ancient Romans, someone was *justus* if he or she abode by the laws of the land and the law handed down by venerable tradition. The symbol of justice, at least in the main Roman tradition, is a faceless, impartial person, usually female, holding a balance in her hand, and weighing out to each according to what he or she has merited. Never mind the fact that justice for the free citizen of Rome was injustice for the slave. After all, the slave was not a full human person!

The Greek tradition, being more philosophically inclined, was quite different. For Plato, justice is a generic word, not for just one of the virtues, but for virtue (heroic goodness = *areté*) in general. Aristotle sometimes thought with his master that justice meant all virtue, and at other times that it was only one of the four cardinal virtues along with prudence, manliness, and moderation. He defines justice in book 5 of his *Nicomachean Ethics* as "that state of character which renders men disposed to act justly, and which causes them to do and to wish that which is just." In other words, it is a personal rather than social reality. It is a hexis, a personal character trait, acquired by good upbringing and intense training, in an individual human being. Aristotle, when he came to think about social questions, found his own definition inadequate and proceeded to revise it as follows:

> Justice, in this sense, is perfect virtue, though with the qualification that it is virtue in relation to our neighbours. Because of this the view is often held that in the list of virtues, justice occupies the top place.[121]

Aristotle's less known work, *Peri Areton kai Kakon* or *On Virtues and Vices,* gives a slightly more elaborate definition of *dikaiosuné* or righteousness, justice, as a virtue:

> To justice belongs the readiness to give to each according to his desert, to conserve family customs (*sozein ta patria ethé*), as well as institutions and written laws, to behave honestly where interest is involved, and to faithfully execute agreements and undertakings. The priority obligations of just people is towards the gods, then to the *daimones,* then to fatherland and parents, then to the departed (*pros tous katoichomenous*). Following justice is always holiness (*hosiotes*), truth, faithfulness and hatred of evil.[122]

Both the Nicomachean and the Eudaemonian as well as other versions of Aristotle's ethical and political thought, we should remember, we have only from student notes and not from the pen of the Master himself. We can therefore overlook some of the inconsistencies among the various definitions. One thing, however, is noticeable, more in Aristotle than in Plato: a fundamental inclination to conceive justice in individualist terms. This is so in Kant and in much of the Enlightenment tradition. Hegel is certainly an exception, but this individualistic orientation seems to be endemic to the Western tradition, and seems to have been there long before capitalism appeared on the scene.

The Golden Age of Roman Justice

In classical Roman society, as it was later to be in the early Enlightenment society, justice was only for the elite, for the free citizens, for the nobility by birth or achievement or property. Caste privilege dominated every aspect of Roman society in a manner difficult to imagine in the Indian society of today or even of two thousand years ago.

The forms and structures through which this justice for the elite was administered were fully cloaked in mysteries and religious ceremonies. It helped only to salve the conscience of the rulers, to hallow injustice with the aura of divine sanctions, and to make the priestly class protectors and beneficiaries of the unjust system. That tradition rules to this day. Why otherwise the wigs and gowns and cloaks of the judges and advocates in many countries? Why this severe punishment for "contempt of court," even in societies that do not respect other institutions? Even blasphemy and the use of filthy language in public today do not offend the upholders of society, but "contempt of court" does provoke legal punishment, even when such contempt may be quite well deserved. It is all part of the ritual halo with which the judiciary and the academy protects the sanctity of the Establishment.

In Roman society, legal training (as a *Rhetor* or rhetorician), legal honors, and a forensic reputation provided the easiest road for access to power (as it does to this day). The male children of the Roman elite all received thorough legal training, so that as an adult each would be fit to inherit the mantle of power. It was the most important part of the training of the elite,[123] for their central concern was to keep power from slipping away. For the Romans as well as for us, law, justice, the courts, the state, the legislature—all these are more for keeping power secure in the hands of its holders than to maintain or promote real justice for the poor. How many among those who hold power in our nations today really want the poor to secure justice in the world?

As injustice ripened and Greek philosophy spread among the Romans, the need arose to build up some philosophical justification for law in general and for the particular kind of laws the Romans had. Cicero was of course prominent among such philosophers of law. We know him better because his writings have come down to us: he virtually laid down the agenda for the debate about justice as well as the rules of that debate, for the Western tradition. Cicero's thought and categories entered the European Christian tradition through Lactantius and Augustine. He was more of an orator than a philosopher, and what philosophy there was in him came from the Greek Stoics. It is illuminating to look at the Ciceronian notion of justice, in the light of what Kant and Hegel have later told us.

For Cicero, the ground of all justice is the understanding of nature, and particularly of human nature. Carneades had argued that law and justice arise by human convention; that is why the laws of the nations differ from each other. Cicero disagrees:

> True law is right reason in agreement with nature; it is of universal application, unchanging and everlasting; it summons to duty by its commands, and averts wrongdoing by its prohibitions . . . It is a sin to alter this law, nor is it allowable to repeal any part of it, and it is impossible to abolish it entirely. We cannot be freed from its obligations by senate or people . . . And there will not be different laws at Rome and at Athens, or different law now and in the future, but one eternal law will be valid for all nations and at all times, and there will be one master and ruler, that is, God, over us all, for he is the author of this law, its promulgator and its enforcing judge.[124]

Obviously Cicero's perception of universal natural law did not fit the facts of experience. Slavery persisted in Rome and Athens, and the philosophers obviously saw no injustice in it. Cicero, who was also a lawmaker, found no problem with the fact that in the same Roman society there were different laws for the "free citizens" and for others: the *jus civile* for the Romans and the *jus gentium* for those who were not Roman citizens.

Ulpian, in the second century, wanted to solve the problem by positing that there were three different kinds of law: the *jus naturale*, the *jus civile*, and the *jus gentium*. Obviously no one lived by the first, that is, natural law. It seems Rousseau may have read Ulpian, since they both believe that a human being is born free and was enslaved only by the laws of nations and societies. Ulpian's principles were incorporated into the foundation of Roman law by Byzantine Emperor Justinian in 533 A.D. when he formulated the Justinian Code: the *Corpus Juris*, incorporating the *Digest* and the *Institutes*. Natural law here becomes the universal standard against which all law has to be tested. For Justinian's legal counsellors and drafters, this was an obvious Christian position. Had not St Paul said?:

> When Gentiles, who have not the law, do by nature what the law requires, they are a law to themselves, even though they do not have the law. They show that what the law requires is written on their hearts.[125]

It would seem that Cicero of Rome and Paul of Tarsus got their ideas about natural law from the same sources. The Christian fathers completed the picture by using an ancient Jewish teaching about the fall of man as the middle ground, which explains the discrepancy between the natural law written on the hearts of human beings, and their actual practice, including the laws of Romans and Greeks.

Augustine made the distinction more schematic by his most influential doctrine of the two cities, the City of God (*civitas Dei*) and the City of the Earth (*civitas terrae*). The two had their different laws. Only the first was divine, and therefore good. The second was a creation of sinful human beings, and therefore necessarily evil. This was a radical departure from Christian teaching and even from Augustine's own earlier position, which was based on St. Paul's injunction in his *Epistle to the Romans:*

> All should subordinate themselves to the ruling authorities; for all authority comes from God. The ruling authorities are established by God. So anyone rebelling against them is rebelling against what God has instituted.[126]

Clearly, for St. Paul the City of the Earth is instituted by God, not by sinful human beings. Other New Testament writers, with the exception of the author of the Book of Revelation, bear witness to the fact that the Apostolic Church's general teaching was more like Paul's than Augustine's. Paul appealed to Caesar, as a Roman citizen, and was spared his life by Roman law, but finally the same Roman law beheaded him. It was in the context of a church-persecuting state that Paul wrote to his lieutenant Titus, to "remind the people to be subordinate to rulers and authorities and to be obedient."[127] St. Peter echoes this church teaching when he writes:

> Subordinate yourselves for the Lord's sake to every authority instituted among human beings: whether to the king, as supreme, or to governors as sent by his authority.[128]

Augustine rejected this church norm because of his Manichean doctrine of original sin, which has no real basis in the authentic Christian tradition. By doing so, he also rejected the notion of "natural law," replacing it with the concept of divine law, the *jus divinum,* which is in conflict with laws made by sinful human beings.

This notion of the relation between *jus divinum* and *jus humanum* played a major role in the development of subsequent Western thought. Charlemagne's Christendom (ninth century) claimed that it had established the *jus divinum* as the law of the *Holy* Roman Empire; this was the law of the City of God on earth, radically different from the old Roman Empire, which was obviously unholy as it was based on manmade laws.[129]

It was Thomas Aquinas who brought back the concept of natural law, though the idea had been upheld by many in earlier times, like Pope Gratian in his *Decretum* (1140 A.D.) and the professors of law at Bologna. Thomas actually systematized the concept of natural law in his *Summa Theologica*, devoting a full treatise to the the subject of law.[130]

Aquinas's overall contribution to Western thought, in my opinion, is his method of precise definition and systematic reasoning. Modern science follows in his footsteps in this regard. On the debit side, however, precision became the big problem later on: Once a precise bit of truth has been distilled and spelt out, as the scholastics always managed, then one could draw logical corollaries from that indubitable conclusion of *scientia*.

Aquinas developed three levels of law: (a) the divine law, or *jus divinum* in the mind of God, which is disclosed only by special revelation; (b) the same law reflected in Nature as natural law, which can be studied by natural philosophy; and (c) the law of reason in the human mind which, unlike in Augustine, by natural inclination tends to the common good. All three are in basic conformity with each other, though the first alone is perfect, eternal, and unchangeable. Before too long the pope became the custodian of the divine law, and the kings and princes as legislators became the custodians of human laws or civil law.

It was this Thomasian synthesis that the Fathers of the European Enlightenment began questioning: Hobbes and Rousseau, Kant and the Hegelians, each in his own different way.

Western Liberalism and the Concept of Justice

Ever since John Rawls's celebrated work *The Concept of Justice*[131] was published in 1971, there has been an ongoing debate amongst the initiated about the foundations of the Western notion of justice, especially in a secular framework. The problem for secular liberalism is that it needs a rational basis for its concepts, and that basis cannot be metaphysical, since metaphysics is taboo for the liberal. Rawls's work is a heroic effort to provide that basis without resorting to metaphysical concepts like The Good. Nor can it be based on the utilitarianism of the last century, which also stands philosophically discredited for the modern liberal.

Michael Sandel, in his *Liberalism and the Limits of Justice,*[132] assesses the debate that ensued from the publication of Rawls's work. His judgment is that Rawls's effort has not stood the test of time and has not been vindicated by the debate. Sandel would say that the fault is with the liberalism Rawls is trying to defend, not with the justification of it. Sandel calls current liberalism a "deontological liberalism": "an ethic that asserts the priority of the right over the good, and is typically defined in opposition to utilitarian conceptions."[133]

> 'De-ontological liberalism' is above all a theory about justice, and in particular about the primacy of justice among moral and political ideals. Its core thesis can be stated as follows: society, being composed of a plurality of persons, each with his own aims, interests and conceptions of the good, is best arranged when it is governed by principles that do not *themselves* presuppose any particular conception of the good; what justifies these regulative principles above all is not that they maximize the social welfare or otherwise promote the good, but rather that they conform to the concept of *right,* a moral category given prior to the good and independent of it.[134]

One may be permitted to wonder sardonically where this totally "nonmetaphysical" concept of the "right" comes from, independent of all notions of the "good," which modern liberals somehow detest. Both in classical Greek thought and in nineteenth-century utilitarianism, the primacy of justice is based on its relation to the good. For classical Western thinkers justice is not one virtue among virtues, but the primary and most inclusive among the virtues. And "virtue" for the classical thinker is simply another name for the good, just as "value" for our generation often serves as a surrogate for the good. There is every reason to suspect that the commercial-minded bourgeoisie simply replaced the classical philosophical or metaphysical concept of virtue by the modern commercial trading concept of value.

In utilitarianism too, the concept of justice is grounded on the modern philosophical concept of the highest common good, which is equated with usefulness or utility. The utilitarian is usually willing to speak about the good being prior to the notion of justice, provided that good is understood in utilitarian and not metaphysical terms. John Stuart Mill, the most articulate utilitarian of all time, would agree that justice is "the chief part, and incomparably the most sacred and binding part, of all morality."[135] Morality, in turn, is useful, because it makes possible the good of greater social utility or the happiness of the majority. That kind of temporal or instrumental priority can be conceded to "right" over the good, if "right" will be useful to bring about the good.

A "de-ontological liberal" like John Rawls cannot be satisfied with that kind of utilitarian priority of right over good. In fact, the liberal wants the concept of right to be independent of any concept of the good. Otherwise, right would be contingent and not absolute. Modern liberalism is based on the notion of human rights and those rights cannot be dependent on any unreliable metaphysics of the good or changing conceptions of what is useful, but "right" must stand on its own right.

Kant and Right

John Rundel, in his *Origins of Modernity: The Origins of Modern Social Theory from Kant to Hegel to Marx,*[136] seeks to reconstruct and deconstruct the social theories of these three prominent thinkers of the modern era. Rundel's attempt in 1987, just before Marxism broke down in Eastern and Central Europe in 1989, was meant precisely to seek the demolition of Marxism. But in his fairly honest analysis, the whole of modernity, with liberalism and Marxism in one package, gets deconstructed. Modernity for Rundel is a complex of theoretical conceptions and the institutions based on them:

> On the one hand, the category of modernity refers to the historically specific series of complex social forms and institutions that social actors themselves create and inhabit; on the other it is simultaneously a practico-interpretative nexus through which these social forms themselves are constituted.[137]

For Immanuel Kant, Reason is the creator of culture, not a part of nature. Reason is thus independent of nature and the empirical world, ruler of nature and legislator for it. His *Critique of Pure Reason* legislates for the world of objects, and his *Critique of Practical Reason* legislates for the human will, for society, for interhuman relations. Reason lays down the rules and is lord of both nature and culture, autonomous, free, ruling. If Heidegger thinks that our problem is forgetfulness of being, Kant would say that we are forgetful of our kingship, and must wake up to assert it. That is what the Enlightenment is all about. *Mundigkeit* or mature adulthood, means coming forward without timidity or hesitation to take over one's royal responsibility as an adult. Indolence is the only thing that prevents humanity from accepting its autonomy and sovereignty. This notion of "coming of age" underlies all three phenomena: Enlightenment, Modernity, and Secularization.

As Frederick van de Pitte puts it in his *Kant as Philosophical Anthropologist,* "Reality is now man's reality, and the Enlightenment is fulfilled; Man is freed from self-imposed minority—he has the courage to use his own intelligence, and to assume his rightful position."[138] One wonders where Kant gets his anthropology, certainly not from his *Critique of Pure Reason!*

Where indeed does Kant find the basis for his social theory, apart from this kind of curious anthropology that seems to defy reason? Kant had taught the physical sciences at the university, and from his understanding of Newtonian physics, he derives his famous metaphysical concept of "unsociable sociality." His second dissertation was on *Monadologia physica,*[139] written in 1755, upon which he based his public *disputatio* of April 10, 1756; it shows that the young Kant had accepted the picture of the world in Leibnizian terms as a system of spatially interactive monads as the stuff of matter. Every monad has a double activity, to attract other monads, on the one hand, and on the other, to repel other monads in the region from occupying its space. The interaction between these two forces defines extension in matter:

> *Corpora per vim solam impenetrabilitatis non gauderent definito volumine, nisi adforet alia pariter insita attractionis, cum illa coniunctim limitem definiens extensionis.*[140]

Abandoning the Newtonian concept of inertia in matter (*materia iners*), Kant posits a dynamic, interactive theory. For him the idea of inertia is a purely subjective perception that is accidental:

> Every physical thing, the way it appears in space, at rest and devoid of tension, is purely accidental and already a subjective human product. The substantial side of matter lies behind materiality; it is made up of the energy centres which generate the incessant conflict within matter. Everything material is thus in contention and in motion.[141]

Kant's view, though of Leibnizian inspiration, is not the same as that of Leibniz.[142] It is derived rather from his understanding of theoretical physics. In his academic career, Kant had taught twenty-one four-hour classes on the subject,[143] and he had developed his idea that in matter there is constant strife between the attractive force and the repellent force. It is this idea that later becomes translated into social theory as "unsociable sociality," a heavily metaphysical concept, not drawn from "Pure Reason", but from pure pseudo-science! So much for the beginnings of critical rationality!

In 1784, thirty years after the dissertation on monadology, Kant applies this principle to society, in his *Idea for a Universal History*,[144] written during the period when he was lecturing in physics. Just as matter has the interplay of attraction and repulsion, individual human monads also have two basic drives, one toward association and the other towards individuality, isolation, and particularity. Politics and notions like "right" are grounded in the former tendency, that is, of socialization, which is a form of association. This interplay of proximity and distance-seeking constitutes the "unsociable sociality" that is the motor of politics. Thus for Kant, strife and antagonism constitute the basic nature of nature and history, in the cosmos and in society. Struggle is a creative process, and is part of the endowment given to the universe by its Creator. Struggle and conflict are thus part of natural law, and are not to be avoided, for that is the way the created order moves forward. Strange indeed is the way of philosophers who seek to build metaphysics on the foundation of pure reason and peace on the basis of war and conflict!

Destruction is part of creativity in nature itself. Kant says in his *Metaphysical Foundations of Natural Science*, published in 1786, that destruction starts out from mundane bodies nearest to the center of the universe and spreads, "gradually farther, so that by the slow decay of motion, all of the world that has run its course will in the end be buried in a single chaos."[145] Meanwhile, parallel to that destruction, new creation is going on, scattered elements condensing to form new suns. Every developed world is thus always "confined midway between the ruins of destroyed nature and the chaos of unformed nature." This is the structure of the universe as a whole: it is eternally becoming.[146]

So, peace is not "natural" to a nature that is violent and warlike. Peace has to be won by reason, not spontaneously granted by nature. Kant is no pacifist. For him war is an indispensable cultural instrument in order to enforce justice or right. It is a mechanism of providence[147]; it improves the mind[148]; it preserves virtue[149]; promotes courage and equality; and above all secures freedom, the premise of morality. But Kant also recognized the negative elements in war, "the worst evil that can befall the human race,"[150] which always revokes the purposes of humanity. So Kant's final verdict on war is that it is the socially manifested ruin of mankind, against which reason casts its "irresistible veto: There should not be any war."[151] It is in his *Metaphysics of Morals*[152] that Kant gives his detailed analysis of the metaphysics of justice, his *Rechtslehre*.

And there is the problem for liberalism: Kant's understanding of justice is based on metaphysical assumptions that modern liberals cannot accept; Kant's concept of virtue or the Good, is based in turn on a prior understanding of justice or right. The *Tugendlehre* forms the second part of his *Metaphysics of Morals*,[153] depends on the *Rechtslehre*. And the concept of justice is in turn based on the categorical imperative, which demands that one should do only that which one wills others should do to oneself.

Behind it all lies the rugged individualism of Kant's bourgeois thinking:

> The character of the species, as it is indicated by all the experience of all ages and all peoples, is this, that taken collectively [i.e., the human race as a whole] it is a multitude of persons, existing successively and side by side, who cannot do without associating peacefully and yet cannot avoid constantly offending one another. Hence they feel destined by nature (to form) through mutual compulsion under laws which proceed from themselves, a coalition which, though constantly threatened by dissension, makes progress on the whole.[154]

The fallacies in Kant's conception of justice are enormous as well as numerous. In the first place, he thinks of the individual as first existing, and then subsequently forming societies; this is a monstrous travesty of what we can observe. In our experience, no individual comes into being without a preexisting society (at least father and mother), and no human being can become human without the process of socialization, which demands the preexistence of society before the individual comes into being.

It is common fallacy in much of Western thinking to assume that the existence of the individual subject temporally precedes intersubjectivity; they have difficulty recognizing the brute fact that human subjectivity cannot be formed without intersubjectivity, that social intersubjectivity is the matrix in which a human infant becomes a person. It is this fallacy that leads to the notion of a "social contract" as the basis of society, the naive Kantian assumption that persons first find themselves existing, and then are forced by necessity to form societies; this is the way some people understand both church and society, as voluntary associations of preexisting individual persons. Kant also contradicts himself when he asserts as a fundamental principle that human reason legislates for itself in freedom, and then goes on to say that circumstances compel them to associate socially.

The maxim that characterizes the Enlightenment notions of liberty and justice is this fundamental right of individual persons to the "recognition" of their personal autonomy. According to Kant, individual human reason is capable of thinking and legislating universally. It is this universality of the individual reason that leads it to recognise also the equal rights of others; hence the principle that each person is to be recognized, not as a means to other people's ends, but as an end in himself. On the basis of this recognition of universal and equal rights of individuals, liberalism is ready to construct a social theory and a theory of justice.

In Kant's theory, people can be means to other people's ends, but if, and only if, in the same movement the people so used are also regarded as ends in themselves, that is, with their free autonomous consent. Thus the social contract among autonomous free beings becomes also the principle of democracy, a public realm where the things (*res*) of the public, or *res publica,* or republic, are recognized. Civil legislation that is restrictive of the freedom and autonomy of individuals thus becomes justified by the fact that such restriction receives the rational and free consent of the citizens. Kant says nothing here of those who want to withhold consent, their individual autonomy, and freedom. It is enough to have free discussion and decision among the people or their representatives; this is the principle of democratic political life. This is why the "fundamental human rights" are so fundamental to liberal thought. The "right" to dissent, question, protest, criticize, publicize, organize, and so on is grounded in the transcendental freedom and autonomy of the individual subject. This is why neoliberals insist on the priority of "right" over justice, since the concept of justice is founded on this individual right. And neither justice nor right is founded on any notion of the common good, but solidly grounded in the freedom and autonomy of the individual.

Rundel summarizes the view of Kant:

> The sovereign ground of right establishes freedom as the basis for human existence, which is expressed through the equaland open membership of all in a civil society. The legal validity of the constitution originates solely in the externalisation of the concept of freedom. For Kant, the civil state regarded as a lawful state, is based on the following principles:
>
> 1. the *freedom* of every member of society as a human being;
> 2. the *equality* of each with all the others as a subject;
> 3. the *independence* of each member of a commonwealth as a citizen.[155]

Two things are worthy of our notice in all this. First, Kant has taken some liberty in editing the slogan of the French Revolution, not as *liberté, egalité,* and *fraternité,* but as freedom, equality, and *independence.* To concede the concept of brotherhood or sisterhood would be to depart from rugged individualism. For the French, *liberté* includes independence, liberty and equality without some familial sense of social belonging together can be disastrous; for Kant, however, sociality springs from individuality.

The second monstrous thing about Kant's notion of right is that it is limited to the full citizen, who is truly autonomous. Only the citizen (i.e., burgher) is colegislator and has the right to vote. In order to have the right, he must have financial autonomy, either in the form of property, or one of the higher professions that do not entail depending on someone else for one's living. Others, such as servants, journeymen, artisans 'of the lower sort' (i.e., the petit bourgeoisie), handymen, tenant farmers (i.e., peasants), even tutors who live with a family and share their bed and board, and all who make their living in their master's household lack civil personality and so cannot vote.[156] No wonder a man with a better moral conscience like Karl Marx wanted to be done with this *Burgheraufklaerung* and yearned passionately for a genuine *Arbeiteraufklaerung* (Workers' Enlightenment)! And again, no wonder that an intelligent modern liberal like John Rawls would not want to be saddled with such an ideology in the name of Reason, and would prefer to be a deontological liberal!

The Rawls Debate on Justice

For John Rawls, Kant's justification of right is faulted for a totally different reason—that it is based on a transcendental idealism. Rawls's major effort in *The Concept of Justice* was to liberate the priority of right over good, which he accepts, from its foundation in a philosophy or metaphysics that is unacceptable to a modern liberal. He would like to secure the concept of right within "the canons of a reasonable empiricism" or "within the scope of an empirical theory,"[157] for empiricism and rationality are the two Articles of the Creed for the modern liberal. As a good liberal, Rawls is committed to the value priority of justice:

> Justice is the first value of social institutions, as truth is of systems of thought. A theory, however elegant and economical, must be rejected or revised if it is untrue; likewise laws and institutions, no matter how efficient and well-arranged, must be reformed or abolished if they are unjust. Each person possesses

> an inviolability founded on justice that even the welfare of society as a whole cannot override.[158]

Rawls does not seem to be aware that none of these statements come from reason or experience. They are not scientific statements of rational empiricism, but merely articles of a creed. Rawls is aware that his foundations are flimsy and weak; so is his definition of justice, though he is more aware than Kant of the social dimension. He would simply like to set aside questions of meaning and definition, with which liberals usually have little patience, to get on with an empirical theory of justice:

> As we have noted before, justification [i.e., of a theory] is a matter of the mutual support of many considerations, of everything fitting together into one coherent view. Accepting this idea allows us to leave questions of meaning and definition aside and to get on with the task of developing a substantive theory of justice.[159]

Critics generally acknowledge, though somewhat reluctantly, that Rawls has failed to achieve his purpose, namely to do the groundwork for "a substantive theory of justice," whatever the word *substantive* means in the context of a theory. According to most critics who followed the debate in the last two decades, Rawls has failed to provide de-ontological liberalism with an adequate theoretical foundation. He has sought that foundation in Anglo-American Pragmatism-Empiricism, with its rabid distrust of metaphysics and speculation.

Of course, most liberals would not even worry about any theoretical foundations whatsoever: there are many such social activists today. Even the "liberation theologians" have been busy tailoring a theology to fit their preperceived goals of social justice, rather than working out a sustainable philosophical or theological foundation for the Christian responsibility for social justice. Most of these would say that it is an intellectual-spiritual disease to be so preoccupied with theory. At that point they are all Marxians: "Philosophers have explained the world; the point is to change it." They would leave reflection to the postactive phase, when theory can be based on adequate practice. But many social activists are getting tired of action without reflection, and are beginning to entertain grave doubts about the validity of this exclusive concern about social justice. So the ranks of the rightists, quietists, and consumerists keep growing.

Rawls began his work in that postaction phase. He was anxious to gain some theoretical justification for this quest for social justice.

The Kantian foundation has proved to be philosophically or scientifically indefensible, neither has the other and more Anglo-American alternative, utilitarianism, stood the test of time as a basis for justice. Theology and metaphysics are taboo for the secular liberal. Pragmatism seemed a prospectively more fruitful source, and all that Rawls demanded was that people would simply accept the notion of individual right as a self-evidently true one, and proceed to delineate justice as basically fairness, which, for most Anglo-Americans, is more acceptable than any metaphysical notions of categorical imperative or social contract.

The autonomy of the individual is a precious concept for the successful businessman; so is fairness, particularly on the part of others, especially the competitors in business. Individual freedom to compete in free trade and commerce in the free market, equality of opportunity (even if not in fact), freedom from governmental or other external intervention in moneymaking and power-building activity—these are precious values cherished by the business community. If theory does not fit these values, then to hell with theory! If academics can find a theory that justifies and promotes these values, the business community, the academy, and the media controlled by the moneymaking and power-building classes would support and underwrite such a search for theory, but they can get along very well without it.

Our famous "critical rationality" should help us see through the historically conditioned and interest-laden nature of theories of justice such as those of Kant and Rawls. They are based on fundamental fallacies of thought, such as assuming the priority of the individual over society rather than holding together persons and society as inseparable parts of an integral whole. Equally fallacious is the assumption that society is constituted by a social contract among equal individuals as if individuals were primary and society secondary. The vision of society as composed of preexisting individuals is theoretically analogous to the notion of the body of an organism as composed of preexisting cells. No biologist would want to argue that the cells existed first and then decided to constitute a body. Cells are formed and cells die out, but the body goes on as one, despite the fact that none of the cells of infancy remain in the adult. No one would want to argue that the interests of the individual cell has priority over the interests of the body. On that premise it would be wrong to shave or scrub your skin with a towel, for in both processes cells are being lost. We do not wish to press the analogy too far, but it can help us see the mutually supporting and nourishing role of persons and societies. Any notion of justice must take into account this mutual symbiosis.

Six Theories of Justice

Ms. Karen Lebacqz, a rather astute young theologian in America, has made a more impressive attempt to list the prevailing theories of justice in her *Six Theories of Justice: Perspectives from Philosophical and Theological Ethics.*[160] In a second work, *Justice in an Unjust World,* Ms. Lebacqz gave a critical summary of the six theories, and what follows is a summary of that summary:

1. *The Utilitarian approach.* It is less individualistic, more concerned about the common good as a utility not antithetical to justice. Lebacqz rejects this view, however, as not providing adequate special protection to the poor and the oppressed, which for her is the essential aspect of the biblical vision of justice. Neither is the utilitarian view sufficiently geared to adequate and effective measures for correcting injustice and liberating the oppressed, again a central aspect of the biblical view of justice, according to her.
2. *The Rawlsian approach.* Rawls leaves some room for at least partial improvement in the situation of the poor and the oppressed, but his view is not grounded in their liberation as the primary interest of justice. "Justice requires liberation, not simply improvement within an oppressive structure."[162] While basically accepting Rawls's definition of justice as fairness, Lebacqz questions his pacific approach to justice as a matter for rational deliberation but not as deliberate action for "new beginnings." She therefore dismisses the Rawlsian view, not because it is theoretically defective, but simply as inadequate "to a world in which rationality itself is distorted by sin." Rawls also errs, according to her, in seeking to separate political from economic justice.
3. *Nozick's theory.* Robert Nozick wrote his *Anarchy, State and Utopia*[163] as a rebuttal of Rawls, and won the National Book Award in 1975. Nozick, like Kant, stresses freedom, but it is largely freedom of the market place, freedom of fair exchange. One can see why it would bag the National Book Award, since it defends the system. Lebacqz rejects Nozick's view, not for that reason, but because it lacks a critical assessment of how the present system and its presumed freedom have actually been effective in creating justice or injustice in the past and in the present. Besides, Nozick offers no room for the "Jubilee Vision" of the Old Testament, so central to Ms. Lebacqz's view as well as mine. This vision we shall

discuss later. Nozickism is also individualistic in its approach, inadequate in its treatment of human social relationships.

3. *The vision of the US Catholic Bishops' Conference.* Our author endorsed the second draft of the *Pastoral Letter of the American Roman Catholic Bishops' Conference on Economic Justice for All,* published in October 1985[164] since it is also moved by a biblical vision, though not quite the Jubilee Vision. The pastoral letter affirmed that "biblical justice . . . is not concerned with a strict definition of rights and duties, but with the rightness of the human condition before God and within society." It is also guided by the principle of a "preferential option for the poor," a notion now popular in Latin America and elsewhere, which holds that in a socioeconomic situation where other conditions remain the same, the claims of the poor must be the decisive priority. She points out that for the Roman Catholic bishops the notions of creation and covenant provide the fundamental matrix for thinking about justice; as for herself, as a good Protestant she would rather base her view of justice on the notions of covenant and God's liberating actions in history, such as the Exodus narrative. She regrets the absence of the Jubilee Vision and the failure to envision a "radical break from the past."

5. *The Niebuhrian view.* Prof. Reinhold Niebuhr, the well-known American Protestant social prophet of a few decades ago, would have agreed in many respects with the Catholic bishops' view. However, for Niebuhr, love was the norm, on which the notion of justice is based, as an approximation to love, or an accommodation of it in the social context.[165] This our feminist theologian finds unacceptable. Love and justice, she says, cannot be so separated to make justice somewhat of a second-class citizen. Neither does Niebuhr deal with the theme of liberation. Of course, Niebuhr wrote more than half a century ago.

6. *The Miranda view.* Jose Porfirio Miranda, a "liberation theologian" from Latin America, has sought to correct these defects in Niebuhr and bring him up to date, in his *Marx and the Bible: A Critique of the Philosophy of Oppression.*[166] According to Miranda, God is known, not in abstract reflection, but in the actual practicing of righteousness and justice. Active participation in the struggle for justice is a necessary precondition for the knowledge of God. Lebacqz concurs largely in this "liberationist" rather than liberal view. Her own approach, however,

> differs from that of Miranda in three respects: Miranda does not recognize the Niebuhrian principle that every achievement of justice will necessarily be imperfect, and therefore he does not provide for perpetual questioning and restructuring of all socioeconomic structures; Miranda's approach is based on a biblical word study of *mishpat,* which is only one of the biblical words for justice; Ms. Lebacqz would prefer her own feminist methodology of "narrative" or "her-story," where you do not try to persuade people to organize for action by arguments of reason, but by telling the stories of the millions of people who can speak about their own suffering and oppression out of firsthand experience.

Ms. Lebacqz's own approach is typical of Western liberalism; it is aware of its own lack of sufficient philosophical basis, but seeks to make a virtue of that lack. She would prefer to start with narratives of current injustice, and from these directly appeal to the human conscience. She has no theoretical model of her own in terms of which to assess the six theories that she so ably summarizes. Insofar as the appeal to conscience works in practice, without any assistance from theoretical models, this methodology is judged to be pragmatically true. She too is a deontological liberal for whom to think too deeply seems eminently dangerous. In her we see the dilemma of the European Enlightenment—a compulsion to formally reject all metaphysical reflection and all dependence on authority on the one hand, and the inevitability of still having to pick and choose from the rejected traditions of Christianity or classical Rome and Greece. There seems to be no final norm above individual taste.

Justice in Hegel and Marx

Hegel set forth his theory of the state and justice in his *Grundlinien der Philosophie des Rechts* (*Outline of the Philosophy of Law/Justice/Right*).[167] T.M. Knox's standard English translation is entitled *Hegel's Philosophy of Right,* since there is no single English word that can carry the three meanings of the German word *Recht*—law, justice, and right. The original text was published in 1821, and formed the basis of his lectures for the next ten years. The main argument is in paragraphs 257 to 313. As Hegel expounded his text, his classes were attended by "even majors, colonels and Privy Councillors," as Hegel himself wrote to his friend Creuzer.[168]

Hegel certainly was no deontological liberal, but its exact opposite—an ontological monarchist. His political philosophy is the opposite of modern liberalism not merely in its defense of monarchy, but in its political economy solidly (some would say, airily) founded on ontology and metaphysics, or protophysics.

It is his philosophy of nature that gives Hegel the foundation for political thought as it did for Aristotle, but that philosophy of nature is in turn grounded on a philosophy of Spirit, which sees reality dialectically, in terms of the Subjective Spirit confronting the Objective Spirit of Nature or the manifest universe, to find the other alienated from oneself, and seeking reconciliation in the Absolute Spirit. The Subjective Spirit emerges out of nature, confronts nature as its object, but as object of its consciousness. The duality is only gradually overcome, and overcome by the mind which rises above the dual perception. It overcomes nature by creating social and political institutions, not just by some subjective process, but by imparting Spirit to objective nature.

Hegel's conception of the state is based on justice and morality; these in turn have two aspects: individual and social. Both are simply aspects of "the march of God in the world" through personal and social history. The dialectic is between the individual will and the will of society that the individual is forced to recognize as he recognizes that his own personhood is dependent upon recognition by others. Human freedom is the ground of justice. Justice is a spiritual (*geistige*) reality:

> The basis of right [justice] is, in general, the Spiritual (*das Geistige*) and its precise place and startingpoint (*naehere Stelle und Ausgangspunkt*) is the Will (*der Wille*), which is free, so that (by it) Freedom works out its substance and determination, and the judicial system (*das Rechtssystem*) is the domain of actualized freedom, the World of Spirit brought forth from itself [i.e., from Spirit], as a second Nature.[169]

Thus, for Hegel, justice is not simply a set of social relations, but freedom actualized in history. This certainly is not an Enlightenment idea and does not fit in with liberalism.

Kant's morality, for Hegel, is not sufficient; its categorical imperative fails the test of consistency. For example, if one considers the question of "helping the poor" as a moral issue, by the categorical imperative it will be shown to be immoral. For, if everybody helps the poor, then there would no longer be any poor, and the action of helping the poor would be found to be impossible and self-contradictory when universalized in accordance with the categorical imperative. Hegel wants to relate Kant's *Moralitaet* (personal morality), to the higher principle of *Sittlichkeit* (social ethics) or the moral principles that guide a people or a nation.

The state does not abrogate personal morality. The right of individuals to certain personal satisfactions cannot be taken away by the state, nor can the state legislate all individual moral actions. Individuals already transcend personal morality in the institution of the family, where each acts only in relation to the interests of the other. Economic life, with buying and selling, as well as the division of labor in society, also introduces relational aspects into personal morality and universalizes it. This is the area of *Sittlichkeit* or *Voelkerecht*, in which a new system of ethics comes into being, to be guarded and enforced by the law and the constitution, by the police, the judiciary, the legislature, and the executive. Thus the state arises in the normal course of the *Weltgeist* or World Spirit advancing in history.

The state also brings into existence new classes or levels of society—the *Staende*, the Estates, each with its own specific rights and duties. Hegel saw three estates in existence: an agricultural class, a business class, and a civil service class. Thus far, the analysis seems convincing. It gets more difficult when Hegel distinguishes between an active, decision-making group and a more passive, collaborating group within each class; the leaders and the led, so to speak. A bicameral legislature, with representatives or leaders of the landowning class in the upper house, and the decisionmakers (i.e., bourgeoisie) among the commoners in the other, becomes part of the state structure, which as a whole, is the concretization of freedom and justice in history.

When it comes, however, to the question of who is to arbitrate among the interests of the various classes, Hegel would say that it is the task of the state, but would go on then to locate the center of the state in the sovereign, responsible, but still arbitrary will of the king or the emperor. This was obviously a judgment of Hegel's that came, not so much from any philosophical necessity of the system, as from a study of existing European states, among which he found the enlightened constitutional monarchy of Prussia the best model. Hegel was no supporter of either the *ancien regime* of prerevolution France or even of the postrevolution Bonapartism of that country. Hegel was for a constitutional monarchy, hereditary and not elective. He wanted two houses of parliament, one for the hereditary landowning peers, and one for the corporations and other bodies of society. The second would be elected, but the first hereditary. The nobility or aristocracy would form the upper house, while the more numerous bourgeoisie would have their elected representatives in the lower house. Power is thus controlled by the three primary "estates": the landed aristocracy, the bourgeoisie, and the executive or civil service class, while the fourth estate of the press or the media keeps the "educated class" informed.

The people themselves, capricious and wayward, cannot be included in the structure of power until they become educated and enlightened. But above the power structure sits the one monarch whose will is final in all matters of dispute brought to him. The monarch is sovereign, and no one can question his will. Of course, his sovereignty is limited to the bounds of his own nation. It finds its dialectical antithesis in other sovereign states confronting it; adjustments would have to be made among these sovereign states in terms of treaties and contracts, which together would constitute international law.

Hegel found no need for a universal sovereign authority to which the states could appeal. The final arbiter in disputes among the states would be history itself, and war would be a legitimate instrument in settling international disputes when rational means of settlement fail. In Hegel's time, history had given the verdict in favor of the Lutheran Protestant State of Prussia with Frederick the Great at its head. It was the final state of the evolution of human social living, and Hegel could not see how even history could go beyond it, though he did not totally deny that possibility.

Hegel seldom used the word *Gerechtigkeit,* which would be the equivalent of our "justice." His key word is *Recht,* which as we have said before, can be Right (*droit*), as in "human rights," or "civil rights," but can also be a general term encompassing not only the judiciary, justice, and jurisprudence, but also personal morality (*Moralitaet*), social ethics (*Sittlichkeit*) and even world history (*Weltgeshichte*), as Hegel states explicitly in the second *Zusatz* of #33 in the German edition of his *Rechtsphilosophie.*

The Marxian Critique

Against Hegel's freezing of human freedom in this form of the Prussian state, Marx, Engels, and many others who cared about what happened to people could not but revolt. Marx's *Kritik des Hegelschen Staatsrechtes (Critique of Hegel's Philosophy of Right)*[170] was unpublished in his lifetime. Marx is always in his true element when he engages in polemic and critique against other people's views. He was rather weak on constructing systems, but strong on demolishing them. But he was rightly appreciative of the depth of Hegel's work and paid it the highest compliments:

> The criticism of the German philosophy of right and of the State, which was given its most logical, profound and complete ex-

> pression by Hegel, is at once the critical analysis of the modern state and of the reality connected with it, and the definitive negation of all the past forms of consciousness in German jurisprudence and politics, whose most distinguished and most general expression, raised to the level of a science, is precisely the speculative philosophy of right.[171]

Marx's concern, however, is not with critique, but with praxis. How do we overthrow the Prussian state, which in Marx's time was full of contradictions? That is the question Marx raises in his introduction, which was already published in the *Deutsch-franzoesische Jahrbuecher* (Paris, 1844). Hegel had died in 1831, at the height of his fame as the "professor of professors." Europe had very few wars since Napoleon's defeat before Paris in 1814 against the four major powers—Britain, Russia, Prussia, and Austria.

The Peace of Paris, negotiated among the four powers and the Vatican, had led to a judicious and mutually agreed upon balance of power in Europe between the six main centers of power: London, St. Petersburg, Berlin, Vienna, Paris, and the Vatican. In 1830 and 1831 several revolutions and uprisings had taken place in Germany and Italy, but without affecting the regimes in Austria or Prussia. Hanover, Brunswick, Saxony, and Hesse-Cassel managed to secure liberal constitutions. Greece and Belgium had obtained their independence. Turkey, the main enemy of Europe, had been rendered powerless. Europe had its tensions, first between Russia and Britain, often mediated by France, then among all the leading European powers; but it was the great age of diplomacy—Talleyrand in France, Metternich in Austria, Palmerston in Britain—and diplomacy became a real instrument of peaceful settlement of international conflicts in Europe and the colonies.

Peace in Europe was a necessary condition for her expansion and conquest in the rest of the world, except that some colonies could be easily taken away by Britain from the Spanish and the Portuguese, and new markets captured in Latin America by supporting wars of independence against these two weakened European nations.

On the other hand, in Asia the British opened up the Chinese market for Europe through the Opium Wars (1839–42) just as Marx was writing his critique of Hegel's Political Economy; the British had also managed to tighten the hold on the Indian market. Wealth was flowing to Europe from Asia and America, powering the Industrial Revolution; and the bourgeoisie were the major beneficiaries of the resultant economic boom. Monarchies in Europe were at that time largely enlightened, and knew that they could not survive in power without the full support of the moneymaking bourgeoisie; the middle classes were happy with the kings and queens, for they not only looked after their own aristocratic interests, but also protected the interests of the traders and the manufacturers, the craftsmen and the professionals, the members of the civil service, the guilds, and the academy. The monarchy helped sanctify privilege with a divine aura, and as it happened, to take the brunt of the dissatisfaction of the oppressed and the exploited.

The case of the poor was, however, quite different. Here Marx, unlike Hegel and Kant, became their advocate, particularly the urban poor, who were victims of oppression and exploitation by the bourgeoisie and were fast becoming restless and discontented. The poor had two possibilities: escape to America "where they had no king," or revolt against the monarchies and aristocracies who held the power to suppress their interests. The bourgeoisie were also becoming discontented with the ruling aristocracy. As the educated classes grew in numbers, they felt they could handle the ruling function much more efficiently than the aristocracy. As Eric Hobsbawm puts it:

> The revolutionary wave of 1830 . . . marks the definitive defeat of aristocratic by bourgeois power in Western Europe. The ruling class of the next fifty years was to be the "grande bourgeoisie" of bankers, big industrialists, and sometimes top civil servants, accepted by an aristocracy which effaced itself or agreed to promote primarily bourgeois policies, unchallenged as yet by universal suffrage, though harrassed from outside by the agitations of the lesser or unsatisfied businessmen, the petit-bourgeoisie and the early labour unions.[172]

It was in this context that Marx wrote his critique of Hegel's *Philosophy of Right*. Marx saw clearly the philosophical underbelly of the economic-political system which oppressed and exploited the poor and the underprivileged, and he went for that underbelly with sharp weapons and consummate skill. He realized that first he would have to dispel what he called "the logical, pantheistic mysticism"[173] that was the foundation for Hegel's political philosophy. The attack on "speculative philosophy" and on religion is on the same ground, that they are mystifications to cover up the injustice in society. The real is the rational, Hegel held. What gives at any given historical moment is the Absolute Idea manifesting itself in time; this is, according to Marx, the worst justification for the evils that are present in the moment and for the abuse of power that is regnant in the status quo.

If Hegel is right, Marx pointed out, then people are mere pawns in the game that the Absolute Idea plays in history. It is this Absolute

Idea that through human activity creates decisive formations and institutions like family, society, and state, by its own inexhorable laws of dialectic development in history. According to Marx, family and civil society are existing active realities that go on to create the state; for Hegel, family and civil society are two spheres of existence inherent in the Idea, and it is the Idea as active subject which goes on to create the state, transcending and absorbing the family and civil society at a higher level of synthesis. Marx accuses Hegel of distorting facts like family and civil society into the products of some mystical entity called the Idea. And the state is sanctified as a necessary and higher product of the Absolute Idea, transcending family and civil society and absorbing them into itself. All this sanctimonious legitimation of the state derives from the mystical notion of an Absolute Idea working itself out in actual history. Hence Marx's unrelenting opposition to idealism and religion as the two inveterate enemies to be relentlessly combated. They are enemies because they are friends of our common enemy, injustice.

The second enemy that Marx wants to combat, on behalf of the poor, is the monarchy that Hegel and the church justified, sanctified, and glorified. Hegel brings in the concept of the sovereignty of the state as something intrinsic to it and provided by the Absolute Idea, and then quietly makes the transition to say that the monarch is sovereign, because the state has to express its intrinsic quality of sovereignty; and thus the sovereign monarch whose authority cannot at all be questioned becomes the expression of this intrinsic quality of the state.

Marx, of course, cannot accept this feudalist metaphysics in any form. Justice, for him too, works itself out in history through the class struggle and the emergence of the classless society. But Marx refuses to give any metaphysical status to the state as the embodiment of justice and freedom. Hegel was opposed to the then rising idea of the "sovereignty of the people," which he dismisses as "one of the confused notions based on the wild idea of the 'people'."[174] "If by 'sovereignty of the people' is understood a republican form of government, or to speak more specifically . . . a democratic form, then . . . such a notion cannot be further discussed in face of the Idea of the State in its full development."[175] Marx laughs at this idea of identification of state and monarch, and posits democracy as the true essence of the state:

> Democracy is the truth of monarchy, monarchy is not the truth of democracy. Monarchy is necessarily democracy in contradiction with itself, whereas the monarchical moment is no con-

> tradiction within democracy. Monarchy cannot, while democracy can, be understood in terms of itself . . . In monarchy the whole, the people, is subsumed under one of its modes of existence, the political constitution; in democracy the constitution itself appears only as one determination, and indeed as the self-determination of the people.[176]

After having given battle to the two enemies—idealism-mysticism and monarchy—Marx goes for the third enemy, private property, which gives sanctification to the power of the bourgeoisie. The manuscript remains incomplete at this point, but the argument against private property is everywhere in Marx's other writings, especially in *Das Kapital.*

Marx's *Critique of Hegel* was written in 1843, five years before the people revolted against oppression and exploitation in 1848. The working class had not yet been organized, except in Britain and the US. The Workingmen's Party in the US was set up in 1828–29, and the proletarian trend was in the Owenite Cooperative movements of 1830. Neither of these was radical-revolutionary. In general, Europe and America were going along various lanes of the moderate-liberal road. Insurrection and revolt had often occurred, but an organized revolution of the 1789 type was still something feared by the common people. The 1830 uprisings had been brutally suppressed, and the people remembered.

1848, the year of *The Communist Manifesto,* was also the year of general revolution in Europe. Marx and Engels were right in visualizing the "Spectre of Communism" that haunted Europe and frightened the privileged. The condition of the laboring poor was appalling, and Marx and Engels were not exaggerating. The poor were getting poorer, at least in a majority of instances, and their prospects were gloomy. Marx and Engels concurred in this prognostication of gloom for poor working-class people, as Malthus and his ilk had done before. The contrast between the rich and the poor became more visible as the rich became increasingly exhibitive in their display of wealth, while the poor starved and went naked.

The industrial revolution changed the form of this rich/poor conflict into an employer/employee conflict, or capitalist/working class conflict. The working-class consciousness was just rising on the eve of the 1848 revolutions. The trade union and the general strike were new concepts and called for organization, reflection, and strategy. The working class gradually found a new consciousness, transcending the mere selfish interest of a higher wage, to yearn and work for a new order of society in which there would be no poor or exploited, transcending nationalism to become truly international, since workers of all lands found themselves in the same struggle and had to support each other. Remaining basically religious at heart, but dissatisfied with traditional religion which supported the status quo, the working people gradually came to embrace a new secular ideology based on science, progress, evolution, and reason.

Socialism and humanism were new names for the new ideology, for which Marx and Engels became the primary articulators and prophets. The new Enlightenment was on—the Workers' Enlightenment—as opposed to the Bourgeois Enlightenment. The state has to wither away, but justice is still the final goal of history. Liberalism cannot accept this inevitability of justice emerging at the end of history, but its doctrine of progress is a trivialized version of the philosophy of history shared in some aspects by both Hegel and Marx.

Liberalism cannot escape metaphysics, however much it may claim to shun it. Our analysis has shown, we hope, that it is not merely in the methodology of knowledge, but also in determining principles of social existence, that the European Enlightenment and its foster children, secular Marxism and liberalism, encounter insoluble problems.

Chapter Nine

Science, Technology, and the Enlightenment: Will They Go On Reinforcing Each Other Indefinitely?

We have discussed elsewhere[177] the problem of the relation between modern science and the technology based on it. There was a time when we could speak of "pure" science and "applied" science, as if they were neatly separable in space and time; today we know that science cannot function without technology and has often to precede it (e.g., the science of high-energy physics depends on the technology of the particle accelerator). We also know that almost all science has some technology in view even at the research stage, and research is funded with that in mind. Science and technology has become a gigantic enterprise, with billions of dollars of investment, millions of personnel, thousands of institutions, hundreds of vested interests, all integrally related to the neocolonial, global system of militarism, exploitation and profit making. Science and technology as an enterprise is far from free and is in need of liberation from the forces that keep it from being at the disposal of the welfare of humanity.

In this chapter, however, we want to highlight the knowledge-distorting aspects of modern science and technology, not its socioeconomic and political-military aspects. Science and technology, the most treasured product of the European Enlightenment and Western civilization, grew up in a Europe of adventure and expansion; and in Western civilization, the Enlightenment and the development of modern science and technology have been mutually reinforcing each other for the past two centuries or more. Transcending science and technology seems a necessary aspect of going beyond the European Enlightenment. They are closely interwoven.

It is a curious thing indeed that modern science, with all its splendid triumphs and magnificent achievements in the articulation of hidden truth, is still unable to say precisely what science is. Even the philosophy of science, which of course is not a scientific discipline and should therefore be freer than science, cannot come to an agreement about the dividing line between science and nonscience. Philosophers of science like Sir Karl Popper look down with some disdain at traditional epistemology and the questions it can put to science about the nature of the reality with which science is dealing, or about the very approach to knowledge it pursues. Popper would even dismiss traditional epistemology's preoccupation with the knowing process (à la Kant and Husserl) as irrelevant to scientific knowledge.[178] "The method of science is the method of bold conjectures and ingenious and severe attempts to refute them," writes Popper in his *Objective Knowledge*,[179] manifesting Western liberalism's great capacity to avoid inconvenient questions and to resort to a naive commonsense realism that provides simplistic answers which look so patently self-evident. The aim of science is "to find satisfactory explanations of whatever strikes us as being in need of explanation." By explanation (or a causal explanation) is meant a set of statements by which one describes the state of affairs to be explained (the *explicandum*), while the others, the explanatory statements, form the "explanation" in the narrower sense of the word (the *explicans* of the *explicandum*). Scientific explanation, says Popper, with disarmingly naive simplicity, is "explanation of the unknown by the known."[180]

It is fascinating to observe how closely related Popper's philosophy of science is to the Darwinian theory of evolution. According to Popper, scientific enquiry begins neither in experience, nor in observation, but in "problems." Problems and puzzles face human beings; inadequate solutions are offered and are refuted by others; conjectures of other and possibly better solutions are proposed; there is a struggle for survival among the various solutions; the fittest survive; and the process goes on. This is, in my own words, the understanding of Sir Karl Popper about what science is.[181] In his own words:

> The theory of knowledge which I wish to propose is a largely Darwinian theory of the growth of knowledge. From the Amoeba to Einstein, the growth of knowledge is always the same; we try to solve our problems, and to obtain, by a process of elimination, something approaching adequacy in our tentative solutions.[182]

Popper, like a good modern deontological liberal, always manages to reduce tough metaphysical questions to easy pragmatic problems. Epistemology for him is the study of scientific problems and how they are handled by human beings; a study of the role of argument, evidence, testing, theory, experiment, and so on. He admits that the "world" is a web woven by spiders called human beings. It is their secretion, it is largely autonomous; we humans constantly interact with it and it grows. Popper substitutes Plato's eternal world of ideas, the *kosmos noetos,* with a manmade cosmos of theories and experiments, or rather an 'objective' evolving "third world" of scientific propositions, tested by theory and experiment, errors eliminated, new theory formulated and tested, leading on to a new set of propositions, ad infinitum. Is there any theory of truth behind this procedure? Certainly there is: truth is consistent in itself; it is compatible with "facts"; and it is compatible with other certified knowledge. Popper does not stop to ponder long about the basic assumption behind the three affirmations about truth: that truth is proposition. And then he proceeds to argue that compatibility with facts would provide a sufficient ground for attaining "verisimilitude" or close-enough-ness to the truth.

It is these basic assumptions pervading the European Enlightenment that constitute its bane. Alfred Tarski's famous definition of truth, which Popper unquestioningly accepts,[183] is based on the assumption that statements and facts are mutually commensurable in the artificially created metalanguage of logic's algebra. According to Tarski, if one wants to speak about Statement S and Fact F in the same breath, we must have a metalanguage, that is, a language about language, which makes possible the mutual interchangeability of S's and F's.

It seems important for us to grasp what science tries to explain, and what it means by explanation. Modern science knows deep down that there is something radically wrong with its explanations: that they do not really explain. A former generation of scientists who were quite sure that their explanations were sufficient, used inductive-statistical models without much deeper questioning. If in a sufficiently large number of cases phenomenon B would in all or almost all cases follow action A, then it would be reasonable to assume that every time we do A, B will naturally follow as cause and effect. C. G. Hempel then amended the inductive-statistical model to propose a deductive-nomological model, in which one should always add a numerical index to indicate the degree of inductive support a particular explanation has; some have stronger inductive support than others.

Wesley Salmon at the University of Arizona then proposed a revised model, the statistical-relevance model, which admits that an explanation is not a logically tight argument, but roughly an assemblage of some relevant evidence along with an assessment of the degree to which the *explicans* explains the *explicandum*. In the distressingly abstruse American debate that has followed these explanations of what an explanation is, the tentative outcome has been C. G. Hempel's Epistemic Relativity Thesis, which says that in all inductive explanations there is a measure of relativity in the conclusions, "relative to a given knowledge situation."[184]

The British discussion, in which several prominent American philosophers of science like Thomas Kuhn and Paul Feyerabend participated, though dominated by the large Popperian presence, has been slightly more productive. The general conclusion is that scientific knowledge is neither "objective" (pace Popper) nor "proved." Scientific knowledge is useful, operational knowledge, which has, thanks to the technology based on it, many impressive and useful achievements to its credit. But as the late Prof. Imre Lakatos put it:

> The proving power of the intellect or the senses was questioned by the Skeptics more than two thousand years ago; but they were brow-beaten into confusion by the glory of Newtonian physics. Einstein's results again turned the tables, and now very few philosophers or scientists still think that scientific knowledge is, or can be, proven knowledge. But few realize that with this the whole classical structure of intellectual values falls in ruins and has to be replaced: one cannot simply water down the ideal of proven truth—as some logical empiricists do—to the ideal of 'probable truth' [referring to Rudolf Carnap] or—as some sociologists of knowledge do—to 'truth by [changing] consensus' [referring to Polanyi, Kuhn, etc.].[185]

That is indeed a powerful statement from a sober professor of logic, to the effect that despite the blissful ignorance of many, the classical structure of intellectual effort that has characterized the West for millennia now lies in ruins.

Others are more optimistic about the outcome, with the characteristic attitude of "No big deal, we will still muddle through." Listen, for example, to Larry Laudan, a recent American writer on the subject:

> Both Kuhn and Feyerabend conclude that scientific decision-making is basically a political and propagandistic affair, in which prestige, power, age and polemic decisively determine the outcome of the struggle between competing theories and theo-

> rists. . . Having observed, quite correctly, that the Popperian model of rationality will do scant justice to actual science, they precipitately conclude that science must have large irrational elements, without stopping to consider whether some richer and more subtle model of rationality might do the job.[186]

Something more noble and more subtle may indeed do the job, but what is the job? To explain and conquer, or to live nobly? That is the question. We should deal with both aspects of science: its sociopolitical power aspect, and its deeper, more problematic, mind-deforming aspect. The optimists about the future of science have for their religion a belief in science, and hold on to it in absolute loyalty and devotion, an attitude not only to be admired but also to be rather compassionately understood. The Age of Enlightenment, whose last days we are now traversing, is also the Age of Reason and Science; it is still an Age of Faith as well, faith in reason and science. The enemy of that faith is the downfall of the naive realism that the Enlightenment had temporarily made respectable. So now if the religion of science and reason is to survive it must reluctantly embrace nonrealist theories of science. These render science less distinct, more modest, and increasingly pragmatist, since all theory is proving to be inadequate; and there is general agreement, at least among discerning scientists, that any scientific project setting out to know "reality as it is" is foredoomed to failure.

One of the major landmarks in critical Enlightenment thinking is this acceptance of the fact that naive realism is without scientific basis. Increasingly, perceptive thinkers, some scientists among them, are realizing that science, based on an understanding of reason reduced to the Aristotelian logic of noncontradiction as something infallible and on empirical testing as the foolproof method, has been standing on two very shaky pillars. The philosophical choices left for modern science when it leaves naive realism are all too few, and not too attractive in terms of the certainty factor that was once its claim to glory and dominance.

First there are those who stick to empiricism, but no longer uphold the naive realism on which it was formerly based. Like Popper and the Popperians, these would denounce any claims to absolute truth, claiming modestly to be mere problem-solvers and not sages; though then by backdoor methods they would give the impression that nobody else comes closer to the truth than they. Popper created the concept of verisimilitude, the idea that science, in its evolutionary progress, is with every step coming closer to the perfect truth, though always short of it, inevitably. These are the Neoempiricists or Problem-solving Pragmatists in latter-day philosophy of science.

Secondly, there are the more sophisticated Post-Empiricist Deconstructionists like Richard Rorty,[187] Richard Bernstein,[188] and Nancy Cartright[189]; perhaps Jacques Derrida also belongs to this group, which is very diverse within itself. The thing that unites them is that they are all pragmatists, and would not like to ask any metaphysical or even deeply epistemological questions. Joseph Rouse discusses many of these in his *Knowledge and Power: Towards a Political Philosophy of Science.*[190] Rouse's main points are: (a) that science is to be seen more as a field of practical activity than as a theoretical endeavor, and (b) that the epistemological and political (power) dimensions of modern science cannot be separated from each other. He cites from Richard Rorty's *Philosophy and the Mirror of Nature:*

> We are the heirs of three hundred years of rhetoric about the importance of distinguishing sharply between science and religion, science and politics, science and art, science and philosophy, and so on. This rhetoric has formed the culture of Europe.[191]

In other words, Rorty gives up on the demarcation problem of science, and affirms boldly that science cannot be so neatly distinguished from other kinds of human activity. Science is a realm of human activity closely bound up with culture, economics, and politics, but perhaps also with human pettiness, greed, and power-seeking.

Richard Bernstein, on the other hand, moves away from noncontradiction logic, to espouse not its polar opposite, dialectical reason, but something in between, a more pragmatic, dialogical community logic:

> Central to this new understanding is a dialogical model of rationality that stresses the practical, communal character of this rationality, in which there is choice, deliberation, interpretation, judicious weighing and application of "universal criteria" and even rational disagreement about which criteria are relevant and most important.[192]

The robust self-confidence that characterized the science of yesterday is no longer there. Its theoretical foundations are immensely shaky.

Habermas and Universal Pragmatism

Habermas's universal pragmatism is more comprehensive, more erudite, and more conversant with the larger debate going on outside the English-speaking world. The most competent, if not the most lucid presentation in English of his work is in Thomas McCarthy's *Jürgen Habermas*.[193] Thanks to Beacon Press in Boston, the bulk of his work has now been rendered in English, the chief works being *Towards a Rational Society* (1970), *Knowledge and Human Interests* (1971), *Legitimation Crisis* (1973), *Theory and Practice* (1973), and *Communication and the Evolution of Society* (1979).

Habermas (born 1929) has a prodigiously catholic European mind, though he does not manifest much awareness or appreciation of non-European thought. Habermas is perhaps unique in current Western thought, in that he ambitiously seeks to provide a Western critical rationalist framework for conceiving and dealing with the whole of reality in an ostensibly comprehensive nonspeculative theory like that of Kant. It is universal, he claims, because it is not fragmented by specialization; at this point he seems unaware of his own cultural parochialism and talks very much like a child of the Enlightenment, very European liberal, seeking to defend critical rationality at any cost. It is pragmatic because he seeks to stay away, unlike Hegel, from speculation. He moves from British preoccupations about linguistic analysis, through the concern about speech in French Structural Linguistics, to his own supreme category: communications-competence or the (according to him) uniquely human capacity for communication through language, symbols, actions, and so on. He is concerned not with epistemology, but with the problem of "legitimizing" our speech and actions for the sake of effective and impediment-free communication. He wants us to forget the question about how we know, the basic question of epistemology, though he tries to do justice to it. It is for him more important to be clear about how we validate our statements and actions, whether propositional, imperative, or ideological.

Validation or legitimation of speech and acts is a social act, an act of communication. This is so important for Habermas as an ex-Marxist, that he would like to move from Marx's redefinition of *Homo sapiens* as *Homo faber* towards a new redefinition of the human being as *Homo* communicator. For Marx, the fundamental epistemological category was social labor, which enables human societies to interact with nature to which they belong and in that process both to humanize nature and to develop human nature in a single process of metabolism, or *Stoffwechsel*, with objective nature.

This is the *Menschwerdung* or Human Becoming of Hegel, not as pure *Denkarbeiten* or thought-work, but as socially organized practical-theoretical labor. For Marx, it is through social labor that humanity perpetuates itself as a species-being. And for Marxists, both science and philosophy are involved in the same task of human social becoming through this interaction with nature (science and technology) and interaction among humans (political economy). Science studies these processes of the forces and relations of production in detail; philosophy simply makes the broader generalizations based on scientific knowledge.

Theory, in the Marxian view, which Popper unconsciously shares, is answering questions raised in the course of practice and not existing prior to practice. At this point the Frankfort School as a whole, and Habermas especially, feel that Marx underestimated the role of theory. He failed to see that social labor was based on the capacity for social communication, and authentic communication is not possible just through shouting at the top of your lungs, not just through the possession of a common language or shared linguistic capacity; it calls for legitimation or validation of that which is communicated.

Habermas here tries to break away from the old British debate about verification and falsification and all that. Authentic communication requires acts and statements that are validated, but this legitimation of communication operates at various levels: in relation to the lowest level of dealing with objective external reality, the physical sciences and technology use their own validation criteria based on experimental demonstration and operational effectiveness; in relation to social reality, the validation criteria of political economy have to deal with questions like what kind of a state is valid, or what human rights are legitimate. At the third level, above all this stands the question of social value choices, which cannot be decided upon according to the value criteria of political economy; it requires a higher level of analysis, and since there are no objective criteria for deciding what is good, every good that is proposed has to be critically analyzed. There is nothing short of complete consensus as the final criterion, but that consensus must be arrived at through hindrance-free communication. One has to psychoanalyze every communication to test its authenticity, to what extent it is driven by concealed falsehood or smaller interests.

This critique of critique is a process of infinite regress, but there is no way out. Habermas's system has the further advantage of not separating the three critiques of Kant into three departments. Communication is the common thread that runs through all processes, including physical evolution, organic evolution, and social formation. There are organizational laws of intercommunication among inorganic atoms and molecules, in which they form larger units and then group together to form cells and organisms. Even at the lowest level of physical or biological reality, without some process of law-governed intercommunication the stars and solar systems could not have come into being, with life in various forms or no life at all on these celestial bodies.

In this view science is seen in its proper perspective, as one of the manifold activities of human societies, not in terms of some heroic individuals ascetically and assiduously pursuing truth, but rather as an enterprise of specific human societies with all the human passions of interest, greed, lust for power, and the desire to dominate swaying and distorting their every activity, including that of science and technology, which always remains integral to the political economy of each society.

Habermas can be counted among the more credible of the upholders of critical rationality and therefore of the European Enlightenment, precisely because he assiduously avoids all metaphysical and even epistemological questions, and gives a comprehensive science-based commonsense view of what is going on in our kind of reality. He is every inch a deontological liberal.

Heidegger and the Hermeneutical School

It is at this point that Heidegger's hermeneutic critique of science comes in. Habermas obviously has been through that critique, but is largely unimpressed by it. Even when Heidegger seeks to shock with the sentence: "Science does not think" (although adding, as an afterthought, "in the way thinkers think,")[194] he is embarking on his project to find the essence or *Wesen* of Being. Heidegger looks for the *Wesen* or Essence of Science, of Technology, of Language, of Truth (*Wahrheit*), of Grounds or Reasons (*Wesen des Grundes*), and of Nature, all as subprojects on the way to the fundamental project of seeking a response to that question of questions about the essence of Being itself, not just the concept of Being, but Being in itself.

The scientific, theoretical attitude to the world, according to Heidegger, rises from the human *Dasein's* anxious concern about the various things or essentials at hand, amongst which and with which it has to live, in its temporality of being-in-the-world. Humanity has to come to terms with beings-in-the-world in order to cope with them, to be free from their threats, to be able to master them and use them for the *Dasein's* purposes. Science may claim, with Kant, that pure reason wants to know them as objects for no other purpose than that of knowledge. Representing the objects through concepts is science's concern; but it has a deeper underlying concern: the *Dasein* is always circumspect; it is ever looking around to see how others would act; and by creating a system of destinations and a system of natural laws, science creates a network of if-then perceptions that are motivated by its own quest for security in a world of temporality, where the other can always be a threat.

Man begins by handling things as tools and in the process of wielding them gets perceptions about their quality: for example, this hammer is heavy. From this it is a short step to regarding not the hammer as such, but the concept of heaviness as an abstract intuition, from which one can proceed to a generalization like the "force of gravity." But behind such abstraction lies the project of Being, which seeks to find itself through the being of humanity. Mathematical physics thus becomes the ground-science, for it provides the total structure for experience.[195]

Modern science, according to Heidegger, is the last stage in Western humanity's forgetfulness of being, the two earlier stages being, à la Comte, Western religion and Western philosophy. As he points out, and as Popper illustrates, scientific truth is seen either as *Sachwahrheit* (the truth of things) or as *Satzwahrheit* (the truth of statements).

In medieval Aristotelian-Thomistic thought, the criterion of truth was always *"veritas est adaequatio rei et intellectus,"* the adequation or correspondence between the thing and the intellect. This view of truth is based on the prior assumption that the true idea of a thing always subsists in the mind of the Creator, and when the human mind makes contact with it, it receives the truth. In modern times the mind of the Creator has been replaced by abstract reason, but the structure is the same. Since *Sach* and *Satz* are still different from each other, modern science makes *Satz* or proposition the representation (*Vorstellung*) of *Sach* or thing. The scientific proposition claims to place before us (*Vorstellen*) the thing or the fact, through a representation which claims to be the fact itself, or perhaps of its unveiling as truth. We have to respond in freedom to this truth of Being unveiled through beings, in letting them be. In such letting be, only the particular is unveiled, the whole remains concealed. In taking the truth of the particular to be truth itself, the human *Dasein* conceals the truth of its own being as well as the truth of the other; and the *Dasein* itself becomes false.

The same is true of technology, according to Heidegger. He is not concerned so much with the power consequences of *techné,* of how technology becomes the source of increased manipulative power for human beings and societies and how they misuse it, as with what technology represents in the development of the psyche of Western man. He is concerned about the dreadful present moment in history when the whole of the history of Western man reveals the forgetfulness of Being and the consequent emasculation of the human spirit. Its restless craving for manipulative power and mastery over everything is the symptom of an advanced disease—the eclipse of Being in the soul of the West.

Heidegger's *The Question Concerning Technology*[196] is as penetrating as it is hard to penetrate. In an attempt "to open our human existence to the essence of technology," he shows the development of technology as something not to be understood functionally, but rather symptomatically. Technology is human activity instrumental to achieving human purposes, but that is only "the instrumental and anthropological definition of technology." It is not its essence. Technology is *poiesis,* that is, a making, or bringing forth, or drawing out of something that was not present before into 'presencing' itself. That which now becomes present and was formerly absent must always have been there, concealed. Technology thus leads out the concealed into unconcealedness.

We have no English equivalent for the German word *Entbergung* that Heidegger uses for this process: it means removing the protective cover that concealed it before. *Verborgenheit* is concealment; *Entbergung* is unconcealment. In Greek, *lanthano* means to conceal or hide or veil; *alētheia* is unconcealment, the manifestation of that which was hidden or veiled; it also happens to be the Greek word for truth. *Techné* is the bringing forth of that which was hidden, and as such a mode of truth. To quote Heidegger:

> Technology is a mode of revealing. Technology comes to presence in the realm where revealing and unconcealment takes place, where *alētheia,* truth, happens.[197]

Modern technology too is a revealing; but a revealing with a difference. It involves an element of defiance of that which is (Nature, Being), forcing it to yield up its secret for our possession and use at will. It is not only drawn out of its concealment, but stands by at our beck and call; it is our slave, "completely unautonomous," waiting to do our bidding.

Now Heidegger moves to a clever piece of linguistic legerdemain which is difficult to achieve in English. Technology takes the mountain or river and makes it a slave, no longer an object of our knowledge, but a "standing reserve" that gives us what we want when we want, like producing paper for our newspapers or providing electric energy to run our machines and light our homes. This making the world our 'standing reserve' or *Ge-stell* is the work of man through modern technology. But what makes man do it? Man seems to be helpless to avoid dominating nature and making it his obedient slave: He is driven to it, but by whom? What concealed presence is doing this to Man?

Man's ordering power reveals itself through science and technology; as Heidegger says: "Modern science's way of representing pursues and entraps nature as a calculable coherence of forces." But before that, "physics, indeed already as pure theory, sets nature up to exhibit itself as a coherence of forces calculable in advance; it therefore orders its experiments precisely for the purpose of asking whether and how nature reports itself when set up in this way."[198] In other words, science is set up (*gestellt*) in such a way that technology can render nature man's standing reserve or *Gestell.*

Technology is not an afterthought of science; it is not the case that first we came by scientific knowledge and then thought up some technological uses for it. Many scientists think that this is what happened and so they calmly and serenely abjure all responsibility for what technology has done. The essence of modern technology has already been present, in a concealed way, in the birth of modern physics, which was only a herald of technology. All comings into being, all unconcealments, happen in this way. Their essence is already present in previous processes, but in a concealed way. Technology, Heidegger says, is not applied science; technology is the real essence of science and precedes it. Technology is the "final cause" of science, and a final cause always precedes the effect, and the essence of technology as well as of science is not the pursuit of truth, but rather making nature our standing reserve. The coming into presence of modern technology, its unconcealment, has as its precondition the coming into presence of modern physics, which precedes modern technology in time but is, in fact, instrumental to it.

But let us return to the question asked earlier and left unanswered: Who set it up this way? Does this coming into presence, this unconcealment of modern science and modern technology (in that chronological order) "happen somewhere beyond all human doing"? Of course not, "but neither does it happen exclusively in man, or decisively through man."[199] Is humanity then, as Hegel's thought has been caricatured, a passive unfree realm in which the Absolute plays its games of concealing and unconcealing?

This, for Heidegger, is the great arena of freedom, and the place of supreme danger if one chooses wrongly. The unconcealing of science and technology unconceals the way humanity is going forward. Humanity can choose to be pushed to the brink along this path, of deriving all the principles of human activity from the process that is now revealed, or humanity can choose to stand in openness to the process that is being revealed, and instead of being carried along by it, choose to "be admitted more and sooner and ever more primally to the essence of that which is unconcealed and to its unconcealment, in order that he might experience as his essence his needed belonging to revealing."[200]

Heidegger at this point brings back the distinction between the "correct" and the "true." Science and technology reveals the correct, but not the true. To follow the correct may be to lose the true. What is now unconcealed is Technological Man, the orderer who makes nature his standing reserve rather than his object as in science. This gives him the possibility of conceiving his own essence as the Supreme Orderer to whom everything is standing reserve, exalting himself "to the posture of lord of the earth," which is what modern secularism is all about.

> In this way the impression comes to prevail that everything man encounters exists only insofar as it is his construct. This illusion gives rise in turn to one final delusion: It seems as though man everywhere and always encounters only himself. . . In truth, however, precisely nowhere does man today any longer encounter himself, i.e. his essence.[201]

That posture "banishes man into that kind of revealing which is an ordering. Where this ordering holds sway, it drives out every other possibility of revealing. . . As compared with that [higher] kind of revealing, the setting-upon that challenges [Nature, to defy it and control it], thrusts man into a relation to that which is, that is at once antithetical and rigourously ordered." Humanity thus, by preoccupation with the technological-scientific revealing that it has mastered, conceals the revealing itself, which is where unconcealment, or truth itself, comes to pass.

Heidegger holds that it is not technology itself that constitutes the danger, but the concealment of the essence of science and technology, and therefore of a "more original revealing," thus denying humanity the opportunity to experience and heed "the call of a more primal truth." Heidegger then goes on to quote his favorite poet, Hoelderlin:

But where danger is, grows
The saving power also.

It is precisely in recognizing the danger in the scientific-technological development that humanity has the possibility of being saved from it. What is this "saving power"? How does that saving power grow, because of the perceived danger? And what does it mean to be saved? To be saved means to be kept from perishing, to be guarded and nurtured, to be granted the possibility to endure without losing oneself. How can we be saved? By paying attention, not to the marvels of technology, being mesmerised into forgetfulness of Being in the process, but to the concealing and unconcealing power behind the manifest and in the manifest. Plato, in his *Phaedrus,* called it the *ekphanestaton,* that which shines forth most purely, the good, the beautiful, the true, that which is revealed in true poetry and art, which is also the true essence of technology. Heeding to the call of Being as the *ekphanestaton* is the beginning of the experience of saving power. The essence of technology is the unconcealing of humanity as the great orderer. It is a way station on the way to our turning around from looking at ourselves as the orderers, to focusing attention on the greater unconcealing itself that is going on in us and through us.

Heidegger thinks that modern technology has a definite view of reality of its own. It does not simply use technique instrumentally to attain certain prechosen human material ends; in that process it gradually transforms Being into something that human beings can manipulate and make instrumental to their purposes. Science simply prepares the way for this process by first reducing everything to "objects of study." Harold Alderman summarizes Heidegger this way:

> Technology is thus much more than simply a practical application of science. It is the unique mode of making beings manifest which provokes "nature" into delivering what is required and demanded by man. In this provocation, the Being of the manifest being is simply what man makes of it. However, prior to their manifestation, technological beings must first be moved into an ontological position from which they can be manipulated most efficiently. The fundamental step in this movement is accomplished in the mathematical ground plan projected by the sciences, where beings are objectified as objects of study. A being for science is only what can fit into the mathematical scientific net constructed by man himself.[202]

Heidegger's question has hardly been heard by most of the Western world—or by the rest of the world for that matter—not to speak of being heeded by many. He is asking us whether we want to equate the world of technology, in which we are masters and mistresses, with the world of Being itself? Modern technology, Heidegger writes, is a technology of overpowering and domination, and is preceded by a science that objectifies everything, in order that all things may be overpowered and dominated. It creates a certain outlook and approach in our civilization, which, while revealing many potentialities previously unsuspected both in human beings as well as in "nature," also makes us want to objectify and dominate everything around us. In that process many other ways in which Being reveals itself to us are lost. He sees that western civilization is now in a stage where its nature as domination is being revealed through technicity and technology.

This should not be taken to mean that Heidegger wants Western civilization and the world to abandon science and technology, or to assume a simple, romantic, rustic life-style. The unveiling of the true nature of science and technology serves its purpose only when humanity sees that scientism-technicity leads us to the illusion that it is handing over to us on a platter the true nature of Being, so that we do not have to look for it elsewhere. Science and technology exacerbates and accentuates the West's centuries-old forgetfulness of Being. Heidegger seeks to unveil its true nature so that all can be aware that they are now even more forgetful of Being than before the advent of modern science and technology.

* * * *

Science and technology and the European Enlightenment have been reinforcing each other till now, but they need not go on that way for long. It was Reason that took the throne when the authority of church theology and tradition was deposed by the Enlightenment, and it is Enlightenment rationality that is in trouble today.

Science and technology has indeed manifested the creative power of that kind of rationality. It has created an impressive world of technological marvels that nothing else could have created. But it is out of that very technology and out of the philosophical assumptions which underlie it that new questions about the method Reason uses to get knowledge have arisen. Enlightenment Reason, which enthroned "Critical Rationality" as the queen of modern civilization, has been shown, by that very critical rationality, to be full of unreason at several points. There is no reason therefore to take it for granted that technology and the European Enlightenment will indefinitely go on reinforcing each other.

The bright light of the Enlightenment not only obscures the night sky, but, it seems, also positively distorts the world we see by that light. To that distortion we must now turn, in order that we can really look beyond that bright light, to gain perspective on what we see by the blinding light of the day. It seems we cannot take for granted what we see by daylight!

Chapter Ten

Reason's Unreason: Ten Questionable Assumptions of Enlightenment Rationality

Critical rationality obviously accepts the principle that reason should always criticize itself, constantly review its conclusions, and make sure that no unexamined assumptions have crept into the process of reasoning. When it comes, however, to the fundamental method of procedure of critical reason, this principle seems often to get ignored. In this chapter we shall examine a few of these assumptions, and abiding by the very canons of critical rationality, exercise our right to criticize the critical method itself.

These assumptions seem to be the ground on which both Western liberalism and Marxism stand or fall. We will take ten of these fundamental assumptions and examine them. Some may assert that these assumptions are inescapable and therefore should not be questioned at all. We counter this by pointing out that other cultures have based themselves on other assumptions, not that the assumptions of other cultures are intrinsically superior. But acknowledging the fact that there are other assumptions possible invalidates any claim of inescapability.

The present author, being reasonably at home in the Indian tradition, can only draw instances from that tradition to show some of the many possible alternatives to the usual Western position. Any Westerner with a modicum of interest in non-Western traditions can easily acquire the competence to compare these different possibilities.

It is even more important that the West makes an effort to acquire that competence. There is no other way for European civilization to overcome its horizon-confining and reality-distorting parochialism except to open itself—even if it appears difficult at first—to some Asian-African cultures, including the Arab, Indian, and Chinese ways of perceiving and dealing with reality, as well as to its own ancient traditions like the Native American, the Shamanist, the Greek, and the Christian. If we point to some of the inconsistencies in the modern tradition of critical rationality, it is not to demand that the West abandon the critical tradition altogether, but only to plead that at least some Western people make a genuine effort to understand the human heritage in a less narrow-minded way. In that process the critical tradition will itself be altered; the fecundity of thought in the West is proverbial; if it exposes itself, it will also absorb, and in that process find some healing; it may also lose some of its cherished false certainties.

The ten assumptions we review here are mutually interconnected: they depend on each other, and it becomes difficult therefore to treat them separately. Any discussion of one of them inescapably touches another or even all of them. But let us first briefly list them, so that we can have a comprehensive look:

1. Naive realism about the nature of reality
2. Truth, Concept, Idea and Proposition
3. Language as a vehicle of truth
4. Epistemology as a guarantor of veracity
5. Conscious reason as the instrument of knowing
6. Causality as explanation
7. Measurement-based Science as a way to precise knowledge
8. The Universe as self-existent
9. Time and Space as given
10. Change, evolution, development and progress.

1. Naive Realism

Naive realism is the assumption that there are subjects and objects, that the subject can know the objects as they are, and that what cannot be known is not real. There are people who think that to abandon such naive realism is to embrace some notion of the world as illusion. This fear is so deeply ingrained in the Western mind that most Westerners are afraid to doubt the reality of the phenomenal world, despite the fact that modern Western science and philosophy themselves have shown the antinomies in the realist worldview of the West.

Naive realism and an equally naive illusionism are not the only two alternatives between which we have to choose. The Indian tradition, for example, has examined a whole gamut of alternative possibilities in the course of its centuries-long development.

The most glaring example of illusionism in India known to the West is the doctrine of *māya* as developed by the great Indian philosopher Sankara in the eighth century. His is certainly no naive illusionism; rather, it is an outright negation of naive realism, and a very sophisticated and involved conceptual structure that undergirds the doctrine of *māyāvāda.*

The epistemological foundations of Sankara's philosophy we will leave for a later section when we discuss the epistemological assumptions of the West. Here, we will only take a quick look at his ontology or cosmology. It is encapsulated in the formula: "*Brahma satyam, jagad mithya, jivabrahmaiva napara.*" Translated, that means: "The Absolute alone has true being, the universe is unreal, and the human soul is none other than the Absolute."

Interestingly enough, the word *māya,* or illusion, is not applied to the universe in that formula, but the more powerful word *mithya* which literally means vanity, nonbeing, falsehood, useless, emptiness. But elsewhere Sankara develops the concept of *māya* at great length, as one of the foundational pillars of his system. The word preexisted Sankara, though not in a philosophically clarified sense. In common parlance *māya* means illusion, the sort that magicians foist on their observers during their performances. *Māyājāla, Māyāvidya, Jālavidya,* and *Indrajāla* are all more or less synonyms for the art of the professional magicians or tricks performed by sleight of hand or mass hypnosis.

Māya, for Sankara, is not a natural illusion like a mirage or a rainbow; it is a trick played by the Absolute, who is the Master Magician of the Universe. *Māya* is a power of the Absolute, a *śakti* that It exercises, very much on the analogy of a mass hypnotist creating illusions in the minds of the observers.

No analogy can of course be perfect, especially any finite analogy by which we seek to understand the Infinite. In *māyāvāda* there can be no observers other than the Absolute; and what is observed is also not something else than the Absolute. It is the same One Absolute Consciousness that appears both as perceiving subjects and as perceived objects. But the Absolute does not have to undergo any modification or transformation in order to appear simultaneously as subject and as object. There are no three realities like God, Man, and World. There is only One without a second.

This might sound absurd to the Western mind, but exercise your critical rationality, and see. If the Absolute is both the *all* and the Absolute, how can there be something other than the *all?* How can there be something in addition to the Infinite or outside of It? Infinite means without finis or boundary. How can the Infinite have an outside? The Infinite has neither inside nor outside, since It is not spatially or temporally extended or bounded.

God, if He or She or It is infinite, cannot create something outside of Itself or in addition to Itself, such that there is God first and then the Other—that is, the created order. Such duality is logically impossible, hence the very name of the philosophical system—*advaita* or nondual. It is not so absurd: logically, it is quite tight.

Why does it sound *prima facie* absurd then? The problem is in our minds, ruled by nescience or *avidya.* Duality and multiplicity are illusions created by the nature of our mind. It is naive realism that is absurd. The illusion created by the nonknowledge in our minds is actually our bondage; it is from this bondage that we should seek liberation or *mōkša,* for our desires and our actions are powered by our nonknowledge and are perilously misleading. Naive realism is fatal; it leads to human entrapment in the endless cycle of births and rebirths. But critical rationality cannot save us from the peril; it can, however, show us how naive naive realism is. The remedy itself lies beyond the conceptual, beyond the inescapable dualism of discursive and rational thought.

Enlightenment rationality and its naive realism keep the three distinct—knower, known, and knowledge (*jñātā, jñēya and jñāna*). There is another power in the human mind that can lead us beyond to this perfect unity, a liberation from nescience and the attainment of true science: *parāvidya* or transcendent knowledge, in which all dualities are overcome, and the knower, the known, and the knowledge become one.

Critical questions can be put to Sankara, and the tightness of his logic may prove to be more apparent than real. We are not interested here in defending Sankara or in commending his line as the only alternative possible to naive realism. Our purpose is only to affirm that there have been alternatives and millions of people have lived by these alternatives. We need to understand these other positions and should not dismiss them too lightly as incoherent or illogical.

In the West, Plato and Plotinus were not naive realists; neither was Hegel or Heidegger. Hegel actually seems to have taken off from Sankara, and posited the Absolute Idea as the sole reality, though he certainly did not dismiss the temporal process as pure illusion.

Hegel's Absolute Idea, however, unlike in Sankara, is in one aspect at least subject to dialectical development through the temporal process, and has to achieve its own full identity through that process. This would be abhorrent to Sankara who regarded the Absolute as absolutely free from the need to change and develop, since It is eternally perfect and not in need of attaining perfection through any temporal process. For Sankara, time and space are themselves part of the illusion arising from *avidya,* and cannot have any power over the Absolute. But Hegel's is another alternative to naive realism that still deserves patient study.

The simple fact is that naive realism is philosophically untenable, though there have been numerous attempts in India (Nyaya-Vaiseshika school, Sarvastivadins, Carvaka, Madhvacharya, and so on) to justify it philosophically. These attempts cannot be deemed to have succeeded. Modern practical theory has shown how the objective existence of discrete objects is impossible to establish.

One of the great physicists of our century, Erwin Schroedinger, has shown us also the fallacy in thinking of the individual subject as capable of comprehending reality. One of the assumptions of naive realism is that individual minds do exist and are located in the body. The old idea of conceiving the brain as the locus of the individual mind seems to have gone out of fashion. Now it is the body-mind as a single composite entity, but still it is of the individual body-mind that the scientist speaks. Schroedinger said this about such a view, in 1958:

> We have entirely taken to thinking of the personality of a human being . . . as located in the interior of its body. To learn that it cannot really be found there is so amazing that it meets with doubt and hesitation; we are very loath to admit it. We have got used to localizing the conscious personality inside a person's head—I should say an inch or two behind the midpoint of the eyes. . . It is very difficult for us to take stock of the fact that the localization of the personality, of the conscious mind, inside the body is only symbolic; just an aid for practical use.[203]

Descartes was a naive realist, who could easily classify all reality into *res extensa* and *res cogitans* or extended things and thinking things. He conveniently overlooked the fact that the thinking thing (the subject) was also an extended thing; his naivete lay in the assumption that he could objectify the conscious subject or thinking being as a *res* or thing. Today we know that consciousness escapes objective study, because the moment one makes the essential subjectivity of consciousness into an object, it ceases to be itself, since it is by nature subject and not object. Further, the mind-body problem is such that we are unable to locate mind or consciousness in the individual body.

In science itself, individual subject-based naive realism is giving place to nonrealist accounts of science itself: Post-empiricist (Rorty, Foucault), or Neopragmatist, or social-dialectic (Bernstein?). Giving up the defense of naive realism, they now resort to a subject-object dialectic, which is also social or communitarian. Richard Bernstein puts it this way:

> Central to this new understanding [of science] is a dialogical model of rationality that stresses the practical, communal character of this rationality in which there is choice, deliberation, interpretation, judicious weighing and application of 'universal criteria' and even rational disagreement about which criteria are relevant and most important.[204]

In all these new departures one observes the gradual abandonment of both naive realism and its individualism. The community character of mind is being increasingly recognized, and the old mid-fourteenth-century debate between Thomas Aquinas and Siger of Brabant at the Sorbonne is finding a new relevance. Siger taught the unity of the mind of the human race and denied the plurality of individual minds. For Thomas it was necessary to affirm the individual mind as identical with an individual soul that was immortal. Naive realism follows Thomas, but not for metaphysical reasons. Today, with the Jungian theory of the collective unconscious and the unity of all minds through the ages, the individual mind is being perceived as possible only in a community of minds. Western thought, however, can affirm the community character of mental activity even in science, but remains unwilling to go all the way to affirm that all minds together constitute one single reality.

Naive realism is losing ground in its belief not only in the distinctiveness of the individual mind, but also in the objectivity of the object. The idea that there is an objective nature independent of us, and that it is composed of a finite or infinite number of particles, is no longer viable in physics. Space is no longer homogeneous and Euclidean; it is no longer infinite and infinitely divisible, nor is it immutable and absolute, independent of its content. Euclidean geometry is not the only geometry possible, as even Bertrand Russell and Henri Poincare in recent times believed. Space is not independent of time nor vice versa. Together, they constitute but four of the possibly more than four dimensions of reality as we observe it. Four-dimensional time-space is not an inert, independently subsisting entity. Unfortunately, our two-dimensional logic is itself derived from the experience of bodies in motion in a homogeneous time-space. If time-space is inert, it can be so only in relation to something outside it, for motion and inertia are relative concepts.

Reality, both at the microphysical and the megacosmic levels, is not visualizable or conceptualizable. The concept of "object" can exist only at the middle level of our "normal" perception, but not at the micro or megalevels. Jean Piaget showed us, forty years ago, that the human infant during the first eighteen months of its existence has no concept of an object; that concept is acquired through our experience of the macroworld. When we speak or conceive of the universe as a megaobject, we are illicitly transferring a category that applies only at the middle or macro level. There is no single, rigidly cohering, "block universe," but only an open, undetermined, potential or probabilistic multiverse, which cannot be made an object of our thought or our perception.

Naive realism belongs to the age of classical Newtonian mechanics, but since it fits in with the middle level of our macroworld experience, we still cling to its outmoded ideas as universally valid at all levels.

The Western world itself has shown us how indefensible naive realism is,[205] but since our scientists, philosophers, and thinkers have not yet succeeded in giving us a coherent and convincing description of the universe that fits with all three: classical mechanics, quantum theory, and the theory of relativity (both special and general), we still cling to naive realism and to its individualistic subject-object dualism and atomism. Our politics, our economics, our sociology and our anthropology, as well as a large part of modern science, are still based on that naive realism. And our cultural creativity remains stunted and unproductive. The "light too bright" seems to have blinded us to the glorious potentialities inherent in us.

2. Truth, Concept, Idea, and Proposition

Truth is a quest, not a concept, not an idea or a proposition. And it is not a quest for something objectively given; neither is it a quest for knowledge in the narrow sense. Truth is a state of being rather than a statement of fact. Truth is being without falsehood, light without the admixture of darkness. Truth is what is, not what is stated.

What is stated above is not truth. It is a personal affirmation about truth, which needs validation. Such validation would not be of truth itself, but only of a proposition about truth. Truth itself does not stand in need of validation, but is self-certifying. Truth provides its own validation. Propositions about truth may be valid or invalid. A valid proposition about truth can be a help in the quest, but is itself not the object of the quest. The object is a state of being, the attainment of a right relation to what is, a being in the truth, a state of being properly grounded and established in the truth, beyond all subject-object dualism, and beyond the threefold distinction of knower, known, and knowledge.

In the Greek tradition, truth or *alētheia* has had various meanings in its history. Heidegger, for example, focuses on its etymological meaning: from *lanthano* meaning to veil or conceal. Adding the negative prefix a- to the noun form *lētheia* (veiling, concealment), one gets *alētheia* (unveiling, unconcealment) as the "true" meaning of truth. In fact, most of Heidegger's work is devoted to coaxing the truth out of its hiding place and to making truth reveal itself. And he does bring out the hidden *Wesen* or essence of many realities, including science, technology, and the human *Dasein*. The skill and dexterity of thinking that Heidegger uses to unveil hidden realities is indeed impressive.

But his ultimate quest is to bring the human *Dasein* to grasp (or be grasped by) the "truth" of Being Itself, which is not the same as the being of beings. Being Itself is finally unconcealed as the abysslike ground of all beings, the ground of metaphysics and of ontology itself. His lecture, *The Essence of Truth* (*Vom Wesen der Wahrheit*, 1930), and his essay, *Plato's Doctrine of Truth* (*Platons Lehre von der Wahrheit*, 1947) mark his initial struggles to unconceal the nature of truth itself.

Heidegger questions the usual conception of God or the Absolute as "the highest Being." This involves placing the Ultimate Being in the same category as beings in time and space. Beings in time and space are present to us, in the present time, either at-hand or to-hand; that is, present to us in such a way that we can objectify them, know them, and ultimately control them. By thinking of Being Itself in the same category as beings, with the qualification that It is the highest being and is eternally present to us, we objectify Being Itself. We anthropomorphize Being Itself, and simply place It at the apex of the class of beings. We do not ask the questions: What is Being Itself? Why are there beings rather than no being at all?

Western metaphysics has always been on the quest for an idea of the Ultimate Being, but that Being is not an idea or an object about which ideas can be formed. By asking metaphysics to ask the question about its own ground, Heidegger wants us to abandon that quest in the realm of ideas. Thinking can unconceal some very deep questions, for which there is no answer that can be given in the form of ideas. There has to be an immediate "appropriation" of Being through an experience that transcends ideas, propositions, and verbal language. Thinking and metaphysics can lead us on to that experience, but do not bring it about. Thinking, with the aid of language, propositions, and ideas, is the *Holzwege,* the forest trails that we must tread. It can lead us to a clearing in the woods, where we can only wait expectantly, without language, ideas, propositions, and even thought, for the truth, which is Being Itself, to unconceal itself.

When it does so, there is not much about it that we can put into language. One sees or experiences (not thinks) It as *Selbigkeit* or Selfness or Selfsame, which unselfishly and self-renouncingly gives Itself to us in love and virtually creates in us the same reaction of total and unreserved renunciation in self-giving. As Heidegger puts it in the closing words of his *Der Feldweg* (1953): "Everything addresses renunciation toward the Self-same. Renunciation does not take. Renunciation grants."[206]

It is certainly inappropriate to think of this experience as an appropriation of Being by the individual *Dasein,* though many Heidegger scholars have been inclined to do so. The unconcealment of Being "happens" in the human *Dasein,* that *Dasein* is the "place" where the Presence appears in the historical "now," and "abides." The abiding itself sends forth the human *Dasein* to its historical destiny; it does not take away the experiencer of Being out of history, but the "presence" in the *Dasein* is part of history's movement toward its destiny.

Heidegger's thought is certainly a radical turn in Western philosophy, a turn even less followed than it is understood. There is, as far as I know, no organized Heidegger movement; few indeed must be the number of those who actually seek this Being-experience along the paths he has charted. Apart from its relation to history, language and thinking, the Heideggerian quest is not fundamentally different from that of Sankara in India twelve centuries ago. Heideggerianism has not become a religious movement, but it contains almost all the elements necessary for one.

Despite all this, however, the understanding of truth that has prevailed in the Western tradition differs from the etymological meaning of *alētheia,* and from the originally Parmenidean meaning of *ousia* or Being. Parmenides, whom Heidegger reconstructs, thought very much along the lines of the *Upanishads* and Hindu thinkers like Sankara. Being is, unoriginate, indestructible, never was, nor will be, says Parmenides in his fragment preserved for us by Simplicius (*Diels B 8*). It always is, One altogether; it did not come from non-being, nor is it to become something. It is homogeneous, indivisible, continuous, perfect, motionless, abiding, resting, unvarying. This is truth, *alētheia;* every other thing is mere seeming, mere opinion (*doxa*), dualist naming.

Parmenides denied time, the void, plurality, and all becoming. As for Sankara, these are but "seeming," or mere appearance. Quoting the *Upanishads,* the *Brahmasutras* and the *Gita,* Sankara also attributes the same characteristics to the Absolute, though not as descriptions or qualities, and later to deny that these descriptions are in any sense adequate for the comprehension of Absolute Being. What Heidegger calls *Selbigkeit* or Selfness, Sankara calls the Self, the *Paramatman,* the Brahma, the One Unchanging Absolute, who is the cause of and agent in all events. He classifies reality into two classes, the *paramārthika* or ultimately real, and the *vyāvahārika* or pragmatically and operationally real, the sort of reality with which modern science deals. But these are not two realities: it is the former that projects Itself as world and as individual humans through the power of *Māya.*

According to Vedanta in general, true reality is that which cannot be sublated or subrated (removed by a subsequent perception). One sees a wax statue and judges it to be alive; subsequent experience, such as the perception of its nonmovement, nonresponse, subrates the original perception and makes you see that it is only a wax figure and not alive. Every time-space experience can be sublated (*bādhita*) by subsequent experience. The transcendent experience of the Absolute cannot be so sublated by any subsequent experience; it therefore is the only truth at the absolute or *paramārthika* level.

This is an alternative perception of truth; it still is not truth, but only an affirmation about truth. It claims to be based on an original experience of *ršis* or seers in ancient times. The *Vēdas* or scriptures bear witness to this truth. Its final validation can be only in the experience of truth, not in any external evidence that perception or inference can adduce. The *Vēdas,* or the testimony of the scriptures, is also part of the *Holzwege* (forest paths) to which Heidegger bears witness. They do not certify that truth but only invite you to tread the path of discipline, thought, and meditation that ultimately leads to the self-certifying experience. Ideas, propositions, prescriptions, exhortations, and so on belong to the second (*vyāvahārika*) level of reality, and their function is to lead one to the self-validating experience of the first (*pāramārthika*) level.

The purpose of this exercise has been to illustrate the fact that there are other ways of approaching the truth than the ones that Enlightenment rationality prescribes for us. The European Enlightenment follows a more unimaginative understanding of the Greek notion of truth, that it is a statement that corresponds to fact and is consistent with other facts. This is the Tarskian definition of truth that Karl Popper and others unthinkingly adopt.

The Hebrew understanding of Truth as *emeth* or *emunah* is radically different from the pedestrian Greek and modern understanding of truth. *Emeth* does not mean a proposition or statement of fact, but "that which is," the name that Yahweh gave for Himself to Moses: *Ehyeh asher ehyeh,* meaning "I am and will be what I am and will be." Truth is that which eternally endures, that which is firm, steadfast, and finally reliable.

The absolutization of propositional truth, which can be conceived, known, uttered, written down, transmitted, understood, possessed, analyzed, stored, and inscribed with ink or pen on paper, is a trivialization of truth that needs to be overcome, if civilization is to have a more secure foundation.

3. Language as a Vehicle of Truth

Language is one of the prized capabilities of humanity, without which human existence would not perhaps be possible. It is a proprium of humanity, that which seems to distinguish the human being from animals and things. Other animals do have rudimentary language; human language is the most developed that we know of. It belongs to human identity, and it unites as well as divides human groups. Language and linguistic communication constitute the essence of human society, yet not all communication is through language or literary symbols. There is for example the silent communication between mother and child, before the child develops linguistic capabilities. There is also communication through silent movies, photographs, musical instruments, art and architecture, weeping, laughter, the look of the eye, the posture of the human body, through gestures and signals. In fact, symbolic or ritual communication seems to have played a larger role than literary or linguistic communication in early societies. Myth and ritual may use language, but their function transcends mere literary communication.

One of the characteristics of the Enlightenment rationality is the tendency to overplay the roles of language and the conscious mind. Theoretically we know, at least since Freud, that there are other levels to the human mind. We know about the "unconscious" that affects the movements of our conscious mind, but we still think of the unconscious as a marginal factor in the mind. Language belongs to the conscious mind. The unconscious speaks through dreams and archetypes more than through literary language.

Western civilization has come to put a higher value on rational, linguistic expression than on intuitive, emotional, imaginal thinking and communication. This is a tendency that goes at least as far back in Western civilization as Augustine of Hippo, for whom the "Word" is the pure and higher form of truth and the image or sacrament merely an accommodation to our bodily nature. The sacrament for him is *verbum visibile* (visible or sensible word) while the *verbum invisibile* (invisible word) is spiritual and superior. Protestant thought revived this Augustinian exaltation of the "pure Word", and hence its greater emphasis on the preached word or the sermon than on the sacraments or liturgy.

Much in our thinking and communication is nonlinguistic, that is, nonconceptual image-thinking, whose logic is more associative than causal. It may use language but is essentially centered around feelings and images, drives and desires, as well as inhibitions and repressive tendencies in the psyche. Archetypes and myths belong to this level, which is much more decisive than conscious linguistic thinking in directing our desires and actions. So does poetry and art, drama and literature, as well as much of good religion and culture. These give better expression to our "deepest inwardness," to borrow a term from Hoelderlin, than all kinds of discursive language, including the one I am using now in writing this.

The conscious, rational, analytic mind is a newcomer in the history of the human consciousness, and we are overfascinated by its great achievements in the area of science and technology, and less in the fields of the human sciences. Language is the preferred tool of this conscious mind, about which the psychologist Whitmont writes:

> The images arise as carriers of messages which are lacking—at times dangerously lacking—in consequence of the one-sided views and convictions of consciousness. The rising pressure of images is the defense reaction of a self-regulating, balancing psychic system. . . But why images rather than concepts? Why, if the one-sided or exaggerated positions of consciousness are formulated in conceptual terms, is the compensating reaction not couched in similar terms? . . . To understand this we must renounce another cherished prejudice, namely that consciousness and its concept-based, abstract frame of reference is the totality of the psyche, or even the standard pattern or standard unit for psychic functioning. It is merely a late-coming upstart. Not only are the conscious concepts partial aspects of the psychic totality, but consciousness based upon conceptualised men-

> tal functioning is a relatively late, secondary form of mental development.[207]

The tragedy of Western civilization is its tragicomic attempt to grasp all truth with this conscious mind and its favored instrument, language. Anglo-American linguistic philosophy, which started out as a kind of positivism and ended up as second-order linguistic analysis of first-order linguistic statements by others, is perhaps the most comic of these Western enterprises seeking to capture truth within the net of logic and language. The French philosophical pilgrimage from existentialism to structuralism and then on to deconstruction is another comic instance of the futility of seeking to capture truth in language and concept. In America, it was Reader-responsism as a popular literary technique that led to deconstruction as a principle of literary criticism. In Germany, the hermeneutical movement marks the move of philosophy to focus on language, text, and interpretation as its basic task. It is perhaps less comic because it retains the quest after meaning as essential to hermeneutics.

Rajnath, in his illuminating introduction to deconstructionism in France and America, has this to say:

> The most subtle form of anxiety of deconstruction one discerns in deconstruction itself. On the one hand, it is by its very nature inimical to institutionalisation and, on the other, it seeks to institutionalise itself. Deconstruction today finds itself in a situation where it has already been institutionalised with students trained on deconstruction having joined faculties. If deconstruction acquiesces in this routinisation, it ceases to be deconstruction; and if it continues to subvert it, it not only opposes itself but loses all hopes of institutionalisation. Either way there is reason for anxiety.[208]

Deconstruction has one thing to be said in its favor. Besides exposing many of the dualisms and unjustified evaluations of Western thought, it seems willing to acknowledge what Blake, for example, recognized long ago: that image is a more comprehensive term for the communicational medium than the word.

> Five windows light the cavern'd Man.
>
> (William Blake)

Language is one image that gets to our ears and eyes, in the form of speech or writing. But there are also tactile images that our skin takes in, smell images for the nose, and taste images for the tongue. Language is certainly not the only sight-image that we take in; nor is it the only hearing-image. By reducing communication to language and visible or audible symbols, we are limiting the scope of the human. Deconstructionists seem to recognize this in their opposition to the very arbitrary dualism of "signified" and "signifier," which becomes for structuralists a convenient tool for divorcing the "sign" (which is what language means to most structuralists) from the signifier and from the one who reads the sign.

Deconstructionists also lampoon Western scholarship's paranoiac preoccupation with "sources" as if nothing had happened in the past that did not leave an archeological or written witness, so that posterity could examine it and inform itself. Literary critics like J. Hillis Miller have begun to argue that instead of language being something constituted by humanity, it is constituting human beings and their societies, not always in the most salutary fashion. The Western notion of the individual self is itself thus a creation of language:

> The self is a linguistic construction rather than being the given, the rock, a solid *point de depart*. . . There is no literal language of consciousness, the self being itself a figure or an effect of language.[209]

I am aware that I am writing all this about language by using language. Language is a prison in which we should not padlock ourselves. Language can show us the limitations of language, and thereby provoke us to seek liberation from the prison. Truth lies beyond language and logic and there is no reason why we should not seek liberation from the prison that Enlightenment rationality has fortified.

4. Epistemology as a Guarantor of Veracity

Habermas, in a sense, represents the culminating point in the European Enlightenment's process of absolutization of epistemology and language.

Kant, as we have seen, was preoccupied with epistemology, since that was where Hume's sharp sword of sensationalist skepticism was most threatening. If Kant is the father of critical philosophy, he, along with Descartes, takes credit for making epistemology the touchstone of truth. But in Kant, normative epistemology functions strictly only at the subject-object level of pure reason, of the first *Critique*. Clearly Kant's attempt was to liberate ethics and aesthetics from the domination of pure reason. Kant's epistemology was in fact a prelude to the system in which two-thirds is based on intelligent speculation rather than on the epistemology of pure reason. It was Habermas who sought to reduce epistemology to "validation criteria" for "Communication and the Evolution of Society," and thereby to create a new epistemology of universal pragmatics that would be normative for all levels of human knowing, willing, and feeling.

Husserl's phenomenology had also sought to make epistemology normative for all activity of the human consciousness, including will and judgment, though he did insist that phenomenology was not epistemology, but something more, namely a ground-science, a noetic or knowing system that was to be the basis of all sciences, physical, organic, or human. Epistemology it certainly was, pace Husserl's protestations to the contrary, as Habermas's mentor and colleague Theodor Adorno had pointed out in his scathing piece: *Against Epistemology.*[210] And it is an epistemology that hides its antinomies and generates too many mythical entities like *'noēma-noēsis'* and "transcendental epoche." For Husserl the epistemological question was: What ought to be the content of experience in order that it may have objective validity?[211] He discounts questions like: How is experience possible? or What is the general content or form of experience as such? He wants to distill out the timeless and universal content of experience, or rather to legislate for all experience universally without reference to any particular experience in the real world. But the universal law of experience that Husserl wants to set up as the unquestionable first premise of all experience is itself drawn from experience and can be validated only on the basis of experience. What claims to be *a priori* is in fact *a posteriori.*

Our concern here is with the function of epistemology as such, not with particular epistemologies like those of a Kant or a Descartes or a Husserl. Its function is obviously the validation of knowledge, by laying down rules for all knowledge. But, as Hegel pointed out, whatever epistemological criteria we set up for valid knowledge, these criteria themselves would have been obtained by a process other than the application of these criteria which are regarded as normative for all knowledge. No epistemology can in fact be validated by itself. This is the Achilles' heel of all modern systematic thought. Every attempt so far in modern Western thought to impose an epistemology as an absolute validation criteria falls under this criticism and collapses. Epistemology is an arbitrary absolutization—this applies to the sophisticated criteria of Habermas as well.

It was Adorno who took up Hegel's point and showed us how there is no absolute "First" that is indubitably given and from which we can proceed with system-building. No epistemology is absolutely given or self-evident. This attempt to absolutize epistemology as an unquestionable first, and then to make it the unshakeable foundation of all knowledge, seems doomed from the start.

This of course is an inevitable consequence of the repudiation of all external authority, which characterizes the European Enlightenment. One consequence of that repudiation is the hypocrisy of rejecting all tradition, and then quietly proceeding to operate with concepts drawn from Platonic (e.g., *eidos, noema*), Aristotelian (category structure, logic of identity, and noncontradiction), Heraclitean (dialectic) traditions. Gadamer in his *Truth and Method* has shown us, through his concepts of "horizon" and *Wirkungsgechichte*, how tradition is inescapable for all human beings, whether they be deontological liberals or Marxists or just old-fashioned theologians and metaphysicians.[212]

Epistemology in the Indian Tradition

Just for the purpose of seeing how another tradition faces the same problem, let us look at the question of epistemology in the Indian tradition. Exhausting the subject would demand several volumes to itself, since epistemology or *Pramāṇavicāra* is a central and highly controversial element in Indian thought.

The Samkhya tradition seems to be one of the oldest in India, perhaps antedating the Buddhist tradition, which began in the sixth century B.C. Unfortunately, our documentation for Samkhya comes from a much later period, the development of what is known as Classical Samkhya (as distinguished from Early Samkhya) in the first century of our era. There are several indirect references to the Samkhya-yoga in the *Katha* (fourth century B.C.?), *Svetāśvatāra* (third century B.C.?), and the later *Upanishads*. The main early sources are the great Indian epic, the *Mahābhārata*, (an epic that has grown through the centuries by constant accretion) and Asvaghosha's *Buddhacarita* (ca. first century A.D.?). The two sections of the *Mahābhārata* that speak of something like the later, classical Samkhya system which we know from Isvarakrshna's *Sāmkhyakārika* (dated ca. 300–500 A.D.), are the *Mokšadharma* and the *Bhagavadgita*, which again are dated around 100 B.C. to 100 A.D. in the case of the *Gita* and about the first to fourth centuries A.D. for the *Mokšadharma*.

The most important thing about Indian epistemology, whether in the Buddhist, Jain, Brahminist, or other Hindu traditions, is the question of the purpose or end of knowledge. Many fail to see this fundamental difference between the European Enlightenment tradition and the Indian tradition, because they overlook this aspect.

Knowledge or *jñāna* is neither an end in itself nor a tool for technological control of the external world.

The Indian tradition agrees with Habermas in emphasizing the "emancipatory interest" of knowledge, but in a sense quite different from that of Habermas or of Sartre, for whom the emancipation is simply from the Unknown or the Other as a threat or limit. The word for emancipation, not in the early Vedic, but in the later Hindu or Brahminic tradition, is *mōkša* or *mukti,* meaning "release"—from the bondage of nescience and from the consequent entanglement in the cycle of births and rebirths. Knowledge is for release from the bondage of nonknowledge, because the latter has disastrous consequences for human existence. This is so also in the Buddhist, Jain, or Samkhya traditions, though they may not always speak of *mōkša* or *mukti.* It all depends on what it is that one seeks release from, what one recognizes as the fundamental problem of human existence.

The fundamental function of knowledge then is existential-emancipatory rather than ancillary to intellectual satisfaction or control of the external world. Epistemology or *pramāňavicāra* becomes significant only in that existential context. Correct epistemology is necessary because it can lead to the knowledge that liberates, not to knowledge that "captures" truth and helps control the world.

But how does one get to that correct epistemology? Can it be established on the basis of the same method? Yes, much better than in Enlightenment epistemology, but it is basically an existential decision based on one's better judgment rather than on any indubitable first principle. But once established, it confirms itself in experience if it leads to the desired emancipation.

Inevitably, the consequence is a plurality of Indian epistemologies. The basic term is *pramāṇa,* which actually means measure or measuring stick, analogous to the western concept of *canon,* which also literally means a reed or measuring stick. The Sanskrit root is *mā,* which means measure as a verb, from which come the nouns *māna* and *mānam;* and adding the prefix *pra-* (which means 'onward' or 'forward') *pramāṇam* becomes a guiding measure for progress in knowledge.

In the Indian tradition there is no uniformity in the names and number of the *pramāṇas.* The number can vary from two to six in the various systems. The totally atheist, secular, Carvaka system has only one *pramāṇa,* namely *pratyakša* or that which is open to the senses of perception. The Buddhist logician-philosopher Dinnaga has two principles and two alone, namely perception (*pratyakša*) and inference (*anumāna*). The major controversy between the Buddhist, Jain, and other systems that reject the authority of the Scriptures on one side and the Hindus on the other was about the third *pramāṇa,* which is variously described as *śabda* (sound or word of a Guru or a *Rši*), *śruti* (that which is heard), *āgama* (that which has come down to us, or tradition), *āptavacana* or *āptaśruti* (reliable, fitting word or that which is heard). All these are in fact synonyms for the scriptures as well as for the words of the wise and the experienced.

The Nyaya system of Indian philosophy adds another *pramāṇa* or epistemological principle—that of analogy—to the three that most systems accept: perception, inference, and scriptures, or the words of the wise. Later Samkhya and Vedanta, as well as Yoga systems, operate with these three principles. The Purvamimamsa system adds another two to the four of Nyaya: *anupalabdhi* or *abhāvapratyakša* (nonperception or perception of absence), and *arthāpatti,* or circumstantial inference or implication.

The number of *pramāṇas,* which can go up to nine in some cases, is not as important as the rigor with which the principles are applied. Buddhists like Dinnaga are very strict in excluding the principle of external authority; in practice, however, they could not function without depending to some extent on the teachings of the Buddha, which they sometimes very cleverly include under inference. Sankara, on the other hand, while accepting the three principles, also insists that perception and inference are valid only for the knowledge of the temporal world, about which scripture, according to him, has nothing to say; or, if it says something contrary to perception and inference about the sense-world, such dicta have no authority. As for the transcendent world, scripture is authority only in the sense that it can bear witness to the ultimate truth. Scripture cannot effect the knowledge of that transcendent truth, or *mōkša,* which does not come about from something extraneous to it like scripture.

In theory, both the Buddhist Enlightenment and the European Enlightenment exclude and proscribe external authority, particularly the authority of the scriptures or religious authority. Both modern Western thought and early Buddhist thought had this in common: that they sought to base themselves on two epistemological principles, namely *pratyakša* and *anumāna,* or sense-perception and inference. Buddhism very soon abandoned this to give quasi-scriptural authority to the teachings of the Buddha, and in effect replaced one set of scriptures with another. Western secular thought scrupulously sought to avoid accepting any new scriptures to take the place of the old, yet it developed its own unwritten code and criteria of validation, justification, methodological falsification, or empirical verification, which functions as a third epistemological principle regulating the use of critical rationality. In addition to the three, certain elements from the tradition keep cropping up in Western philosophy and science.

Early Buddhism did not conceptualize knowledge itself in a simple subject-object dualism, but used a totally different eighteen-element scheme for what we now call objective knowledge. The three fundamental units are objects, senses, and consciousness, each of the three being sixfold. Objects are visible, audible, smellable, tasteable, touchable, and mental—thus sixfold. There are six senses, corresponding to the six kinds of objects; and also six mental faculties in consciousness for cognizing the six types of objects of the six types of sense; the sixth sense is mind, *manas,* or the instrument of thought as distinguished from cognition or *vijñāna* (Pali *viññāna*). Mental objects are classified in the same category as sense objects.

The wide variety within Indian epistemology has only been sampled above. The purpose is simply to affirm that epistemology is a special choice within a system of thought and can vary from system to system. Epistemology cannot validate itself before other systems. The test of the system is not in the demonstrable reliability of its epistemology or ontology, but whether or not it leads to real emancipation. Enlightenment rationality has of late recognized the emancipatory aspect of knowledge, especially with Habermas's *Knowledge and Human Interests.* But the emancipation is conceived only in terms of the Other or the Unknown as a threat or limit to the subject's own existence and domination over others. In other words, Enlightenment rationality conceives the purpose of knowledge as total power over all things. The civilization created by that rationality has rendered us innumerable services to be acknowledged with great gratitude, but it leaves humanity basically unemancipated.

Epistemology, with which modern Western thought begins, is a brave and bold attempt to do without external authority. But basically it is an effort that has failed. The scientific knowledge it has yielded remains unproved and with very little ultimate validity, except for operational purposes. Epistemology has proved to be no guarantor of truth.

5. Conscious Reason as the Instrument of Knowing

We have already stated the limitations of conscious reason as an instrument of knowledge when we discussed the problems of language. We need to dwell on some things that other cultures have to teach us about how to go beyond conscious reason in order to come to the experience of ultimate reality.

Sankara recommends concentration on a single object of meditation, something that begins with the conscious mind and soon leaves it behind. Meditation has to be continuous—like a thread of flowing oil; and for a long time: *tailadhārāvatu samānapratyayapravāhēna dirkhakālam.*[213]

There are so many forms of meditation: one is *nama japa,* or the continuous repetition of the divine name, usually a special name of the divine being given to the disciple by the guru, like *Om Sivamayam, Om Narayanaya nama, Om Christo nama,* or any other that the guru knows to be dear to the disciple. A second form is *praṇavavidya* or repetition of the single syllable *"om."* There are numerous other methods, but the purpose is the same: going beyond the dualism of the conscious mind. Meditation has to be preceded by a strict discipline of self-control and of overcoming the drives and passions: *vāsanānāśa* or *indriyanigraha,* and the overcoming of the dualist consciousness of *avidya* or nescience, which is the major obstacle in going beyond the conscious mind. The senses turned towards the outside have to be turned inwards. The right kind of meditation needs the guidance of a guru, since one can be led astray by one's own unconscious drives and passions even during the act of meditation.

Dhyāna, or meditation, does not necessarily lead to final emancipation since that is totally uncaused, not something that comes at the end of a program or project. Meditation can help one to go beyond the conscious mind and to develop some unusual mental powers or *siddhis;* but it does not automatically bring about emancipation from *avidya.* Even when one has gone beyond the conscious mind and has discovered new potentialities and powers for the mind, one can continue to be in nescience, within the world of *māya.* The final release is an act of grace when one's agenthood is abolished and one experiences total identity with the all, not by the conscious mind, but through *atindriyajñāna* or knowledge beyond all organs of knowledge. That release is true Enlightenment, true realization, true vision, the blissful beatitude of *samyagdarśana.*

Critical rationality of the European Enlightenment has practically blocked the possibility of this other Enlightenment by conceiving the conscious individual mind as the whole of mind. The West has failed to heed the views of its own savants like William James and Carl Gustav Jung in this respect. In recent times there has been a willingness to explore new aspects of mind, that transcend the individual and the conscious. Maharishi Mahesh Yogi's transcendental meditation techniques have convinced many in the West about the possibility of exploring the transcendental mind. Some of the explorations have used the very techniques of European Enlightenment rationality to monitor and check transcendental experiences.

The literature on the subject, admittedly of uneven quality, is fast proliferating. Coming from competent Western as well as non-Western authors, some of it repays careful, critical (but not totally skeptical), patient, and open-minded study.[214]

6. Causality as Explanation

Scientific explanation seems so heavily dependent on the principle of causation, that once we question the notion of causality as such, the whole scientific enterprise becomes shaky. Most of modern science is about how things and events come to be; for if we know what causes them, we can at will reproduce the effects by engineering the causes. If we know, for example, that water at one hundred degrees centigrade will cause or become steam, or at zero degree ice, then by bringing about the required temperature in water, we can create steam or ice. And if we know the dynamics of how steam has expansive and therefore motive power, we can make steam cause the kind of movement (steam engine) we want. Causality in modern science has an integral relation to its basic intent, namely engineering or technology.

There is no use protesting that science and technology are two different things. As Heidegger has clearly shown in his *Die Frage nach der Technik* (*The Question Concerning Technology*), modern science has reduced the Aristotelian notion of fourfold causality to a nonteleological, mechanical, emaciated causality. Modern science did not come into being in a pure vacuum as the unadulterated quest for truth for its own sake. If science precedes technology, this does not mean that the origin of science has nothing to do with technology.

In Greek the word *aition* did not mean instrumental causality as we today conceive the notion of cause. *Aition* had more to do with origination rather than instrumentality. How did a thing or an event come to be? This was the question for which the fourfold causality was Aristotle's answer. Here is an earthenware pot. How did it come to be? Since it is a human artifact, the form of it was in someone's head before it came to be. That is the formal cause. Then there is the material cause, clay. Third there is the artificer, the potter, who is its efficient cause. There is a purpose for which the pot is made, to contain something; that is its final cause. The Aristotelian fourfold causality did not have a mechanical framework for reality as modern science has. And when science makes a prior decision that reality is a machine with interconnected and interacting parts, then causality becomes a question of which part acted on the other part. Efficient causality becomes the overshadowing center of modern science's understanding of causality.

When the medieval European theologians spoke of God as *causa sui* or Its Own Cause, they were not using the word "cause" in an instrumental sense. They were thinking in terms of origination. All things in the world, as well as the world itself, are caused by, in the sense of having come from, something else; but God is not originated by something else. This is what they wanted to say. In classical causality, the maker or originator has the central role; in mechanical causality, there can neither be a personal maker nor a personal purpose: it is the machine that does it, independently of the maker of the machine, and machines do not have a purpose or teleology of their own. A machine simply acts on the basis of its own built-in causal structure. There is no point in asking who made the machine or for what purpose: the machine exists in itself, and we stand outside it trying to understand it in terms of efficient causality. Similarly, there is no point in asking where we came from, either. The theory of evolution, some people think, answers that question adequately: the same machine produced us and our minds, even the minds of people who can stand outside the machine and understand it. And everything is to be understood in terms of causality alone, because the law that governs the machine is "natural law," the law of efficient causality, the law of the machine called "Nature."

David Hume in the West had raised some questions about the logical structure of causality, but mechanistic science found it convenient to ignore such unanswerable questions. Simply because B in most observed instances follows A, there is no strictly logical reason to assume that B is caused by A. Such an assumption can only be an inductive inference, making generalizations based on a limited number of observed instances. But since this *post hoc, propter hoc* (following this, therefore because of this) formula works operationally, modern science and the philosophy of science saw no need to pursue the issue further, until quantum theory came along.

Very few knowledgeable scientists today would deny that mechanical causality is unable to explain the behavior of quantum phenomena. Bell's Theorem (1964) "proved" nonlocal, noncausal interaction of "wavicles" (or those energy packets that behave in some ways like particles and in other ways as waves) across space. John Clauser's 1972 experiment at Berkeley has empirically confirmed it. A change in the spin of a wavicle can take place instantly as a response to what happens to a twin wavicle miles away (in our kind of space) without any message or signal passing between them.

Most of us still function with a worldview and a causal understanding of reality that fits Newtonian mechanics much better than the new perceptions of the Special Theory of Relativity or of quantum theory. The Copenhagen interpretation of theoretical physics even today seeks to fit together the Newtonian and the quantum-relative worldviews into a single system that would still use the framework of classical Newtonian metaphysics and mechanical causality. Centuries of conditioning make it difficult for us to change mental habits that we know with part of our minds to be already obsolete.

At least fifteen centuries before Hume raised the question in the West, in India the Buddhist philosopher Nagarjuna (ca. 150—250 A.D.) had raised the question about causality and causal understanding of reality. The Samkhya system had taken causality to be a universal underlying feature of the cosmos, much as classical Western physics did, but even Samkhya did not posit real change through causation; the effect is already inherent in the cause, and the cause simply comes to light in the effect. There is neither a temporal nor ontological gap between the cause and the effect.

Nagarjuna questions this view by asking whether the cause ceases to exist when the effect begins; varying answers are possible. If you take a seed and a sapling, the seed has ceased to exist as a seed in order to let the sapling exist in its place. Or alternatively, either the seed is contained in the sapling, as milk is contained in yogurt, or the seed, the cause, was destroyed by the coming into being of the effect, the sapling. If the cause is in the effect, then the effect is the same as the cause, which is not true. If the effect is other than the cause, how can the cause create something different from itself? Using the negative dialectic of the Prasangika method, Nagarjuna refutes the very notion of causality.

Causality is one of the Four Noble Truths that form the foundation of Buddhism and the Buddha's own teachings. The primary observed fact is *duhkha*, unrest or suffering. The reason (*hetu*) for *duhkha* is desire, passion, *rāga* or *tṛṣna*. The cutting off of unrest or pain or suffering is possible only by the cutting off of its originating cause, namely desire. How then can one deny causality itself?

Nagarjuna's answer is a sophisticated one. Causality itself is a time-space concept, belonging to the temporal world or *samvrtisatya*. Both desire and its effect, unrest, have no transcendent existence. They do not belong to the ultimate level of truth, the *paramārthikasatya*. Causality itself belongs only to the temporal order and that.is why the very concept of causality is so full of logical contradictions.

Western thought has exalted causality to such a high level that it becomes the central principle of scientific explanation. And in science itself, at the microlevel, causality becomes problematic. Physicists now speak of nonlocal, noncausal interactions. Others retreat to a notion of statistical causality, holding that while the behavior of the individual wavicle cannot be predicted, the behavior of wavicles in the aggregate can be predicted with a high degree of accuracy.

The distinguished physicist Wolfgang Pauli could not face the possibility of causality being abolished, for he rightly saw that the whole structure of modern science would collapse if causality were to be abandoned. He sought therefore to see some correlation between the two realities—the material world and human consciousness—with the help of his friend C. G. Jung. They could not agree totally, for Pauli was starting from the physics side and Jung from the psychology side, and physics still knows little or nothing about consciousness and the human psyche. There was a time when the great physicists did see that the world could be understood only in terms of the complementary duality of matter and psyche.

Niels Bohr, Max Born, Werner Heisenberg as well as Wolfgang Pauli saw this complementarity but could not explain it in terms of physics alone. They criticized Cartesian dualism, but could not transcend it in terms of physics alone. Even the Copenhagen interpretation, which put primary emphasis on the classical materialist-mechanistic framework and sought to incorporate quantum physics and therefore human consciousness as a primary and fundamental "spiritual factor" into it, was criticized by Soviet physicists in the 1950s as being too idealistic, and not compatible with the Marxist dogma of dialectical materialism. Bohr abandoned the metaphysical quest to go beyond the apparent dualism, in order not to displease Soviet physicists like Fock, and in order to maintain the unity of the international scientific community. Bohr developed a phobia against the term "realism," which at that time was a dogma in the scientific community.[215]

However, Wolfgang Pauli, a Nobel laureate in physics, was determined to tread the metaphysical path to resolve the apparent duality, and because of it found himself alienated from his friends Bohr and Heisenberg. In collaboration with Jung, but not totally agreeing with him, Pauli published that unusual work: *Naturerklaerung und Psyche*[216] in 1952. Both agreed that the Jungian concept of "archetypes" may "function as the sought-for bridge between the sense-perceptions and the ideas, and are, accordingly, a necessary presupposition even for evolving a scientific theory of nature."

Jung, on the other hand, advanced the idea of "synchronicity" as a necessary explanatory principle in addition to causality. The hypothesis was that at any given time, there is a correlation between one's inner psychic world and the outer world of events. It has been scorned or ignored by physicists; but it remains a great insight of our time. The problem, however, is that it has not been possible to devise an experiment that would empirically "prove" it.

Causality, we may conclude, is one of the idols of modern thought, which has been created by the illegitimate absolutization of time-space and matter in a mechanistic framework, and would have to be fundamentally qualified if we are to find our way forward in seeking foundations for new civilizations. The taboo against teleology in scientific explanation can only be the consequence of an insane commitment to the mechanistic model. Synchronicity is rejected mainly because it introduces purpose into the cosmic process. Nowadays it has become fashionable in scientific circles to get around the problem of teleology by talking about "stochastic" processes, which in effect mean teleological orientations in reality. People are only just beginning to realize that some of the things that matter in our universe are not made of matter: for example, identity, difference, relation, quantity, quality, and compassion. Causality without teleology is a dogma, a dangerous and superstitious one.

7. Measurement-Based Science as a Way to Precise Knowledge

If causality is the sole principle of explanation in modern science, precise measurement seems to be its other claim to truth. Even the human sciences had at one time resorted to measurement as a mark of its scientific respectability: econometrics, psychometrics, but not, as far as I know, sociometrics or anthropometrics. Measurement and quantification seem to be essential for planning and computing in government programs, and international organizations are looking for precise parameters for such intangible entities like culture and the quality of life. To a certain extent it can be done, but experience shows that the parameters seem to need constant revision, and never yield full satisfaction.

Measurement is always of a finite space-time entity; the infinite is by definition unmeasureable, because measure presupposes limit. Material objects can be measured because they are finite. So can forces, speed, movement, and energy, but always in terms of other finite entities of time, space, and number. Measurement can be objective, that is, in terms of intersubjectively agreed arbitrary entities like inch and meter, joules and volts, seconds and years.

Measuring is a process of putting into classes of equivalence and proportionality, a process necessary for ordering, relating, understanding, describing, prediction, retrodiction, and operative control. This implies interaction among three entities: the object measured, the measuring instrument, and a consciousness that interprets and relates the data yielded by the measuring instrument. It also implies an intersubjectively agreed upon unit of measurement which is constant and uniform and conforms to a mutually acceptable standard objectively maintained somewhere.

The problematic aspect of measurement does not come to light in the classical mechanical frame of reference; the problems begin when we enter the microlevel. Can events in the quantal realm be measured at all? We speak of "constants" in quantum physics. There are two major constants, *c* and *h,* denoting respectively the speed of light in a vacuum and Planck's constant or the unit of a finite quantum of energy involved in quantum or microevents. There may be other constants like *e* for the unit of charge on the electron, or the fine-structure constant and so on. But these are all constancies that we observe in our measurement, in our space-time classical terms. So long as the test body or measuring instrument belongs to the macro or classical realm, which is the only one we can observe or understand, even a universal constant like Planck's, or the speed of light in a vacuum, or other variables like the spin of a wavicle or its electrical charge can only be the result of macrolevel determinations made by our macroinstruments, posterior to the "collapse of the wave function" about which the Copenhagen interpretation speaks. What is measured then is not the wave function of the wavicle, but its post-mortem measurement and determination at the macrolevel.

When an observation is performed on a quantum state, and a finite quantum of energy is added to that end, that state "collapses" into a single eigenstate out of its many possibilities, and it is this collapsed eigenstate that we can measure. If we had not measured it, another eigenstate of the wavicle could have prevailed.

> Quantum theory requires that we renounce the possibility to predict the results of individual measurements, even in principle. It tells us that the future cannot be predicted uniquely from the past. Instead there is a variety of possible futures, each with its own possibility.[217]

Can entities in the quantal realm be measured at all, if measurement means the collapse of the wave function, which seems to imply a transition from the quantum level to the classical? It seems that what is measured is at best just one interface between the quantal realm and the classical realm at a particular point and not the event itself in the quantal realm. If quantal realities are "by nature" unobservable, then they cannot be measured either.

The test bodies used to measure entities in the quantal realm are aliens to that realm; they are natives of the classical realm; our brains also have evolved to deal with the classical realm. This does not necessarily mean that our consciousness cannot deal with events in the quantal realm; it means only that whatever capacity we once had to sense events in the quantal realm is now atrophied, with the development of objective thinking and objective, nonpoetic language and categories. It may mean also that we have not adequately developed the capacity inherent in our minds to deal with the quantal realm. It can be inferred from our experience so far that when we finally get to develop such capacities, we may discover that it is not by objectification and measurement that we can best deal with that realm.

Enlightenment rationality has perhaps put too much stock by a measurement-based science. A new civilization will mean learning other ways of knowing, related to art and poetry, to intuition and imagination, but perhaps also to faith, hope, and love, to rite and ritual, to "religion" and the mystical experience (not mysticism, which is only an ism).

8. The Universe as Self-Existent

That the universe exists in itself and by itself, and that it can be understood in itself, is one of the unexamined dogmatic assumptions of modern science. God is thus for it an unnecessary hypothesis. The whole secular civilization is built on that unexamined and arbitrary assumption. Whether one subscribes to the Hot Big Bang theory (the Friedman model of a zero-mass, high-temperature initial explosion), the less popular Continuous Creation model, or the new Penrose Model of Multiple Possibility Universe, how the whole thing comes to be is a question that goes begging.

Carl Sagan, in his brief introduction to Stephen Hawking's *A Brief History of Time*, says:

> Few of us spend much time wondering why nature is the way it is, where the cosmos comes from, or whether it was always here, . . . and why there is a universe.[218]

I hope my good friend Prof. Carl Sagan himself is one of the few who do. Stephen Hawking, who uses the word "God" so many times in his book does so, at the beginning of his brief history.

Hawking examines Kant's antinomy in his *Critique of Pure Reason* about the question whether the universe had a beginning or not. If it did not, Kant said, every event would have an infinite amount of time preceding it, which according to him would be absurd. If it did, there would be an infinite period of time before the universe, and there would be no reason for its beginning at a particular point of time, which Kant found equally absurd. Hawking quickly identified the fallacy in Kant's thinking. Kant separated the universe and time, assuming that time is a continuing stream, whether there is a universe or not. He could not see that time is only a dimension of the universe, and that time does not exist independently of the universe.

Hawking credits Augustine with the discovery that the concept of time has no meaning before the beginning of the universe. This is excusable in one whose knowledge is largely confined to Western thought. Even in Western thought, however, both Tatian in the second century and Alexander of Aphrodisias in the second and third centuries, had proposed that time is a creation of the "creative mind" or *nous poetikos.* Augustine got his idea from the Neoplatonists and the Cappadocians St. Basil and St. Gregory.

Did the Universe Have a Beginning at All?

Christians and Jews argued long with the Greeks in the early centuries of our era on the question whether the creation had a beginning or whether it is eternal. Origen's (ca. 185–253 A.D.) attempt—and he was not alone—to establish the eternity of creation (many universes one after the other, but eternally) as a piece of Christian teaching failed. The Cappadocians, especially Basil and Gregory of Nyssa, most resolutely attacked the idea of the eternity of creation, and the doctrine that prevailed has been that the universe had a specific beginning, but not in time.

This, however, was not the prevailing Greek view. Most Greeks, beginning with Plato, affirmed some form of the self-existence of *hule,* or matter, if not of the universe as such. If the *demiurgos* shaped the world, it was out of preexistent matter. The argument between Greek pagans and Christians came to a head only in the sixth century, mainly between Simplicius the Neoplatonist and John Philoponos the Christian, both of whom had studied under the Neoplatonist Ammonius (435 to 517?) in Alexandria.

The teacher of Ammonius, Proclus (410–485), *Diadochos* or successor of Plato as the head of the Academy in Athens from 450–485, had written an important work opposing the Christian view that the universe had a beginning: *De Aeternitate Mundi contra Christianos.* This work is lost. But Philoponos's reply, *De Aeternitate Mundi contra Proclum,* published in 529, summarizes the eighteen arguments of Proclus against a beginning for the universe.

The main argument of Philoponos is that if the universe had no beginning, it must have existed for infinity. This means an infinite number of individuals who have existed in that infinite time. But infinity cannot actually exist:

> For if it were at all possible for the infinite to exist part at a time, and so to emerge in actuality, what reason would there be to prevent it from existing in actuality all at once? . . . If it comes into being part at a time, one unit always existing after another, so that eventually an actual infinity of units will have come into being, then even if it does not exist all together at once (since some units will have ceased when others exist), none the less it will have come to be traversed. And that is impossible: traversing the infinite and, so to speak, counting it off unit by unit, even if the one who does the counting is everlasting. For by nature the infinite cannot be traversed, or it would not be infinite.[219]

Richard Sorabji, in his *Time, Creation and the Continuum,*[220] gives us a comprehensive, masterly, but not always accurate account of the debate, and shows the weaknesses in the arguments on both sides. The idea of a beginning that is timeless is difficult to comprehend. Clearly, the Christian teaching contains two such paradoxical and problematic ideas of a timeless beginning: a) the idea of a timeless beginning of the universe, which is the origin of time itself; and b) the idea of the eternal "birth" of the only-begotten Son, born of the Father before the ages, that is, before all time and independent of time.

The Augustinian teaching about time being a creation of the mind, taken over from Tatian and Alexander of Aphrodisias, was not and is not the accepted Christian view. Time exists independently of our minds, as does the universe. Whether it exists exactly as our minds conceive it, or how time or the universe is in itself, independently of our perception of it, are different questions.

In the classical Christian tradition, which the Western church does not always follow, it was Gregory of Nyssa (ca. 330–396), who gave the most philosophically respectable formulation of the distinction between Divine Being and Created Being. Much more than Augustine, for whom psychology was easier than metaphysics, it was

Maximus the Confessor (ca. 580–662) who tried to improve upon Gregory's thought, with rather doubtful results. The basic difference between Gregory and Maximus is instructive in relation to the questions of beginning and end.

Both believe that the created order has a) an *arche,* which means origin, beginning, originating principle; b) a *telos* or a destiny, a goal, a fulfillment to be achieved; and c) an *hodos,* a way, a path, a course to be traversed, from *arche* to *telos.* The difference is that for Maximus the final goal is static, unmoving tranquility and rest (stasis), the course running from genesis (coming to be or beginning) through kinesis (movement or motion) to stasis (cessation of change and movement, standing still); while for Gregory, the origin is a principle—the principle of creation, namely the idea, the will, and the word of the Creator, not only giving birth to the created order, but also sustaining it in existence and leading it to its final *telos,* which is infinite growth in the good. Time and the created order are dynamic all the way, from beginning to end and beyond.

For both, the beginning of the created order is not an event in time, nor is it an event in the past; it is a continuing event by which the created order is sustained now and is being led to its *telos.* The beginning is not in time, as St. Basil most clearly demonstrated. In his famous nine homilies on the six days of creation, he argues that the six "days" cannot be twenty-four-hour days, since that kind of day depends on the sun, which was created only on the fourth day. He also argues that if time is composed of a series of uniform moments, then we can journey through time in a backward motion, traversing each consequent moment in our imagination. Every point in time or moment is uniform, in that it is both preceded and succeeded by another similar moment. Yet, in our journey backwards we finally arrive at that moment of time that is unique: it has a succeeding moment, but no preceding one. This is the moment of creation, for that first second is preceded by He Who Is and nothing else. This is the first moment that Stephen Hawking found fit to skip over, in his majestic *First Three Minutes* (of the universe), as well as in his intriguingly innocent *A Brief History of Time.*

Gregory of Nyssa makes the distinction clear between He Who Truly Is (*ho ontos on*) and those things that simply are (*ta onta* or *ta panta*). The *ousiai* or is-nesses of the two beings are radically different. The first is self-existent, owing its Being to none other, unextended in time and space, always that which It Is, not needing to become something else. The second is not only not self-existent, but is nothing without the wisdom, will and word that brought it into being, sustains it, and leads it to its *telos.* Nothing in the created order, either part or whole, is without beginning or without an other-derived and other-dependent existence. The latter is dependent and contingent upon the former, and is not to be counted as an entity existing alongside or beside It. There is only one reality, in which there is a self-existent, unextended (*adiastatos*) *ousia,* and a time-space extended, other-derived existence, not outside It, but with It; the latter can exist only in relation to the former; without It it is nothing. The ordinary Western Christian theism that regards God and Universe as two different realities will not do for Gregory.

What we have sketched above is by no means the whole of Gregory's very sophisticated thought that I have somewhat amply discussed in my *Cosmic Man.*[221] It certainly is not the final truth, but a philosophically respectable statement about the conceptually ungraspable Ultimate Reality and the relation of the universe and ourselves to It. It should be supplemented by and compared with a whole plethora of alternate views that have been held in the history of humankind. What is philosophically less respectable would be naive realism's unexamined assumptions about the self-existence of the universe. Other cultures have had other assumptions, less naive than those of modern thought.

9. Time and Space as Given

Are time and space real entities? Do they exist independent of our consciousness? Whatever they are, space and time provide the framework of our existence. Only reflection reveals some of the problems involved. Naive realism can carry on as if there was nothing to reflect about in space and time, except the way we use words and concepts. But all cultures, at one time or other in their process of formation, have had to make some conceptual decisions about the nature of space and time.

There has been, so far as I know, no compendious and all-comprehending study of how various cultures have looked at time and space across the ages. Christians and Platonists have not been the only ones to discuss these issues. We shall start out by looking at two of the ancient Indian systems—Samkhya-yoga and Abhidharma Buddhism—particularly in relation to time. Both systems are pre-Christian and come from the same period and region. The very fact of their coexistence despite basic dissimilarities helps us to see the inevitability of pluralism in conceptions of time and space. Both are symbol-systems by which large groups of people have tried to construct meaning for human existence. The fact that these two systems of conceptualization of time and space met with passioned opposition from each other as well as from later systems like Vedanta and Madhyamaka should alert us to one fact: these questions arouse so much passion precisely because they touch the source-springs of our very existence.

The fundamental notions of Samkhya are:

a) *Puruša,* or transcendent consciousness;

b) *Prakrti,* or the unfolding world process confronting consciousness; and

c) The interface between the two: *sannidhi* (presence), *samyoga* (conjugation or combination) and *sarga* (evolution and creativity).

Everything takes place in the context of this interface between consciousness and world. Even the twenty-three tatvas, or principles or categories that make up the world, arise only in the context of the interface. Time and temporality also belong to this interface, in which consciousness faces the evolving world and leads it to its full manifestation. The Samkhya-yoga tradition, however, does not include time and temporality among the categories of understanding at all, because they are not directly experienced either by the external or the internal organs of the human being. *Kšana,* the moment, is there. So are present, past, and future, in our consciousness. But Samkhya does not try to weave them together into an entity called *time* as a fundamental category or object of human experience.

Vyasa, in his commentary of Patanjali's *Yoga Sutra,* says:

> The flow [*pravāha*] of these [moments] has an order [*krama*] and is continuous [*avichhēda*]; but moments and their orderly succession cannot be compiled [*samāhāra*] to form an object or *vastu.* Time being of this nature cannot be construed as an object, but is a product of the mind. It is a consequence of verbal knowledge [*śabdajñāna*]. The moment is objective and is dependent on the order. Orderly sequence of moments is called time by the yogins who know.[222]

Or to quote a contemporary writer, S. K. Sen,

> For our knowledge of anything we must ultimately refer to our experience. In our experience we find events or actions but never time as such. Therefore, we may say that pure or empty time

as such is nothing or non-existent. It is nothing apart from actions or events that are revealed in experience. If it is anything, it is one with them.

Of course, the Indian form of realism (not so naive) held the opposite view, that *kāla*, or time, is an independent Real, pervading the whole universe, giving basis for perceptions like before and after, prior and posterior, simultaneous and nonsimultaneous, present, past, and future. The Nyaya and Vaisesika systems that coalesced around the tenth century, along with Tarka, constitute India's Logical Analysis, or Scholasticism. The Samkhya-yoga represents an earlier and much more profound perception, not based on any scriptures, but not opposed to the scriptures either. It is a way of thinking and perceiving not aimed at knowledge for its own sake, but for seeking a way out of the *duhkha* or unrest of the present existence.

So is the Abhidharma doctrine of Buddhism, codified by Vasubandhu in his *Abhidharmakōśabhāšya*, which played such a major role in the formation of Chinese Buddhist philosophy in later centuries. The Abhidharmika school was avowedly antischolastic, regarding the Sutras or the teachings of the Buddha as more relevant than the logical systems of the Sastras. But they were not averse to the use of logic where it would help. It therefore did later develop some outstanding logicians like Dinnaga and Dharmakirti. Abhidharma schools, not always uniform in their approach, flourished in India from the fourth to second centuries B.C.

Initially, their ontology was rather simple, focusing on the right understanding of the *dharmas* or fundamental existents, depending on the Four Noble Truths taught by the Buddha: Unrest, Origination of Unrest, Stopping the Originating Cause, and the Way to Nirvana or real cessation of suffering and unrest. Epistemology, as in all nobler Indian traditions, is ancillary to soteriology. Knowledge or cognition (*vijñāna*) is always contingent on two factors: *višaya/ālambana* or sense-object/mental object, and *citta* or *vijñāna*, i.e. consciousness or cognition. Abhidharmikas would generally agree with Husserl that consciousness has always to be consciousness-of. These objects of consciousness are the *dharmas* or existents; they go through change in past, present, and future, but the changes are produced by each *dharma*'s own *svabhāva* or own-nature, which has its own *karitra* or causal efficacy. The objects can change their *avastha*, or state of being, at any given time, as well as their relation to other *dharmas;* but the individual *dharma*/existent persists through all its *avasthas* or states. Each existent has its present, past, and future, it goes through the three times; but it does not abide permanently; it comes into being and goes out of being. The three times through which it travels therefore have no ultimate validity. The past, present, and future are in no sense real, they are merely three stages through which each existent passes. Time, for the Sarvastivadin Abhidharmika, has no validity apart from the *dharma,* which goes through various *avasthas.*

We have briefly looked at two of the ancient Indian thought-and-perception systems, in both of which neither time nor space have any ultimate validity, except as creations of the conscious mind. Now we take a quick look at two other Indian systems which refuted the above systems: *Vedānta* and *Mādhyamika.* We will not go into details, but simply observe that Vedanta in its refutation of the Samkhya system, does not end up with a higher evaluation of time or space. On the contrary, they are seen as creations of *māya* and *avidya,* and have to be thrown away in order to attain the transcendent knowledge in which neither time nor space exists. Nagarjuna's *śunyavāda* also, after its fierce attack on the *sarvāstivāda* of Abhidharma Buddhism, does not come up with a higher assessment of time or space. In fact, he refutes all attempts to conceptually grasp the reality of anything, including that of time and space. For Nagarjuna, there is neither coming into being nor going out of being, and therefore neither time nor space.

According to Nagarjuna, any of the four possibilities about any entity, whether time or space or universe, would have to be negated. Does it have existence (*bhāva*)? No, you cannot say yes to that question. Then does it not exist? You cannot answer that question in the negative either. Then, does it both exist and nonexist? You cannot say that is true either. Does it then not exist and not nonexist? To say yes to that question would also not be the truth. The truth is on none of the four horns of the *quadrilemma,* the *catuśkoti.*

Nagarjuna's answer to the question about the reality of time and space would be twofold, both in effect meaning the same thing: *pratītyasamutpanna,* and *śunya.* The first word means having cooriginated under certain conditions, and the second means void of any determined content. *Pratītyasamutpāda* teaching is comparatively easier to understand: it means mainly that the phenomenal world is not *māya* or illusion, nor is it objective truth existing in itself, but something that cooriginates when a consciousness like ours confronts whatever it is that comes to our minds and senses as phenomena. What is it in itself? It is *śunya,* zero, the void, without any determinations or modes of being. The world of time and space is *pratītyasamutpanna,* or conditionally cooriginated, and in itself *śunya,* devoid of any determinations.

Of course such a position must seem atrociously nonsensical to many Westerners. Nagarjuna's contemporaries raised all sorts of logical objections to his argument. The most devastating was the argument that if everything is void, then the statement that everything is void must also be void. Nagarjuna's even more devastating reply was: "You are right, because if my statement were not void, then the statement that all is void would not be true. I make no proposition, for propositions of all kinds are also void."

We should not forget the fact that in denying ultimate reality to time and space, these thinkers were referring to a level of reality different from that of our everyday observation. Their insistence is that the phenomenal world is not the ultimate reality, and that we must go beyond ordinary perception to a higher level of reality, where alone the Ultimate Truth reveals Itself.

The European Enlightenment and its fosterchild, secularism, absolutize time-space reality as the only kind of reality that we can deal with. It is this assertion that is groundless and fundamentally misleading. Only as we begin to perceive the contingent nature of time-space reality, not as an absolute given, but as a window through which we can get to a transcendent apprehension of a higher level of reality, do we begin to approach the foundations for enduring civilizations.

10. Change, Evolution, Development, and Progress

Plato in his *Timaeus* (37E–38C) was probably the first in the West to clarify the difference between the is-ness of everlasting being, and the was-is-and-will-be nature of things that are becoming in time; only the latter has a past and a future. Eternal Being eternally is; It does not grow old with time because it has neither change (*tropé*) nor becoming (*gignesthai*), neither movement (*kinēsis*) nor origination (*genesis*).

Time, for Plato, is the moving image of eternity, and has come into being along with the heavens; time will also perish with the cosmos or *ouranos*. Time and the sensible cosmos are characterized by change, *tropé*. Nothing remains static and unchanged. Everything is in flow, in a dynamic process of continuous change. Even Carnot's Second Law of Thermodynamics bears witness to this fact. But the kind of change which that Law speaks of is disintegration from a more evolved or keyed-up state to a less intense state, moving from the orderliness of the cosmos towards the disorderliness and stable equilibrium of chaos and death. Simultaneous with the process from cosmos to chaos, we can also observe the opposite process: order out of chaos, as Ilya Prigogine calls it. Even if one does not believe everything Stephen Hawking says about the *First Three Minutes* or in *A Brief*

History of Time, we can accept the fact that the galaxies and the planetary systems are the result of a cooling process, where lowered temperature reduced the total chaos and brought some stable order into it.

In fact, the theory of evolution, the mainstay framework of modern thought, presupposes not merely the evolution of the species, but also the astrophysical and chemical evolutions that preceded the organic and social evolutions. If the Hot Big Bang occurred ten to fourteen billion years ago, since then there has been a continuous process of positive change from the initial chaos to the evolution of the human brain, the most complexly organized entity we know. Both entropy and negentropy are now operating simultaneously. The two processes go on intertwined with each other—the one from order to chaos, and the other from chaos to order. In a sense, not altogether metaphorical, we can call the two processes death and life. The Second Law of Thermodynamics describes the death-process, from order to chaos, from organization to disintegration, and the laws of evolution—astrophysical, chemical and organic—as well as the laws of social formation, seem to indicate the life-process: from disorder to order, from disorganization to integration. The two processes can be intellectually distinguished, but not quite physically separated from each other. For life, too, in our world, carries death within itself.

Progress is an aspect of evolution, of the life process, but it is neither uniform nor automatic. The equillibria occurring at punctuated stages of the process are not totally stable, and we observe retrogression as an aspect of progression. The life process is stochastic, that is, it seems to have some targets in mind, but often fails to hit the target, and has to retreat in order to try again. Evolution itself seems to operate by fits and starts, by leaps and leap-backs. This certainly is the case in social evolution. Even in organic evolution, Steve Goulding's "punctuated equillibrium" theory does not tell the whole story.

Rupert Sheldrake, in his two books, *A New Science of Life* and *The Presence of the Past,*[224] seeks to correct the picture of a simple linear process of evolution. He suggests that the past is present in the form of "morphogenic fields" that are carried over from the past and which provide the possibilities at any given moment of new forms being shaped. "Morphic resonance" involves the transmission of formative causal influences through both space and time. Nature, so to speak, has its own memory and habits, and learns from experience. This is possible only if the cosmic process is like a living being, and not possible if it were a machine with feedback processing. And we cannot understand an organism in terms of eternal laws. "The cosmos now seems more like a growing and developing organism than like an eternal machine. In this context, habits may be more natural than immutable laws."[225]

Sheldrake points out a basic anomaly in our thought habits. On the one hand, life evolves, but the cosmos for us remains an eternal machine, with unchanging eternal laws, so that we can extrapolate from behavior in the present all the way back to the very beginnings, and retrodict how the whole thing began and evolved, in the first three minutes as well as in the ensuing billions of years. Sheldrake thinks this is a bad habit inherited from our centuries of mechanistic thinking. The cosmic process cannot be understood in terms of eternal law; it should be understood in terms of evolving habit. The cosmos is not an eternal machine; it acts more like an organism which has both memory and personality, the past lives in the present, as does the future also, as anticipation and hope, not only in human beings, but also in the cosmos as a whole. It is in this context that we can understand the words of the Apostle Paul in his letter to the Romans:

> For the eager longing of the created order anticipates the full manifestation of the children of God. The created order has been subordinated to a sort of futility, not because it so willed, but because of Him who so subordinated it, in the anticipation that the whole created order itself shall be liberated from its enslavement to disintegration, for (sharing in) the freedom of the glory of the children of God. We know that the whole creation is till now groaning together as if in labor pains; and not only the creation, but even we ourselves who have been granted the first-fruits of the Spirit, we are also inwardly groaning, as we wait for our full sonship, the redemption of our bodies.[226]

Secular civilization has, however, made a heroic but also rather pathetic decision to accept the presently perceived futility of the world as somehow final. The determined effort to absolutize the world open to our senses as the only possible world, and to deny its contingence and dependence on the Transcendent, can only be the consequence of a desperate unbelief, which was perhaps a reaction to too credulous a faith that preceded it. We persist in that fully insane self-confidence that we shall know and we shall ever conquer; we shall acknowledge no master, we shall bring everything under our mastery through our knowledge and our technology. We shall uncover every mystery, and solve every problem, with our science and technology. God is dead, and we have taken over. Is that how Western civilization wants it? Such hubris can only lead to the tragic nemesis of our self-destruction.

To that hubris and that nemesis we should soon be seeking remedies. Progress and evolution will not guarantee our success. We should learn to put our trust in something slightly higher than just progress, development and evolution. For at the end of it all, there may be life or death awaiting us.

We have sought in this chapter to show how critical rationality itself calls for a reexamination of its own pet assumptions. We have tried to show how other cultures have looked at the problem, mainly to show that alternative approaches to the same questions are possible. If all this seems unintelligible to some Western readers, lack of lucidity in exposition can only be part of the reason. Most Western people have grown up within the narrow confines of a monolithic European Enlightenment tradition without even suspecting that there may be truths with which the Enlightenment is incapable of coming to terms. They suffer not only from the forgetfulness of Being of which their own Heidegger accuses them, but they have forgotten the many valid insights of their own European tradition, before the Enlightenment came to dominate the scene. Perhaps opening themselves to non-European traditions, even as an act of charity, will bring to their minds some of the insights and perceptions of their own wise men of the past.

Another kind of Enlightenment forms an integral part of the European tradition. It is waiting in the wings to burst in on us, as soon as we open our inner eyes, ears, and hearts. It has always been there, like the starry heavens during the day, but the Enlightenment has been too bright a light. As dusk brings the dimming of sunlight, the sky of reality will take on a new aspect. To that Other Enlightenment we must now turn.

Chapter Eleven

TURNING TO THE OTHER ENLIGHTENMENT: THE EUROPEAN TRADITION REVISITED

Heidegger sometimes seems to regard the European Enlightenment with its science and technology as the logical culmination of the whole history of the Western tradition. He himself appears as one who claims not to belong to it, as one who has made a *Kern* or turn away from it. And the strange thing is that he does so by frequent reference to elements within that tradition, be it Plato or the pre-Socratics, Goethe or Hoelderlin. We cannot jump to the conclusion that the Enlightenment heritage exhausts the European tradition.

The European tradition, like all great traditions, is infinitely rich in the variety that it has entertained, engendered, and fostered; no one can hope to catalogue exhaustively the plethora of Europe's cultural wealth expressed, not only in thought and philosophy, but also in art and music, in literature and poetry, in myth and drama, in dance and song, in festivals and rituals, in institutions and attitudes, in elite and folk cultures, as well as in science and technology, architecture and engineering.

Heidegger exaggerates when he describes the whole Western tradition as one where the human observer seeks to stand outside nature and to understand it from outside, as if the world were an object outside him or her, rather than he or she being inside and part of it. This objectivizing trend, which later resulted in the European Enlightenment and its science and technology, is only one among the many strands in the rich Western tradition. It so happens that it is this strand that came to prominence in the eighteenth to twentieth centuries; it has certainly served a purpose, not just for Europe, but in fact for the whole world and for the whole of humanity. It has managed, by its character of "adventure and expansion," to conquer the external world by that powerful combination of scientific-technological domination of the world and adventurous-aggressive territorial expansion into that world.

It is to the credit of Europe that she has been instrumental in bringing all of us together into a single stream of human history, though that may not have been her intention. It seems more a case of serendipity or unintended benefit. It could also be the case, as both Hegel and Heidegger suggest, that something is working behind the scenes, be it the Absolute Idea or Being in process of self-revelation and self-actualization, or to use modern secular myths acceptable equally to liberals and Marxists, physical-organic evolution or just plain history as an agent or moving force. Perhaps science and technology, arising in the matrix of European imperialism, is not an accident. It serves, through colonialism-imperialism and neocolonialism among other things, the purpose of uniting the world, or merging national and regional streams into one single global flow. Even the temporary discomfiture of the Marxist system seems to serve this purpose; increasingly, the world is being united into a single marketplace, a single interdependent economy, one humanity in constant interaction and intercommunication. And yet the same humanity remains divided and working at cross-purposes. Unfortunately, we are unable to do justice here to a theoretical consideration of this dialectic, to spell out a doctrine of Providence or to begin to enunciate a philosophy of history in this modest work. We cannot also go into describing the great wealth of European art, music, and literature, which though today greatly impoverished by the Enlightenment, may very well be the area where the reuniting "New," which must eventually show up, puts in its first appearance.

We want to speak of another Enlightenment that has been perennially present in the European tradition long before the kind of European Enlightenment of which we have been speaking sprang up. This other Enlightenment to which we shall now refer is not peculiar to Europe; it seems quite universal. It did take specific forms in Europe, but these forms actually bear witness to a global process, widespread in humanity, perhaps a development of something in human nature itself.

In the West they call it "mysticism" or "spirituality." Both names are eminently and dangerously distorting misnomers for a reality transcending what is conceived under these names. Some call it religion; that too is a misnomer, when it is taken to mean a department of human activity, a personal choice, an optional interest of particular individuals. In the absence of a better name for something which is so comprehensive and all-pervading as to be inseparable from everything else, we will call it provisionally the "overall religious-cultural outlook."

This may be philosophically enunciated, as in the case of Plato or Plotinus, Aquinas or Augustine, Boehme or Hegel, and Tauler or Eckhart, or held undemonstratively and somewhat hidden as in the case of Socrates and Heidegger. But it is certainly more than what is articulated; it pervades the consciousness of all people, as a concealed and somewhat unexpressed social consensus of which very few individuals in a society are ever consciously aware. Sometimes a poet or a bard, a sage or a literary writer, a painter or a composer, a sculptor or an architect, manages to give utterance to one or other aspect of it, in metaphors and similes, in images and allegories, in stories and anecdotes, in music and drama, in art and architecture. Sometimes a community holds on to it through myths and rituals for which there is no specific individual author. Sometimes it is all attributed to one great soul like Gautama the Buddha or Jesus the Christ, Mohamed the Prophet or Lao-Tze the Sage.

This is not to be identified with Jung's archetypes of the collective unconscious. In fact, the archetypes, which may occur in dreams, actually draw from the concealed consensus of a community's consciousness. That consensus is drawn from generations of collective as well as personal experience and memory in a community. There exists something we could call a "social brain," though it is difficult to localize it. It is a field in which the minds of the present generation participate. Many minds, which from our dried-up Enlightenment point of view lived in previous generations and seem therefore now gone, in fact participate in this field through their own psychic energy and now make an active contribution to the field. This forcefield not only touches our time-space world significantly, but is also every day influencing our world of decisions and actions to an extent far larger than we ever suspect.

A Light Too Bright

The awareness of this other world impinging upon our little time-space cosmos was once very strong in the European tradition; it has been only partially eclipsed, even by such a powerful antireality force as the secular Enlightenment with its critical rationality. But the light of the European Enlightenment today shines so bright that it covers up much more than it reveals. It is like vision during the day and during the clear night: we can see many details of our earth very clearly by sunlight, which we would not see by the light of the stars or of the moon at night. But during that process of seeing by sunlight we give up the possibility of seeing the night sky with its galaxies of stars, the other planets, and the moon.

It is only as the daylight fades and the dusk begins to obscure much of the detail we see by day, that the night sky with all its grandeur and splendor comes into view. Our European Enlightenment is something like the daylight, which makes us see many things that we would not have seen without its help; but in that very process of opening up a detailed and clear vision of some things, the daylight, by its very brightness, eclipses the stunningly vast expanse of the billions of galaxies that lie all around. *It is too bright a light,* this European Enlightenment and its critical rationality. If we lived all twenty-four hours by sunlight we would miss out on most of reality, which "comes to light" only when the sunlight is dimmed, and when even the moon's reflection of the sunlight is not too forceful.

Our waking consciousness is like the light of the day. During the day, it is possible for us to do many things that we could not do at night, except perhaps with some substitute for daylight: hunting, fishing, sowing, harvesting, and most other of our normal activities except perhaps sleeping, dreaming, and procreation. It is also obvious that we cannot stand that waking kind of consciousness continuously without great strain; we need the night to sleep for at least a few hours in order to be capable of that daylight kind of awareness for one more day.

But suppose there were no night when the sun would go down from our sky and leave us in the dark. Suppose we lived in a flat, plane earth where we had full sunlight all the time. We would not in that situation know for sure that the stars, planets, and our own moon existed; our understanding of the universe would be extremely limited, and if some scientist were to come along and tell us that there were other planets besides our own orbiting around the sun, or that there were myriads of other suns or stars or galaxies in the grand universe "out there," we would be a bit skeptical. The night helps us to see much we would have missed otherwise and also to know our own finitude in such a vast universe.

I repeat, the visibility that the eighteenth and nineteenth-century Enlightenment has given us has been like the light of the sun. But if we live in that light all the time, we are likely to miss out on much that is going on in the universe, and be ignorant of other dimensions of our own existence. The European Enlightenment has indeed brought on the *siecle des lumieres,* the age of the *Erklaerung,* the two or more centuries of bright sunlight. We have discovered so much; we have invented many contraptions; we have made numerous sorties into space and into the nature of things. We claim to know much more than our ancestors did; we can answer many questions they could not; we can do much they never could. But does that mean definitely that they knew less than we do? Not necessarily, because this daylight that blinds us now to other dimensions of reality was not so strong for them. They could see the night sky in a way we can no more. And even if we do not immediately understand what they say they saw, it may be useful for us to listen to them again, especially the wiser among them, the sages and the seers.

The Ancient Heritage of Europe

We do not know much about the ancients of Europe before Socrates, Plato, and Aristotle. We have sagas and myths, epics and tales, as well as brief dicta from some of the pre-Socratics; but we know so little of the peoples' life and experience. We comprehend so little of Homer and Hesiod, Dionysus and Orpheus, Bacchus and Thor, Wotan and the myriad other heroes and gods of the diverse European peoples; their world strikes us as strange; the literature tells us about gods and goddesses, their fights and frolics, their envy and strife, their tragedies and comedies. It all must have somehow made sense to the ancients, and to those soldiers of Alexander who carried Homer and Hesiod with them into the battlefield for their daily or weekly reading.

What kind of sense could these myths and sagas make to us today? Shall we translate them into our modern scientific jargon in order to squeeze out their "rational" meaning, or shall we just dismiss them as childish superstitions of an unenlightened age, of the fanciful infancy of humanity? These immortal gods and goddesses, daemons and devils, *we know—don't we—that they do not exist;* we have looked around everywhere in our own little space, in our own bright Enlightenment light and we have spotted them nowhere. So we confidently conclude that they must be fantasies of our ancestors, who we think were mere children compared to us, we who claim to be knowledgable grown-up, modern, mature people! That conclusion would have been all right only if our bright Enlightenment awareness were so finally and universally and for all time normative, which unfortunately is not the case.

Our confidence in the normative sufficiency of our critical rationality can only be our own childish fantasy, of equal strength as that of our ancestors. Sensitive thinkers can see that it is only a modern myth, an article of secular faith that has no scientific basis. We have been brainwashed by the European Enlightenment, by its scientism and technicity, and in that process the universe has changed its shape for us. The ancients had a different constitution of mind, with the result that their universe was constituted differently. They may have discovered less, but perhaps some of them saw much more of what is significant than most of us do today. This interdependence of perceiving mind and perceived universe is itself one of those profound insights on which the sages of old agree with our own understanding in modern physics. We know today that there is no "objective" universe "out there." It exists only on the meeting ground between our own "inner" equipment and "outer" reality. We know that mechanistic-scientific concepts like causality, linear time, three-dimensional space, locality, and objectivity have no ultimate base in reality outside our own time-space limitations of sense and consciousness.

Though John Stewart Bell "proved" mathematically by his famous "Bell's Theorem" (which I do not pretend to understand) in 1964 that the universe is essentially nonlocal, some physicists persist in the hope that we can have a mathematical description of the world "as it is." The logical outcome of Bell's Theorem, it seems to a layman, is that the secular worldview is radically groundless, and that critical rationality cannot ever hope to do justice to our situation inside of reality. We need to explore other areas of our minds, possibilities other than the persistent subject-object dichotomy that provides the frame both for critical rationality and for modern science, if only so we can find our own way afresh through reality. Perhaps a more humble reexamination of what some of our ancestors have thought and said may shed some light on our way.

And these ancestors of ours, whether European, African, or Asian, were always learning from each other. Eusebius, the church historian of the fourth century A.D., tells us the anecdote of Aristoxenos of Tarent, a contemporary of Aristotle in the fourth century B.C. (i.e., seven hundred years or so before Eusebius):

> Socrates met at Athens an Indian who asked him what sort of philosophy he practised. Socrates [in good European style] told him that his investigations were regarding the life of man; he [i.e., the Hindu or Buddhist or whoever the Indian was] began to laugh, and said, you cannot contemplate human things unless you know about divine realities.[227]

I do not believe that Socrates was a "secularist" of the modern type. He was one of these pre-Enlightenment sages who believed in gods and daemons and in initiatory rites into the mysteries of the universe. The picture of Socrates that has come down to us from European Plato studies may give the impression that he was not in our sense "religious"; but he stood squarely in the Pythagorean tradition, which did not believe that "man" was some kind of an autonomous subject, independent of the world and of transcendent reality.

The Greco-Roman Heritage

The postmythological tradition in Europe probably dates from Pythagoras in the sixth century B.C.; he was a near contemporary of the Buddha who also initiated a postmythological tradition in India at about the same time, or even slightly before Pythagoras. Thales and Anaximander of the Milesian school had begun their speculative quest to find the single principle that constitutes and guides the universe, but it was really Pythagoras who systematically laid the foundations of the European tradition, by holding that the *apeiron* or the Infinite Reality had its other pole in our finite world, and that the latter could not be understood without reference to the former. Relation, measure, unity, diversity, harmony, conflict, and so on belong only to the finite pole, though the Undifferentiated One and the Many are two poles of a single reality.

Zeno of Elia already pointed out the unreality of many concepts that later European science took for granted, like movement and location, dimension and plurality. Heraclitus of Ephesus introduced the principle of dialectical change as the fundamental reality of our universe, but also posited the one eternal logos that alone holds together the changing world. The Material Atomists Leucippus and Democritus of Abderā (in the fifth and fourth centuries B.C.), whom Karl Marx came to admire as a young man in the university, posited the theory of eternal atoms, unchangeable, impenetrable, and indivisible. The Atomists also inspired Leibnizian Monadology and Kant's early theory of the universe. Democritus in a sense is the father of both Western liberalism and Marxist scientism, with his insistence that the universe is governed by a fixed causal order which can be objectively known. Protagoras in the fifth century B.C. established the other cornerstone of both Marxism and liberalism by asserting that man is the measure of all things, without going on to ask what the measure of man was.

These are all part of the European tradition, and have perennially influenced it throughout its history. Some of these ideas contemporary Europe may well be able to dismiss summarily, but many call for rather careful attention, since the questions are crucial to humanity and neither modern science nor critical rationality has the competence to provide adequate answers. Most European thought simply chooses to pay no attention to the hallowed wisdom of the ancients. The first step in the birth of a new consciousness in Europe will be the European intellectual world's willingness to go back to a reassessment of previous answers to these questions, and in that process to find out that critical rationality and scientific methods are quite inadequate to that task of assessing and evaluating the answers.

Europe's "Religious" Heritage

Europe, like every other continent, has a rich heritage in which what we today call "religion" was the fundamental constituent. That heritage is not to be confined to the Greco-Roman or northeastern Mediterranean, but was of Celtic, Druid, Iberian, Scandinavian, Teutonic, Varangian, Slavic, and numerous other components.

Of these, the Greeks have left us more written records than any other group, and so their heritage has been better studied. There is no reason to believe that Greek civilization was more advanced than the others simply because they came upon the alphabet a little ahead of the other Europeans, and were therefore able to think and reflect in a different style. It is their "religion" that we know a little better, though far from well.

The Greeks made no distinction among religion, philosophy, and science as we do today. These are *our* divisions of experience into compartments that dissect and distort the truth. There is no separate Greek word for any of the three mentioned. The same is true of the other classical languages of the world, including Sanskrit and Chinese. Even philosophy was an unknown word to the early Greeks, until Pythagoras called himself a *Philosophia* or 'friend of wisdom'—not a *philosophos,* which would only mean 'friend of the wise'.

Scholars see three different religious strands in the early Archaic (ca. 1200–ca. 750 B.C.) and in the Archaic (ca. 750–ca. 500 B.C.) periods of Greek history, perhaps more clearly in the Classical (ca. 500–ca. 320 B.C.) and in the Hellenistic (323–27 B.C.) periods of Greek civilization. It is quite difficult to draw the geographical contours of ancient Greece that included Apollonia and Attica, Cyrene and Epidaurus, Halicarnassus and Idalium, Ionia and Miletus, Pergamum and Seleucia, Athens and Sparta, Phrygia and Bithynia, Asia and Cilicia, Pontus, and Anatolia—some of these in what we today call Asia and Africa.

Early Greek religion had seers and sages, oracles and soothsayers, myths and rituals, sacrifices and taboos, but none of what we today associate with religion: no prophet or messiah, no specialized clergy or sacerdotal caste, no church or scripture, no creed or coherent set of beliefs. As Jean-Pierre Vernant says in the article on Greek religion in the *Encyclopaedia of Religion:*

> It was deeply rooted in a tradition in which religion was intimately interwoven with all the other elements of Hellenic civilisation, all that gave to the Greece of the city-states its distinctive character: from the language, the gestures, and the manner of living, feeling and thinking, to the system of values and the rules of communal life.[228]

The oral and ritual tradition was the bearer of all; poets and artists and common people gave expression to it in music and painting, mime and dance, songs and sagas, theatre and drama, myths and fables, epics and tales of gods and heroes told by grandmothers and nurses to the children.

Three different main strands emerged, under Asian and African influence: the Eleusinian mysteries, the Dionysian cult and festivals, and the Orphic cult. There were other mystery cults of local provenance: the Kabeiroi with their renowned sanctuary in Samothrace, where Herodotos had been initiated; the Kouretes of Crete worshipping the dying and rising Zeus of Crete; and possibly many others.

In the Eleusinian mysteries, which were in honor of Demeter or Deo the Mother (parallel to the Indian Devi, the Mother), the initiate (*mustes,* from which the Greek word *mysterion* and our words mystery and mysticism arose) was exposed to three different types of experiences: the *dromena* (from which our word drama) or things enacted; the *legomena* (from which our word legend) or things uttered; and the *deiknumena* or things exhibited, the *darsana* involving all the human senses—nothing so unmaterially spiritual as we sometimes think.

The center of the Eleusinian religion was the temple or the *temenos,* parallel to the Indian *kšētra,* or the Field, the sacred space which localized the transcendent or divine energy. This space was set apart and was no man's property. Admission was by initiation, and the initiate (*mustes*) advanced by slow degrees of purgation and discipline to become an *epoptēs* or beholder-participant of the mysteries, going through successive stages of purification and illumination.

Animal sacrifice was common to both the mysteries and the Dionysiac cult. The central theme of the sacrifice, never expressly stated, was communion with the Divine in flesh and blood. This gory ritual, at the expense of dumb sacrificial animals, drew forth the ire and satire of the rational mind. The *temenos* and the *thusia,* or the temple and the sacrifice, carried, but did not always convey, a very deep level of meaning. This is the problem with ritual: it carries and conserves as well as transmits to posterity meaning, but does not always convey it consciously to every participant. The temple, the *kšētra* of the Hindus, the *haikal* of the Jews, was the sacred space on earth where the power and energy of the transcendent world operated. It was also the physical dwelling, the abode of the Divine Presence (*shekinah* for the Jews, *pratyakša* for the Hindus), the space where the Divine could be encountered on earth, and offered obeisance and worship.[229]

Animal sacrifice was the supreme obeisance, the offering of flesh and blood of animals in place of one's own, to the Owner of Life. Part of that flesh and blood is consumed by the Divine, usually symbolized by fire, and the other part by the priests and people. Thus through the blood sacrifice, the deepest mystery of existence—the unity in communion between the divine and the human—is ritually experienced and actualized; the ambiance calls for great inner strength in overcoming the frightening nature of the sacrificial act. That fright, that *thambos* or reverential awe, is part of the game, something not so easy for the cool rational mind to accept or go through, but essential for the religious experience.

The Orphic Religion behind Classical Greek Philosophy

Philosophy critically examined the myths and rituals, the temples and sacrifices. The philosophers rejected some aspects as excessive or unnecessary. The whole Orphic tradition was opposed to animal sacrifice. Pythagoras, Plato, Socrates, and probably Aristotle himself belonged to the Orphic rather than the Eleusinian or the Dionysiac tradition. Later Neoplatonists openly espoused the Orphic tradition in their "theurgy" or obeisance to God, which was wholly ritual-liturgical; and even to keen rational minds like that of Proclus in the fifth century A.D., theurgy was more fundamental and primary than theoretical philosophy, which always fell short of the goal of union with the Divine.

The Orphic tradition came from outside to Europe, mostly from Chaldea (Babylonia) and Egypt. The *Chaldean Oracles* was the classical text of Orphism and was widely used both by Christian fathers and Pagan philosophers. Proclus is said to have derived his theurgy from a daughter of Plutarch, which included the power to conjure up gods and goddesses.[230]

Once adopted by Europe, the Asian-African religion of Orphism went through its own morphological transformations, adapting itself to the Pythagorean and Dionysiac traditions that prevailed. We have no Orphic corpus except a number of songs, hymns, oracles, and ritual rubrics bearing the name of Orpheus that developed and grew throughout the centuries, alongside the more orderly and civic religion of the city-states.

Though related to the Eleusinian and Dionysiac traditions, the basic animus of Orphism is anti-Eleusinian and anti-Dionysian. While the two stressed experience and feeling, the Orphic religion was Apollonian, rational, and opposed to animal sacrifice, irrationality, and excess. This was why classical philosophers such as Socrates, Plato, and Aristotle, as well as the Neoplatonists, espoused it.

Socrates and Plato

Plato's academy stands very prominent at the head of the European tradition, though its influence at the beginning was deeply felt more in the Eastern Mediterranean, than in Europe outside of Greece and Rome. Plato himself did not create his thought out of nothing. He took into account what the Pythagoreans and the Heracliteans taught, as well as questions raised by the Parmeneidians and the many Socratic schools of the fourth century B.C., the teachings of the Megarians, the Cynics, the Sophists, the Atomists, the Milesians, the Cyrenaics, and many others. He was also in touch with the wisdom of the Persians, Chaldeans, and Egyptians, and possibly also of the Indians, if not of the Chinese.

Plato was wise enough not to compile a systematic philosophy such as our scholastic temperament so ardently yearns for. He used the dialogical method which avoids propositional finalization of truth, and allows several different ways of looking at an issue to stand facing each other. What some people regard as Plato's inconsistency was one of his major strengths as a sage. Dialogue need not always lead to a propositional conclusion. Dialectical thinking can expose the shaky foundations and inconclusiveness of any philosophical systematization.

Though Plato seemed to believe the Socratic idea that a perfected reason is the true source of all real knowledge, he by no means equated reason with the intellect, or humanity with the individual. Like Pythagoras and others before him, Plato also sought Enlightenment as the chief goal of humanity, but he never held that the light was enclosed within the cave of our finitude. The light came from outside the cave, and all we saw inside was but shadow. What the European Enlightenment and the cult of secularism have done is simply to absolutize the cave and say that that is all there is. The seventh book of *The Republic* can still teach all of us, but we despise the past and take pride in our own mastery of the cave in which we dwell.

But it is also so easy to misconstrue the teaching of Plato about the shadow character of the cave experience, and about a superior world of purely intelligible realities, into the false doctrine of the Two

Cities, one perishing and the other eternal, totally opposed to each other. We can today say, in the light of two millennia of human experience, that Plato also went wrong in locating in the material world the source of all impurity and evil and error in our world. In the *Phaedo,* for example, Plato gives us the wrong idea, that we can and must see all things with the help of reason alone, unmixed with the data yielded by our senses.

He was wrong when he pictured the ideal seer as one "who employs pure, absolute reason in his attempt to hunt down the pure, absolute essence of things, and who removes himself, so far as possible, from eyes and ears, and, in a word, from his whole body, because he feels that its companionship disturbs the soul and hinders it from attaining truth and wisdom."[231]

There is one important thing Plato taught us, which we have now forgotten or disregarded as unimportant: it is the point that there can be no true knowledge without *katharsis,* or a cleansing and purification of body and mind. That purification consists in things that we do and practice in the body, in this world. Plato was probably inconsistent in the way he at times played down the body and the temporal world, and proceeding to insist that justice, prudence, temperance, and courage had to be practiced in the body of the here and now, in order that humans become capable of true knowledge.

In *The Republic* and in *The Laws,* Plato is much more realistic in insisting that the body must be trained and purified in order to prepare the soul for knowledge. In his later life, as reflected in *The Laws,* Plato made religion compulsory, in a manner that seems to us undemocratic today. We should not forget, however, that Plato's academy was a religious brotherhood, which one could enter only by renouncing the world and donning the black robe, the robe that academics, monks, clergy, lawyers, and jurists wear today without a second thought about its original significance as the mark of renunciation of the world. The essential role of *katharsis* (purification) as a necessary precondition for true knowledge was perhaps one of Plato's points that was more than a mere dialectical assertion, to be qualified by contrary or alternative affirmations. And besides, democracy is only one among other values, not the final goal of human existence, nor the only principle of community existence. Discipline is sometimes just as important. Only the committed and disciplined can form genuine community.

Today we can go beyond Plato. We can translate Plato's teaching into our own context by saying that there are things we must do both in our own individual persons, and *also in our societies,* before our knowing can be rectified. It is only when we practice both a personal and a social discipline of self-control and compassion for all; only when we advance further in the establishment of social, economic, and cultural justice both within and among the nations of the world; only when we have begun to make it possible for the peoples and nations of the world to live together as responsible members of a single global community in peace and mutual cooperation; only when we fully see that humanity is one with a single living environment that it shares with other forms of life, that our knowing processes too would be cleansed and rectified.

Our modern science was born in a context of extreme aggression and greed on the part of the European nations, combined with a limited quest for truth and righteousness. And it bears the marks of that ambiguity of intention. Social justice as *katharsis* and preparation for true knowing is something quite strange to our ears, but we must learn that lesson from Plato in a new nonindividualist, nonelitist form suited to our time. The way to learn from Plato today is not simply to retreat into solitary contemplation and meditation. It is also to engage actively in bringing about societies where all human beings can live lives of dignity and freedom in community and seek that which is good and true and beautiful. Not that contemplation, meditation, and the life of prayer are in themselves unimportant; the point is that they begin to be ten times more effective when they go with an active concern for the life of humans and of other beings who share the bundle of life with us.

From Plato Europe and the rest of the world can learn, but not in uncritical credulity. We must learn to be discerning enough to sift the wheat from the chaff; or rather to distinguish between what is central and what is merely doxa or opinion in Plato and textbook Platonism. Platonic dualism, if there is such, is indeed chaff or doxa; Plato's apparent denigration of the body and matter is also to be discounted, as are Plato's ideas about virtue. We cannot allow virtue to be merely personal; we need the practice of social virtue by a people pursuing justice, peace, and the unity of humanity, which are not individual matters. We can learn from Plato about truth, beauty, and goodness, though with a good many qualifications of what he said about their personal and social embodiment. We can do more. We can awaken to the wonder of beholding the One in whom truth, beauty, and goodness, with wisdom, power, and love, become unified in the freedom of pure bliss, and in that beholding, cease from all quest and unrest in approaching that pure rest which is both creative and active, the *theoria* which is also true *praxis* in freedom.

All this and much more we can learn from Plato with great profit. We can learn what we tend to forget today, that passions which militate against the true freedom of the soul and enslave us must be overcome: the bodily passions of hunger and thirst, lust and lewdness, the mental passions of hate and envy, jealousy and strife, bitterness and contempt, greed and pride, sloth and slander, pretension and hypocrisy. But we must also go beyond Plato. We know better today that there are passions of the mob that are more destructive than those of the individual soul. The social psyche can just as much or even more be swayed by passion and morbidity, by greed and aggression, by irrational cruelty and the love of lucre, as also by cunning and deceit, and by the refusal to recognize inconvenient truth. True knowledge and wisdom wait till these are overcome or largely brought under control.

The tragedy of our present knowledge of the world lies precisely in these passions that do not cease to rage in that world. We do not teach the techniques of controlling and overcoming individual and social passions in our universities and schools, and so knowledge languishes; wisdom lingers; science leads astray and technology destroys more than it builds. The person and society together have to reach out towards the true, the good, and the beautiful; only then knowledge yields wisdom as its fruit.

What is the bane of the civilization created by the European Enlightenment and its secular culture? We have separated fact from value and assume that knowledge can be divorced from goodness. We still do not realize that knowledge divorced from wisdom and love can only lead to evil. This is where Europe can learn afresh from its own Plato, that if knowledge is to lead to wisdom it must be accompanied by true goodness and purity of thought and intention.

Socrates, as Plato presents him to us, is indeed another pillar of the Western tradition. We have created our own Enlightenment Socrates, rational, secular, and devoid of worship or mystical experience. Diotima, the woman priestess of Mantinea, initiated Socrates to wisdom. Whether she is real or fictitious is not important. What Plato's Socrates narrates in the *Symposium* as her teaching on the Truth, which is also the Beautiful, is what matters:

> This beauty is first of all eternal; it neither comes into being nor passes away, neither waxes nor wanes; next, it is not beautiful in part and ugly in part, nor beautiful at one time and ugly at another, nor beautiful in this relation and ugly in that, nor beautiful here and ugly there, as varying according to its beholders. . . This above all other, my dear Socrates, is the region where a man's life should be spent, in the contemplation of absolute beauty. . . Do you not see that in that region alone

> where he sees the beauty with the faculty capable of seeing it, will he be able to bring forth not mere reflected images of goodness but true goodness, because he will be in contact not with a reflection but with the truth? And having brought forth and nurtured true goodness he will have the privilege of being beloved of God.[233]

Neither Socrates nor Plato was a secularist who believed that the world open to our senses is the only reality that exists. For them truth, beauty and goodness is One, and that is the goal of the human quest. Why did the Enlightenment separate these into three compartments called pure reason, practical reason and the critique of judgment? Why do people still separate fact and value, art and science, compassion and truth? Why doesn't Western civilization seek its way out of the fatal cul-de-sac into which it has led humanity? Why is it unable to turn to its own wise ancestors seeking help?

It seems the trouble started with Aristotle's rather scholastic characterization of Socrates as one concerned largely with moral virtues, and "as the first to seek of these [i.e. of moral virtues] a universal definition".[234] Aristotle recognised that the definitions were not the same as Plato's 'ideals'; for Socrates did not separate the thing and its form or definition as the Platonists did. But Aristotle misinterpreted Socrates' intention as definitional or scholastically rational. For Aristotle, Socrates was seeking the 'essence' of virtue, "for he was seeking to syllogize, and 'what a thing is' is the starting point of syllogisms."[235] Even Xenophon's *Memorabilia* or Socrates' younger contemporary Aristophanes' *The Clouds* which parodies him "as preoccupied with celestial matters" went as far as Aristotle in distorting the personality of Socrates.

If Socrates could drink the cup of hemlock with good cheer, it was certainly not because he had a very precise definition of moral virtue, but because of a basic perception of the nature of reality itself. While his friends who were Democritan Atomists had a mechanistic, nonteleological view of the universe, Socrates held firmly to the idea of purpose in the universe. "When I have drunk the poison, I shall leave you," he said to his friends, "and go to the joys of the blessed."[236] It is this belief that gave him great courage and strength, and not any rational definition of morality. Socrates can have only contempt for the kind of critical rationality that secular liberalism has created. As Plato makes him say in *The Republic:*

> They have never seen that of which we are now speaking realized; they have seen only a conventional imitation of philoso-

> phy, consisting of words artificially brought together, not like these of ours having a natural unity. . . By every means in their power seeking after the truth for the sake of knowledge . . . they look coldly on the subtleties of controversy, of which the end is opinion and strife.[237]

Plato makes Socrates say in the *Meno* that

> virtue is neither natural nor acquired, but an instinct given by God to the virtuous. Nor is the instinct accompanied by reason. . . then, Meno, the conclusion is that virtue comes to the virtuous by the gift of God.[238]

It is rather tragic that the picture of Socrates developed in the West is by and large that of a rational man asking the right questions at the right time to the right people; this is trying to squeeze Socrates into the confining mold of modern critical rationality. For Socrates what mattered was *phronēsis* or active wisdom, with a fidelity to the vocation laid on us by God, and adhering to that which is good and true and beautiful, not just conceptually, but with one's whole being, and even in the face of death.

Rediscovery of Socrates as one whose fearlessness is rooted in the fear of God can be the first step in the West's finding its way back to the authentic Western tradition of the Other Enlightenment from which it has so pathetically deviated in recent centuries.

The Neoplatonic Heritage

Plotinus (ca. 204–270) has been more influential, in the European tradition as a whole, than is often recognized. Some of my mentors at Oxford tried to cultivate in me some contempt for Plotinus as not only old-fashioned but also as irrelevant, even as irrational, feeble-minded and anti-Christian. I have found Plotinus worthy of much respect and attention from me, and I hope from others whom prejudice would not hold back from direct acquaintance. Many in the West think that Plotinus is the fountainhead of Western mysticism. I cannot agree, both because mysticism as a concept is a creation of the rational Enlightenment and because if by mysticism people mean direct intuition and experience of the Absolute, then Pythagoras, Plato, and Socrates and a host of others were mystics before Plotinus.

Of course Plotinus was not the only Neoplatonist. In fact, in the third century Neoplatonism is hardly distinguishable from Middle Platonism, the successor of Plato's academy, or even from Neo-pythagoreanism. Many of the views of Neoplatonism were shared by other Greek philosophical schools, both Platonist and Stoic; for example, that the human soul descends into this world through the planetary spheres, in which the soul acquires successively greater degrees of impurity and a successively denser 'astral body', a view that even many Christians shared at that time. Even if we distinguish Neoplatonism from Middle Platonism, we have to include in the former not only Plotinus and his disciples and successors like Porphyry, Proclus, and Iamblichus, but also many Christian thinkers in the West, including Augustine of Hippo and Boethius, and Byzantine or East Roman thinkers like Dionysius (the Pseudo-Areopagite) and John Philoponos.

But the influence was and is much wider. R. T. Wallis in his *Neoplatonism,* had this to say about the influence of Neoplatonism:

> A survey of Neoplatonism's influence threatens to become little less than a cultural history of Europe and the Near East down to the Renaissance, and on some points, far beyond. The reason this has not always been recognised is that that influence was often indirect.[239]

That influence is pervasive in three different worlds at least: in the medieval Western, the Byzantine, and the Islamic worlds of thought and experience. Neoplatonic influence is current even in the post-Cartesian world, as is manifest in the poetic creativity of Yeats, Blake, Shelley, and Coleridge, as also in the renowned contemporary English poet, Kathleen Raine. Its indirect influence can be detected in the whole corpus of European mystical poets and writers.

In medieval Western thought, the influence of Augustine, whose Christian philosophy owes so much to the "books of the platonists," was the most prodigious and pervasive and therefore best known. But through many other channels, like the *Liber de Causis,* a work based on Proclus's *Elements of Theology,* and often on the mistakenly attributed authority of Aristotle, Neoplatonist thought became the very foundation of medieval thought. A whole corpus of Aristotelian apocrypha based on Neoplatonist thought developed and passed into the theological corpus of the Latin West.

As early as the fourth century the Pagan Macrobius made Neoplatonism fashionable even among educated non-Christian Romans, through his commentary on Cicero's *Somnium Scipionis.* This commentary was in fact a popularized version of Neoplatonism. The fourth century Latin theologian Marius Victorinus translated Plotinus and made it available for Augustine and other Latins who knew little Greek. With the Latins' general aversion for metaphysics, it was often Porphyry's popularized version of Plotinus that the West could more readily assimilate, since it stressed the moral and ascetic side of Plotinus more than his metaphysics, which Porphyry tended to oversimplify.

Neoplotinian influence on Byzantine thought came mainly through Christian writings, chiefly the brief and succinct formulations of Dionysius the Pseudo-Areopagite in the fifth century; he was wrongly identified with, and thus invested with the Apostolic authority of, the first century Athenian philosopher Dionysius the Areopagite, whom St. Paul had converted to Christianity. Dionysius's extant writings are four: *The Celestial Hierarchy, The Ecclesial Hierarchy, The Divine Names,* and *The Mystical Theology.*

This corpus of Greek writings (possibly by a Syrian writer belonging to the anti-Byzantine Oriental Orthodox) came to the West in the ninth century, and was badly translated into Latin by the Irish philosopher John Scot Eriugena (ca. 810–877); he seems to have learned Greek just to do the translation, but it gave him and others in the West fresh access to the Eastern Christian heritage. This Latin version of the Dionysian Corpus then became the bible of the Western monastic and mystical traditions. In Byzantium itself the Cappodocian Fathers of the fourth century and Maximus the Confessor (ca. 580–662) critically appropriated the Neoplatonist tradition and with radical changes incorporated it in the Christian heritage.

The Byzantine tradition is an integral part of the European heritage; Byzantium was as much European as it was Asian and North African. By a strange twist of history, the Byzantine tradition underwent a double isolation, which led both to its Greek grandeur and its spiritual impoverishment. Its net result was Byzantium's eventual isolation both from Latin Europe and from Asian-African Christianity. It also paved the way for the rapid spread of Islam in the eighth century as an expression of protest against Latin-Hellenist domination. That twist of history merits a brief digression here, since it is one of the decisive features of European history and explains partly the development of Europe's peculiar psyche, which regards Islam and Eastern Christianity as its virtual enemies (the Crusades were directed against both), and sought, unsuccessfully perhaps, to eliminate all Asian-African identity and debt from its consciousness. The development of Neoplatonism in Western Europe, in Byzantium, and in the Islamic world can hardly be grasped without that historical background.

A Necessary Historical Digression

In 330 A.D. Roman Emperor Constantine founded the city of Constantinople on the site of ancient Byzance, and established it as the New Rome, the capital of the Eastern Empire. This Byzantine Empire, by borrowing freely from Asian and African cultures, soon developed a splendor that was then unrivaled. The Western Roman Empire, which went into decline, never forgave the East for that. In spite and frustration, perhaps, the West cut off nearly all direct cultural relations with the East, withdrawing into a sort of splendid but pathetic isolation. This spite and frustration continued to operate in Charlemagne's Christendom and in the Crusades of a later age. It perhaps still operates today, despite the West's technological and economic superiority.

Almost five centuries later, the Latins and Franks sought to exclude the Byzantine heritage from the new European Christendom that Charlemagne initiated in the ninth century. On Christmas day, 800 A.D., Charlemagne was crowned as the first Holy Roman Emperor by Pope Leo III. And with that began the creation of a Europe that consciously sought to be Franco-Latin, rather than Roman. The Roman Empire of the Caesars was a heavily Greek affair, and Asian and African cultures could flourish in it. The Greek language had been the language of culture for Europe. But with Charlemagne, Latin takes over almost completely.

The Carolingian Renaissance initiated the new *Romanitas,* which it identified with *Christianitas.* In keen competition both with the Eastern Roman Empire of Byzantium, and also with the rising and more glorious Islamic civilization of the Caliphates, Charlemagne recreated his own exclusive version of the Roman Empire and of Christendom. As the reborn Romanitas, Franco-Latin Europe identified itself not only with Christianity, but also with the Kingdom of God on earth, conceived in imperial terms, under a new Franco-Teutonic Holy Roman Emperor.

Till about the eleventh century, the term "Romans" was applied to both Greeks and Latins. The Franco-Latins changed this, by excluding the Greeks from the title of "Romans." Laws were promulgated, demanding that the Romans of the East Roman (Byzantine) Empire should be referred to only as "Greeks"; the ethnic title Roman was to be used exclusively for the New Romans of Franco-Latin Europe. Even today the Arabs refer to the Greeks as "Rumi" as they had been known at the time of the rise of Islam.

Both Byzantium and the Islamic Caliphates were thus fitted into an enemy image, suitable for rousing patriotic passions through promoting hatred of aliens. These attitudes came to light at the time of the Crusades, which though ostensibly directed against the Muslim "Kaffir," was just as vehemently waged against Byzantine Christians.

The early Byzantine Empire was an amalgam of Europe, Asia, and Africa, the heritage of Alexander's conquests in the fourth century B.C. Its political capital was on the frontier of Asia, and its intellectual capital was Alexandria in North Africa, named after the Macedonian conqueror. It was a Roman Empire, but the vast majority of its people were Asians, Africans, and Greeks. The early emperors sought to maintain this cosmopolitan character of the empire for more than a hundred years by actively promoting Egyptian, Syrian, Armenian, Chaldean, and other Asian-African cultures, as well as the dominant and all-pervasive Hellenic culture.

In the Byzantine Empire (330–1453) Eastern Orthodox Christianity was the cement of the empire as well as its spiritual foundation, but the Church was riven inside with acute cultural conflicts, mainly between the Hellenists and the Asian-Africans, despite heroic efforts by Byzantine Emperors to keep them from breaking up the empire.

Two symbols of this conflict can illuminate the nature of the struggle. At the level of the people, it was in the sports arena that the competition between Eurasian Hellenists and the Afro-Asians could most harmlessly (though not quite nonviolently) be expressed. The gladiators, the charioteers, the runners, the wrestlers, and so on were neatly divided into two major teams, with distinctive uniforms—generally, the blues were Hellenists and the olive-greens were Asians and Africans. A lot of the steam of cultural conflict was let out this way by the cheering and booing crowds. The other arena was the Church, where the conflict, unlike in the sports arena, could get quite vicious. Allegation of heresy was the weapon with which rival groups fought each other. Obviously, religion evokes deeper feelings and passions than sports.

Around the middle of the fifth century, the theological hairsplitting centered around the issue whether Christ, who was both God and Man, had two natures (divine and human) or one united divine-human nature. The Hellenists generally held to the two-nature formula, while most of the Asians and Africans preferred the one-united-nature view. Theodosius II (401–450), the emperor, himself of Spanish origin, wanted only to see that the dispute did not divide the empire. He promoted education by setting up the University of Constantinople, the first in Europe, in 425 A.D. When the theological dispute about the nature(s) of Christ first reared its head with the in 431 and had Nestorius, the patriarch of Constantinople, condemned for heresy. The dispute went on behind the scenes, but the emperor had more serious matters to attend to. In 435 Theodosius set up a commission to codify the law of the empire; in 438 he promulgated the Theodosian Code, the precursor of the Justinian Code which became the foundation for European law. The former code made heresy a punishable offense.

Emperor Theodosius's elder sister, Pulcheria, who had been regent during the boyhood of the emperor, exercised great power and influence, and was the main support for the Hellenist party. The empress, Theodosius's wife, on the other hand, who never got along with Pulcheria, supported the more cosmopolitan and pluralistic view of culture, and upheld the cause of the Asians and Africans over against the Hellenists. Poor Emperor Theodosius had to umpire between sister and wife, and most of the time he favored the latter. In fact, soon after Theodosius's marriage to a non-Roman, there was little love lost between brother and sister.

A conspiracy, scarcely dwelt upon by European historians, ensued. Pulcheria was in constant touch with the Pope of Rome, Leo I, whose ambition was to set up the papacy as the supreme authority in the Christian church—an ambition which not only Asian-African Christians, but also most Greek Christians stoutly resisted. Pope Leo was not politically powerful enough to directly oppose the emperor's pluralist policy; the pope saw this pluralism as the major obstacle to his quest for universal authority in the Church, since Asians and Egyptians made no bones about their opposition to papal supremacy in the Christian church. The alliance of Pulcheria and the pope was really an alliance between Latins and Hellenists against the Asians and the Egyptians for cultural domination. This alliance played a crucial role in the rupture between Europe and Asia-Africa, and in the history of European development in isolation from Asia and Africa.

In 449, Theodosius, possibly with some persuasion from his wife as well as from the renowned and highly influential Asian "pillar saint" Simeon Stylites, and definitely under pressure from the powerful and politically astute Egyptian Pope Dioscurus, called a church council, whose avowed aim was to curb the rise of Latin-Hellenist dominance in church and empire. It excommunicated Flavian, the Hellenist Archbishop of Constantinople, and insulted Leo of Rome whose memorandum for the council (called *The Tome of Leo*) was not even allowed to be read. Dioscurus, Pope of Alexandria (the title *pope* was first Alexandria's before Rome also assumed it) chaired the council and dominated its proceedings with imperial support. Pulcheria wrote to Pope Leo dubbing the council a "Robber Synod" and the title *Latrocinium* is still used by Western historians.

The Latin-Hellenist alliance was beaten in the first round, but soon hit back with typical European sagacity and brutality. The next year, in 450, the emperor, "fell off his horse and broke his neck" in a hunting accident in his own palace grounds. Such "accidents" seem to have been more acceptable in European "Christian" society than the outright murder of an emperor. Immediately, without even waiting for a prolonged mourning period, the emperor's sister Pulcheria married the aged General Marcion, leader of the Hellenist party, and declared themselves empress and emperor.

In 451 another church synod was held at Chalcedon. This time the emperor and empress saw to it that no bishop chaired the church council. Previous church synods or councils had always been chaired by a bishop, though the Pope of Rome never attended or chaired a council. With a view to ensuring the triumph of the Greco-Latin alliance, the presiding job was given to a team of "imperial commissioners" with clear instructions as to what the council should decide. The bishops were given little option. Leo's memorandum was read and incorporated into the official *horos* or theological definition of the council. Flavian was posthumously reinstated, and Dioscurus was excommunicated. The triumph of the alliance seemed complete.

But the Byzantine and Latin churches, as well as Europe as a whole, paid a very heavy price indeed in subsequent history. They had completely alienated the peoples of Asia and Africa; when a couple of centuries later, another Asian religion with no Greco-Latin domination arose, West Asians and North Africans were able to welcome Islam as a liberator from European domination. During those two centuries and for some time after, Hellenistic Christians oppressed, tortured, and persecuted those Asian and African Christians who were not willing to be totally hellenised. But the resistance was equally determined, and the Egyptian (Coptic), Syrian Orthodox, and Armenian churches of today are the survivors of a struggle that neither embraced Islam nor agreed to be hellenized and latinised like the Maronite Christians of Lebanon.

But the Byzantine Empire suffered both ways. They lost the friendship of the Asians and Africans who had made their culture what it was. Eventually, the Franco-Latins of Europe also turned hostile, as we have already stated. Byzantium thus suffered its double isolation, and though it flourished for a while, capitulated to the Turks in 1453. The Latin-Greek alliance started by Leo and Pulcheria in the fifth century was not strong enough to bring Western assistance against the Turks. Asians and Africans may be excused if they sometimes think not only that Greeks and Latins are equally domineering, but also that they cannot be counted upon as faithful friends.

Here we must end our historical digression and go back to a further look at Byzantium and the Neoplatonic tradition. The point needs, however, to be made here, that Western Europe's access to its own Other Enlightenment will be helped immensely by some willingness on its part to mend the fences with Byzantium and also with the Africans and Asians; for these have traditionally been the sources from which West European civilization has nearly always been renewed.

Eastern Europe and the Other Enlightenment

The Byzantine Empire, the great amalgam of Europe, Asia, and Africa, is also part of the European heritage, though West Europeans and white people in general now prefer to see their Greek heritage as limited to the classical period. Few are willing to recognize that the Eastern Orthodox Christian (Byzantine and non-Byzantine) heritage now forms the patrimony of more than half of the people of Europe who aspire to join the European Community: the Slavic peoples of Russia, the Ukraine, Bulgaria, Serbian Yugoslavia, Moldavia, Byelorussia, the Greeks of modern Greece and Macedonia, the Latin people of Romania, as well as the ancient Orthodox people of Georgia and Armenia. Will Europe be able today to reassess this heritage and appropriate from it much that can correct the one-sidedness of her secular rationalism? Can Europe see that her heritage is not quite identical with the classical Greek and Western medieval heritage? Can she now rediscover the Other Enlightenment that is central to her heritage and was once shared by East and West alike?

Europe's Christian Heritage

For Gibbon, Christianity was the last vestige of Oriental barbarism in Europe. Nietzsche might concur, on a different ground. Theodore White may argue that it was the Judeo-Christian heritage that was responsible for the ecologically unsound Western approach of domination of nature through science and technology. Marxists used to argue that all religion was bad and had to be eliminated in order that humanity may progress. Some of them at least seem to be more discerning these days.

These do not deny that the Christian church, in its various manifestations, both officially organized and underground, has played a major role in making present-day Europe what it is. They differ only in the assessment of the proportion of positive and negative elements contributed by the European experience of Christianity. By Europe I mean more than the people now inhabiting that continent; Europeans have practiced and experienced Christianity in other continents where they have emigrated.

This Christian heritage is a mixed bag. In the first place there are the four large traditions, Eastern Orthodoxy, Latin Catholicism, mainline Protestantism, and the more than one thousand sects of sectarian Protestantism. Within each of these there are varying strands, and some strands are common to all four, like some form of belief in God and in Jesus Christ.

The liberal strand and the evangelical strand also run through all four. The liberal line can flourish even without an organized church, and it takes different forms of expression even in secular society. It is the liberal line in Western Christianity that has been politically and economically relevant in this century. It fits in more neatly with the secularist perception of reality engendered by the European Enlightenment. The Other Enlightenment, which survives in the evangelical strand in all Christian traditions and in the mystical tradition of all religions, is now banned from the public arena, and is banished to the domain of private individual choice.

Liberalism in Christianity is fundamentally different from evangelicalism, in that the former puts humanity at the center of things, while the latter, at least in ideological statements, puts God at the center. In practice, however, evangelicalism also turns out to be man-centered. It seeks primarily "salvation" for the individual human soul, a very egoistic religious goal. The main difference is that the liberals want some kind of salvation for societies in this world, while the evangelicals put their priority on salvation for individual souls in the "other world." The liberal goal of this-worldly socioeconomic salvation is certainly less egoistic than the evangelical one.

It is fascinating to take a quick look at the recent shifts in the professed goals of American liberalism. These goals are chosen with reference to no abiding principle. The rhetoric till yesterday was "America's leadership of the free world"; today it is "the national interest." These goals reflect perceived perils to the American economy: till yesterday it was world Communism as a threat to the market economy on which the prosperity of the middle and upper classes in America were dependent. And America's leadership of the free world was the liberal rhetoric best suited to fighting international Communism. After the downfall of Soviet Communism, the perception changes to the threat of Japanese and European economies as too strong competitors; it is also perceived that Middle East oil is the lifeline of the American economy. Then the "national interest" theme becomes the rhetoric best suited to pursuing those goals with ruthless technological acumen, and still trying to hide the national interests under some label like "liquidating the tyrant."

The tragedy is that liberal humanism, which claims to make humanity central, would like to add two other centralities to that humanity. American humanity is the center of global humanity, and the middle and upper classes of America form the center of American humanity. Liberalism and evangelicalism, the two most powerful strands in Western Christianity, thus betray their own professed commitment to humanity or to God. Evangelicalism professes to question the European Enlightenment in rejecting its dictatorship of critical reason; it would espouse the Other Enlightenment as personal individual faith. But that faith has little to do with the public domain, which is left to the government and the political economy.

Christian mysticism, another form in which the Other Enlightenment is espoused, also keeps the mystic out of the public domain, concentrating attention on the "inner world" of the mystic's experience. How to make the Other Enlightenment relevant to the public domain, and how to make it reconciled with the demands of the European Enlightenment, is the problem that faces us today. Western society has access to both Enlightenments, but no pattern has as yet been developed to keep the two together in healthy tension.

The Other Enlightenment, which in the European tradition can be traced back at least to the Greek "mystery" cults and religions imported from Asia and Africa and adapted to European conditions, found its most refined expression in the great Pythagorean-Socratic-Platonic pagan tradition influenced by Aristotle and the Stoics; and in the Byzantine and Latin expressions of the Judeo-Christian tradition, also imported from Asia and Africa and locally adopted. (Remember that African Coptic monks spread the Christian gospel in Ireland and Switzerland as well as in many other parts of Europe.)

Besides these official expressions, there were also underground expressions of the Other Enlightenment, especially during those periods when the official traditions became oppressive and top-heavy. New socioeconomic classes, struggling for social recognition, often gave birth to new and original, though somewhat impatient, forms of piety. Some of these have much to teach us in finding our way back to a healthy balance between social concern and personal fulfilment in religion.

Three such movements, ignored, persecuted, or condemned by mainline Christianity, would repay some attention: Thomas Muentzer and the Anabaptists, John Wycliffe and the radical Reformers, William Penn and the Quakers.

Muentzer (ca. 1488–1525), since he was opposed to the bourgeois interests of the mainline Protestant Reformation, has received a bad press generally in the West. Martin Luther's outright condemnation of the poor peasant classes that followed Muentzer as "vermin," and his un-Christian exultation over the execution of Muentzer as a "just and terrible judgment of God" have not helped to improve the image of Muentzer and the Anabaptists. The German Peasants' War of 1524–25 when thousands of rebellious peasants in Thuringia and Frankenhausen were brutally massacred by the Christians, remains a major blot on the record of the Protestant Reformers.

Muentzer's main concern from his youth was the relation between faith and history. Born of a well-to-do German family and having obtained a master of arts from Frankfurt-an-Oder, he was fairly well versed in the history of the radical-mystical Christian tradition in Europe; he knew his Joachim of Fiore (Italian Cistercian abbot in the twelfth century who predicted an age of the Spirit, an *Ordo Monachorum* or a Contemplative Order in which all people would be monks, so to speak), as well as his Johannes Tauler (ca. 1300–61) the German Dominican follower of Meister Eckhart and Henry Suso and father of the Theologia Germanica, the theology of Dionysius the Pseudo-Areopagite in its German form.

Muentzer's heroic effort was to reconcile faith with life as it was lived, in church as well as in society. The discrepancy between the faith-claims of the Church and the reality of human life shocked him. He espoused the cause of the peasants, because they were the victims of injustice at the hands of the rising bourgeoisie whom Luther defended. He was a mystic who wanted to purge the world of sin and evil by direct action against the perpetrators of injustice.[240] He condemned, through many tracts, the comfort-loving middle-class Christians of Germany who acquiesced in an unjust social system. In his *A Highly Necessary Defense and Answer Against the Soft-living Flesh of Wittenberg*[241] and other tracts he argued passionately for a society in which all submitted themselves to the spirit of God dwelling in their hearts and in which all lived the holy life. This passion for a society rid of all evil led him to espouse the cause of violence against those who refused to submit themselves to the Holy Spirit—a cause that was justly doomed. But Muenzer was a mystic with a social passion for justice, the kind of Other Enlightenment that Europe as well as the rest of the world needs today, but perhaps grounded on saner and healthier premises and principles.

John Wycliffe, two centuries earlier (ca. 1330–84), was also associated with the British Peasants' Revolt of 1381, and was a firm believer in the need for the Christian clergy (including the pope and bishops) to be poor and to dissociate itself from civil authority. Wycliffe was reputed to be the most learned man of his time (in England, of course, and perhaps also in Europe) and was Master of Balliol at Oxford. He may not have been much of a mystic, but he was certainly no deontological liberal. His theology, however, had more impact on human social institutions than most liberal writings. The key to his thought is in his understanding of *dominium* or 'lordship'. In his two key works: *De Dominio Divino* and *De Civili Dominio,* he put forward the thesis that "lordship" could be bestowed only by the grace of God; all who have the grace of God have the power of lordship in true humility and goodness.[242]

In a society where the dispute was about who had been given the power of God, the state or the Church, the prince or the bishop, and about whether kings received their power directly from God ("divine right" of kings) or through the mediation of the pope as Christ's vicar, Wycliffe in effect said "a plague on both your houses" and insisted that God's power was given directly to the lay Christian and not exclusively to king or priest.

The question was eminently theological, but the answer made all the difference to the future of democratic institutions all over the world. The ordinary human person came into one's own, as the direct recipient of dominium by the grace of God, and not as a "subject" of the civil realm or as a passive recipient of salvation from the clergy. This is another clear case where Europe's Other Enlightenment was not a matter of inner illumination without social consequences.

The third example we can consider is that of the Quakers or Society of Friends, particularly in America. It was a mystical, anti-sacramental movement in seventeenth-century English Christianity, and its social consequences were immense. In 1682, William Penn, the Quaker missionary from England, founded Pennsylvania (which means "the forest land of Penn") and its chief city Philadelphia ("friend of brotherhood"), all on a Quaker basis.

Though they despised art and music as somewhat frivolous and not sufficiently solemn, their passion for help to the poor, social change, and justice was unequalled. The "inner light" of the Quakers could even dispense with the sacraments and the scriptures, but that same inner light also led them to fight slavery and to espouse the cause of black liberation with such great courage of conviction. The Other Enlightenment of the Quakers gave birth to a radical revision of Thomas Muentzer's violent campaign to eradicate evil in society; it was nonviolence that leads to lasting social change, and Quakers refused to do military service. Along with other historical peace churches like the Brethren and the Mennonites, the Quakers have been a consistent peace witness in a war-oriented European civilization.[243]

These illustrations are sufficient to show that Europe's Other Enlightenment is not merely a matter of inner illumination without social and economic consequences in the external world. That Other Enlightenment is not a world-denying mysticism or a socially irrelevant Pietism. It is both inner light and external transformation. It is this tradition of the Other Enlightenment in Europe that we need to examine more carefully, though that cannot be attempted in this modest work. We need to do more work on why that Other Enlightenment failed to take root in the European civilisation, and why the latter had to go after a one-sided and rather regressive secular option.

The Esoteric Tradition

It is only possible, given the limits of length, to barely mention the "Esoteric" or "Occult" tradition as an important aspect of the Other Enlightenment in Europe. Theosophy, theurgy, and alchemy are aspects of this richly varied tradition. Though the eighteenth and nineteenth-century European Enlightenment did make a massive onslaught on the esoteric tradition, it seems to flourish, though often underground, to this day. It had close associations with the Neoplatonic tradition in Europe, but seems to be of independent origin. Its connection with magic and astrology also seems obvious. Its ethos is directly opposed to the European Enlightenment and its secular, rationalist outlook. The intimate connection among God, universe, and humanity as one integral and interacting corpus is basic to the esoteric tradition, and the Enlightenment could arise only by cutting the umbilical chord that connected humanity and the universe to the Divine.

The esoteric tradition not only held God and world together, but also posited all sorts of intermediate beings between the two—a whole world of beings and powers that could be invoked and made to do things for us beyond our own power. Access to these beings and powers is through special initiation and long and arduous training. Its mesocosm or intermediate world reminds one of the Gnostic world of the Greeks and the Tantric world of the Hindus and Buddhists.

What the European Enlightenment has done for us is to make the very concept of a mesocosm appear somewhat ludicrous and superstitious. In fact, however, it may mean only that the bright light of Enlightenment rationality has flooded out our primal capacity for an interior vision that liberates. Jakob Boehme and the Jewish Kabbalah bear witness to the rich and profound potentialities of this esoteric tradition of Europe, which also came from Asia and Africa. Dante and Nicholas of Cusa also drank copiously from this tradition, as did William Blake and Carl Jung later. We can also mention William Law, Emmanuel Swedenborg, Rudolf Steiner, René Guenon, Mircea Eliade, Vladimir Soloviev, Nikolai Berdyaev, W. B. Yeats, Thomas Mann, and a host of others; the whole Romantic and poetic-literary traditions in Europe are permeated with elements drawn from the esoteric tradition. The sacred world of myths, symbols, and rituals, medieval Jewish and Islamic philosophy, the Greek classics, European literature, scientific theory, and philosophy—all rose out of the esoteric tradition and continue to delve deep into that tradition to renew themselves.

It is this Other Enlightenment in Europe that has been ruthlessly flooded out by the bright light of the eighteenth and nineteenth-century European Enlightenment and its dry critical rationality. Not that Europe can today just abandon all the manifold benefits of the Enlightenment and simply trace its way back to the Other Enlightenment. But the way to a healthy understanding of reality lies through a discerning reappropriation of some of the lost treasures of the Other Enlightenment.

That reappropriation can perhaps be helped by Europe conceding that the European Enlightenment is no sufficient guide for humanity in finding its way through life. Once that is conceded, there may be a willingness on the part of Europe also to open itself to non-European cultures and religions. The discerning reappropriation of Europe's own past should go hand in hand with a breaking out of European cultural parochialism and out of the confining parameters of Enlightenment rationality; without that breaking out little can be understood of what goes on outside European civilization, or even within it.

Chapter Twelve

The Twain Shall Be One: On Bringing the Two Enlightenments in Integral-Dialectical Relation to Each Other

Civilizations are never made from whole cloth, we need to remind ourselves quite often. We cannot, as the world's peoples and nations, just sit down and think up a formula and ingredients for brewing a new civilization as if starting from scratch. We have all to start from where we are at present, and start with what we have and what we can get; and do what we can do. History will probably decide the final outcome.

It is also clear that the kind of civilization we now have will just not do. It is too destructive of human potential, and has become capable of destroying itself and humanity in one blow. What went wrong with the present civilization is that it has been built rather one-sidedly on the foundation of the values of the European Enlightenment and its kind of rationality. Both in secular politics and in the secular academy, we have not allowed the Other Enlightenment to play its part adequately.

By introducing the Other Enlightenment into the now secular political and academic realms, would we not be undermining the institutions of democratic freedom that we have so laboriously built up in the past three centuries in the West? Would we not be giving back to religion what we have with such great effort wrested away from it for the sake of human freedom from the domination of the Church? This is indeed a legitimate concern and should not be so lightly dismissed as unimportant or irrelevant. For the moment we will only answer that what we are proposing is in no sense handing over political power to the churches or religions.

We are at a new and crucially transformative stage in human history. The Gulf War of 1991 has simply revealed the nonviability of our present civilization. We need to pioneer in rather bold and imaginative ways. All that is offered in this chapter can only serve as pointers for the direction in which we have to proceed, after a global discussion of these questions being raised here.

Bringing Together the Two Enlightenments

The two Enlightenments are certainly not homogeneous, and it is therefore not feasible to bring them together in some simple way. In fact there seems to be some hostility between the two. There are, of course, competent scientists who also have a deep commitment to religious faith and practice. But in very few of them does one find an integration of the two Enlightenments. What we often find is an uneasy coexistence, and in too many cases the scientist has only a tenuous relation to organized forms of religion; the scientist's religion is mostly a refined belief in some ultimate power or force, to which one feels an inner need to bow in worship, especially if the scientist is poetic enough to be impressed by the marvels he or she often unveils in one's professional work as a scientist.

The incompatibility, if any, between scientific rationality and religious practice, I suggest, is in part due to the kind and degree of religious or scientific dogmatism maintained by the individual scientist. It is the privatization and individualization of religion by the forces of secularism that made the situation worse. If one's faith or religious conviction is a matter of the individual's personal choice rather than of belonging to a community with a common commitment, then the individual takes personal responsibility for one's faith even when he or she has been born into and brought up in it. When it is no longer the common faith of a community that one shares with others, one has to tailor one's religion to one's own personal tastes and interests.

One often forgets the fact that one's scientific convictions are also derived largely from the faith of the scientific community rather than from one's own personal or individual experiments. Can we concede the obvious fact that in both science and religion, one does often go along with the convictions of a community, largely on trust, with individual freedom to protest, deviate, and dissent? If so, most of the conflicts between religious and scientific convictions can be sorted out in a setting of mutual dialogue between informed religious persons and competent scientists.

The more important difference between the two Enlightenments comes from our perception that while the European Enlightenment was rather a social-intellectual movement pervading the whole of a society, the Other Enlightenment would seem to be an entirely personal and individual attainment. The European Enlightenment was certainly the product of a particular time, brought about by a confluence of historical and geographical factors. The Other Enlightenment, on the other hand, seems perennial and universal, as well as more personal than social.

Can the two be brought together in an integral way, even if in dialectical tension with each other? On the surface, there seem to be insurmountable difficulties. How for example, would a state machinery deal with the Other Enlightenment? How would the modern academy or university deal with it? These are questions that can arise only from the unwarranted assumption that the present form of the state and the academy cannot be radically altered. We will see that altering these forms would be part of any solution.

Planning Futures

A decade or two ago there was a rampant rage for planning futures. Futurology became a science on its own, when the concept of long-term planning was taken over from Marxism by Western liberals. It was Marx who claimed that the future was an entity that can be reliably and scientifically prognosticated by understanding the processes inherent in history.

But history has also taught us that, pace Marx, the future cannot always be extrapolated from our knowledge of the past. There are always surprises, the unexpected in history, the unpredictable in future developments. As Fred Polak told us in the sixties:

> The challenge of the future waits, none too patiently, at our very door. If we do not hasten to answer it, we may lose both our freedom to give an answer, and our future too. The future can be a hostile mother, devouring her weak and sickly offspring. . . The very concept of the future inhabits another world to which experience has no access. Neither does Pure Reason, if such a thing exists. Thinking about the future requires faith and visionary powers, mixed with philosophic detachment, a rich emotional life and creative fantasy.[244]

In 1980 *The Global Report to the President* was published in Washington, D.C. It had been commissioned by President Jimmy Carter as a blueprint for constructing the future in the twenty-first century. Taking into account economic, demographic, and environmental variables from all over the world, the report sought to identify long-term strategies for all nations; task forces were set up in scores of countries to look at their own national strategies for the coming century. Most of those prognostications now lie in shambles, hardly a decade later.

One can best see the perils of pure reason's planning in the case of the USSR which also set up a task force around that time. How many surprises has history brought to that country in less than a decade! Most of its planning has now become totally irrelevant; due to unexpected developments stemming only partly from the *perestroika-glasnost* program.

Our computing capacity has grown to enormous proportions, and the number and complexity of the variables we can handle in a supercomputer are simply astounding. And in this past decade some of the most sophisticated projections about the future have been made in Europe, Japan, and America. The GLOBUS Project is one of the most comprehensive in terms of variables, since the Multination Global Model includes trade, domestic politics, and international relations among its variables. It can, besides, be operated on a microcomputer, so that any scholar with an ordinary computer can check and modify it. It was developed by Prof. Stuart Bremer of the Department of Political Science of the State University of New York in Binghampton, at the Wissenschaftszentrum in Berlin.

There is a Soviet Global Modeling Project initiated by the Institute for Systems Studies of the USSR Academy of Sciences, directed by Dr. Victor Gelovani, which is also comprehensive; it takes into account the long-term demographic, socioeconomic, technological, and ecological variables for nine regions of the Soviet Union and the world.

The Institute for twenty-first-Century Studies (1611 North Kent St., Suite 610, Arlington, Virginia 22209) publishes a handbook for twenty-first-century studies listing similar projects all over the world.

Obviously, planning the future is fully in fashion today, and the amount of information fed into these computers does yield some significant conclusions. But the number of variables that the programmers leave out or are unable to handle seem more numerous and not too "computer-friendly." Culture and civilization are not exhaustively quantifiable, though our science and technology has to its credit some brilliant successes in computing not only the future climate on earth, but also the eventual consequences of present or projected patterns of resource utilization and demographic growth.

Planning futures is not a concept to be contemptuously discarded, despite so many failures so far: failure to be precise in prediction and to attain targets in implementation. Planning is pure reason's most brilliant show, and its defects are inherent in the nature of pure reason itself. And just as we are unable to discard critical rationality altogether, we cannot afford to abandon planning futures and resort to a simple strategy or pragmatic ad-hocism, seeking solutions only as problems come up, as many intellectuals today seem tempted to do.

The robust confidence in planning futures, however, seems to be misplaced. In a country like India, there was, some years ago, in the early days of the Rajiv Gandhi regnum, a naive confidence in India "entering the twenty-first century as a technological civilization." History has mocked India, filling it with leaderless despair about the future. The West, too, might have entertained a too-robust optimism about the power of technology to create the future after its dazzling virtuoso performance in the Gulf War. A little reflection has already begun to infuse some sobriety into that technological optimism about the future. It is the very success of technology that makes thoughtful people wary about its possibilities.

Language and the Future

Some Western philosophers like Richard Rorty have already begun to argue that it is not philosophy or pure reason, but literary writing, especially the novel, that will show us the way.[245] Rorty cites, evidently with much approbation, Milan Kundera's *The Art of the Novel.*[246] Kundera suggests, and Rorty nods approval, that the novel rather than philosophy, is the "the most European of the arts." Kundera rightly reminds us that "the eighteenth century is not only the century of Rousseau, of Voltaire, of Holbach; it is also (perhaps above all!) the age of Fielding, Sterne, Goethe, Laclos."

Of course there is no doubt that the modern novel is just as much a product of the age of bourgeois individualism as the European Enlightenment itself. The relation of both the modern novel and critical rationality to romanticism is another parallel worth exploring, though not here. What Rorty the philosopher does is to express his disillusionment with metaphysics in philosophy through the espousal of creative fiction in literature, as an alternative means to show the way forward to the future.

The novel in some ways serves the same function as platonic dialogue. Points of view can be lambasted, refuted, mocked, and ridiculed, just as much in the philosophic dialogue as in a good novel. In these days of movable type and desktop publishing, the novel can get in touch with more people than can a treatise on philosophy, even if the latter is cast in the form of a dialogue.

And it was done most interestingly in the debate between two novels of the last century in Russia: Chernishevsky's *What is To Be Done?* and Dostoievsky's *Notes from the Underground.* Both are partisan pamphlets, Chernishevsky pushing a strictly rationally conceived just society, while Dostoievsky argues for the sovereignty and dignity of the human will that would defy any strict rational structure imposed upon a human being from outside. And indeed, the argument between the two novelists was closely followed by thousands of pre-revolution intellectuals in Russia.

Unfortunately, I do not know of any successful novel in our time that accomplishes this debate about the future global patterns for society. H. G. Wells, George Orwell, Bernard Shaw, and, in an earlier day, Swift and Dickens, wrote largely critiques of British society, and did not even bother about the problems of cultural and religious diversity as well as of peace, justice, and environment, in a global society such as ours today. Rorty exaggerates when he eulogizes Kundera's utopia which he sees as "carnivalesque, Dickensian, a crowd of eccentrics rejoicing in each other's idiosyncrasies, curious for novelty rather than nostalgic for primordiality"—as opposed to Heidegger's utopia which "is pastoral, a sparsely populated valley in the mountains, a valley in which life is given shape by the primordial fourfold—earth, sky, man and gods."[247]

But then, Rorty is not asking us to abandon philosophy and to follow some novel. He is pointing out that Europe has managed better on the novel than on philosophy. One can share Rorty's characterization of Heidegger as one of Nietzsche's "ascetic priests" who seek to dominate by encapsulating everything everybody else wrote into some one idea and then rejecting it totally, in order to "sing a new song" no one has ever before heard.

Rorty does even better in his essay on "Philosophy as Science, Metaphor, Politics"[248] in the same volume, in making the point that the aim of philosophical reflection takes usually one or more of three different lines:

1. The "Scientistic" aim, modelling philosophy on the physical sciences, exemplified both by Husserlian Phenomenology, and Anglo-Saxon Analysis Philosophy
2. The "Poetic" aim (e.g., Heidegger, Hoelderlin), reacting against the scientistic answer through which the European Enlightenment once sought to resolve all problems and issues

3. The "Pragmatic" or "Political" aim (e.g., Peirce, Dewey, Habermas): again a reaction against the scientistic approach, but modeling itself after engineers, technicians, and social workers, rather than after the physical scientists or the poets.

The difficulty, which Rorty does not dwell upon, is that the first and the third lack inner vision and illumination, and put no stress on being transformed from within; within not only the individual but also within the social corpus as it becomes conscious of its own transcendent origin and dependent interconnectedness with all other reality. All three aims overstress speech and action. Rorty himself has come around to recognize the overemphasis on language in Western thought. He can now say, with a cheerful sense of humor, that this preoccupation with language in Wittgenstein and Heidegger, in Derrida and Foucault, as well as in the more run-of-the-mill Analytic philosophers is only a futile attempt to replace the concept of "experience" that was the preoccupation of an earlier age (Kant, Dilthey) but which could not, unlike language, be objectified in the interest of scientific description. Language does not help us to rise, as both Husserl and Carnap vainly tried, to a transcendental "God's eye view of reality," a privileged "first philosophy" perspective in which the interrelatedness of all is perceived with mathematical precision and infallible lawlike logical structures. The attempt to delineate and define the conditions of the possibility of language has been a dismal failure. Habermas, less sanguine about language, seeks still to bring in normative conditions for the validation and justification of speech and action in all social contexts.

All of them, including the Pragmatists, exhibit a sanguine confidence in the power of reflection and action, of language and discourse, of reason and rationality. They all see theory as merely ancillary to practice, and theory as a linguistic act.

Both literature and philosophy seem equally preoccupied with language as the medium of revelation. Philosophy in the West seems now hopelessly rudderless and forlorn, almost blabbering. As the boundary between literature and philosophy narrows and begins to fade, literature, too, seems to lose self-confidence.

Richard Rorty thinks the best we can do is to try to reweave the fabric of our beliefs and desires through the only three means available to us, namely perception, inference and, here is something new, metaphor. This is strongly reminiscent of Indian thought, especially Nyaya philosophy; there, too, the four sources of knowledge are tradition (*āgama*), perception, inference, and analogy (or *upamāna*), which latter is defined by modern Naiyayikas as "the knowledge of an object to be ascertained by means of its similarity to a known object."[249] Rorty's "metaphor seems more sophisticated than Nyaya's *upamāna,* though not so much. Rorty takes off from Donald Davidson's discussion of metaphor.[250]

Metaphor too, after all, is language. But according to Davidson and Rorty, it opens up the parameters of language: "a voice from outside logical space, rather than an empirical filling up of a portion of that space, or a logical-philosophical clarification of the structure of that space. It is a call to change one's language and one's life, rather than a proposal about how to systematize either."[251]

Can a metaphor really do all that? To a non-Westerner this clinging to metaphor as a new linguistic device seems more like a symptom, rather than a cure, of the disease; namely, clinging to language. Why do Western writers torture themselves by this fixation about language, literature, and writing as the cure-all?

Language is indeed a precious human tool; but let us not make an idol of it. Rorty rightly distrusts the essentialism of conventional philosophical language, and wants to open up language and discourse beyond their conventional parameters. He also distrusts the pragmatist insistence that one should scratch only where it itches. Some sort of pragmatist he certainly appears to be; yet he insists that pragmatism is ineffectively seeking to continue the romantic reaction to the European Enlightenment's sanctification of natural science. To this writer it appears that Rorty and many others who do serious thinking in the West today are unable, despite their best efforts, to extricate themselves from the fetters of linguism and pragmatism or actionism.

On Going Beyond Words and Actions

How can we go beyond words and actions, except through words and actions? Whatever one says in answer to that question will be in the form of words and invitations to action. The words that follow are of that kind. They themselves do not represent the reality beyond words and actions; they are at best invitations to act, in order that we may be transformed, both as individuals and as societies.

The key word is discipline. And we are talking not only of so-called spiritual disciplines, important as they are. We speak about a combination of personal and social disciplines, as a way of bringing the two Enlightenments into an integrated package, which alone can break through the secular bind in which we are now caught.

Personal and Social Disciplines

Academics talk about disciplines in the sense of the subject matter of study, a *Fach,* like microbiology or genetic technology. The English word itself comes from the Latin *disciplus,* meaning pupil or student. The Greek equivalent of *disciplus* is *mathetes,* from which we get the word *mathematics,* meaning that which is transmitted from teacher to disciple. And a disciple is one committed to follow the way shown by the guru or teacher.

The Enlightenment culture places but a low value on the guru, thinking reason is a sufficient guide. But a great Sufi sage like Jalaluddin Rumi would say: "Whoever travels without a guide needs two hundred years for a two days' journey." The West's general unwillingness to follow gurus or sages may prove to be extremely costly in terms of time and pain.

But discipline need not be merely an individual relationship—one person's obedience to a superior person as guide. The tradition is, above all, a discipline, a guide for living. The Jews call it *halakhah* or the way to walk. The Hindus call it *Mārga* (way), the Chinese, *Tao* (way); and the Hindu Vedantins spoke of *Brahmacarya,* or walking in the Brahma. The early Christians called themselves *People of the Way.* Buddhism is the *Eightfold Path* or *Way.* In the Muslim Sufi tradition, the Guide, who is called *Shaykh* (Arabic) or *Pir* (Persian) watches over his disciple (*murid*) and guides him through the eight stations of the path that leads to *ma'rifah,* or fulfilment in God.

The European Enlightenment, though not always conscious of it, has always had its own tradition or way—a way that has led to some impressive achievements as well as to some bewildering catastrophes. Some of that way will have to be retraversed, in a painful retracing of weary steps. But the West sometimes seems to have a phobia of discipline as an infringement on one's freedom; yet many in the West are now taking to Eastern disciplines like Yoga or Zen. The zen master will tell you that "one is most free when one is most disciplined." Discipline alone can really make one free. To fear discipline as bondage is to stay in bondage to fear.

But as we have stated several times, discipline today has to be both personal and social. Let us take the eightfold path of Hinayana Buddhism to make the two dimensions clear in our context. Strangely enough, there are a number of traditions where the number eight plays a major role in listing the stations on the spiritual path. Patanjali in his *Yogasutra* (2.32ff) commends *aṣṭāngayōga* or yoga of eight parts:

1. *yama* or restraint
2. *niyama* or control

3. *āsana* or body postures
4. *prāṇāyāma* or breathing exercises
5. *pratyāhāra* or withdrawal of senses from their objects
6. *dhāraṇa* or stream meditation with mantras
7. *dhyāna* or deep meditation
8. *samādhi* or realisation of equillibrium.

This eightfold path does not lend itself easily to a social dimension, and remains purely an individual's path. The Islamic or Sufi path is twelvefold and also meant for the individual:

1. *tawbah* or repentance
2. *wará* or abstinence
3. *zuhd* or renunciation
4. *tsawm* or fasting
5. *tawakkul* or devout surrender to Allah
6. *faqr* or practice of poverty
7. *sabr* or patient hope
8. *shukr* or gratefulness
9. *bast* or ecstatic joy
10. *qabd* or control of ego
11. *mahabbah* or love
12. *ma'rifah* or mystic merging with the Divine.

The Noble Eightfold Path, or *Aryāštāngamārga,* of Buddhism lends itself to social adaptation, which was perhaps not quite evident in the original teaching of Sakyamuni Buddha himself, in his first major sermon at Banaras, preached immediately after his Enlightenment under the Bodhi tree. It is of the essence of Buddhism, along with the Four Noble Truths. In the *Pali Dhammachakkappavattanasutta,* this eightfold path is listed thus:

1. *samma-ditthi:* proper vision, or seeing things as they are
2. *samma-sankappa:* appropriate imagination or capacity to conceive reality
3. *samma-vāca:* appropriate, fitting, speech and discourse
4. *samma-kammānta:* appropriately motivated and right action and conduct
5. *samma-ājiva:* appropriate means of earning one's livelihood
6. *samma-vāyāma:* proper exercise and effort and exertion of one's energy

7. *samma-sati:* appropriate orientation of one's mind and thought to the four noble truths and the eightfold path
8. *samma-samadhi:* fitting and appropriate meditation.

The Pali *samma* is the equivalent of Sanskrit *samyag* which literally means 'fitting well' or auspiciously appropriate. Though the Buddha himself thought primarily in terms of a personal discipline, the social dimension was not absent from his thought. The great emphasis he placed on community or *sangha* witnesses to this conviction that the rectification and transformation of personal attitudes and actions also has a social dimension.

Towards a Social Discipline That is Also Personal

Among the large number of spiritual disciplines practiced in the various religions, we have chosen to dwell at some length on the Buddhist discipline. One reason is that Buddhism is perhaps the least dogmatic of all religions, unlike Christianity or the Vedanta. It is not our intention, however, to recommend any established religion in its traditional form as providing what we need as a new foundation for generating new civilizations.

The first requirement of this eightfold path is *samma-ditthi* or *samyagdršṭi,* or a holistic vision of reality, a good and fitting perspective on things as they are. Modern science used to claim that it had knowledge of things as they are, a claim that is now obsolete. Buddhism offered us, more than two millennia ago, a perspective which least contradicts the insights of modern science, and yet carries high contemporary relevance.

Philosophically this perspective was clarified by the great Nagarjuna in the second century. We will here summarize what we have already described in some detail. To say that the world of our experience is a faithful reflection of an objective world as it exists apart from our perception of it, is simply not true. Naive realism, which lies at the foundation of Enlightenment rationality, is not only false, but eminently dangerous as a foundational assumption for human life and culture. Nagarjuna, as well as the Buddha centuries before him, asserted that all we can say is that given the set of perception equipment with which human beings are endowed, there arises in our consciousness the world of our experience. To call this world "real" or "unreal" or a combination of both, is folly, for our very notion of real and unreal is drawn from our experience of things (*res*) in time and space. The world is certainly not *māya* or illusion; but then neither is it a hard reality as naive realism assumes it to be.

The technical Buddhist term for the nature of the world of our experience is *pratityasamutpāda* or conditioned coorigination; the world of our consciousness arises only when the two conditions meet: the particularities of our perception equipment on the one hand, and whatever there is on the other hand. This is *samyagdršti* or appropriate and fitting vision of the nature of reality.

Such a vision has tremendous consequences for culture and civilization. If properly grasped by people, it does away with our present conceptions of the good as acquisition of power, glory, comfort, pleasure, property, social position, possession of commodities, and wealth. The purpose of social existence and planning cannot, under such a vision by the people, be the kind of material and economic development towards which most of our social effort and state planning are now directed. Some vested interests are deceiving us today with totally misdirected social goals. Producing commodities we must continue to do, because without some production we will all starve and go naked. But our obsession with increasing economic or material productivity would have to be mitigated by a deeper vision that we should produce in such a way as to make the best of our common life and not for personal or group aggrandizement.

Such a vision held by society would radically alter the foundations of our culture, which has been increasingly taken over by the culture of consumerism. We will have totally different notions of what is good, and our social effort, with as well as without the government, will be oriented in a different direction, namely cultural creativity of the good.

But such a fitting vision has to be held by more than just a few individuals. It must become a social vision, with always the freedom for individuals to deviate and follow one's own vision. The social dimension of this vision includes radical negation of the secular assumptions of our state, our academy, and our media, which all seem to function on the basis of a naive realism and a secular dogmatism that have no real basis, with a consumerism and commodity fetishism born out of that wrong perception of reality.

It will have to be a social vision created by literary writers, poets, philosophers, and scientists, seers and sages, and promoted by the media and by the educational system. Many elements will come into play in the expression of that vision, including the perceptions of different schools of theoretical physics, astronomy and biology, but also of the various religious and poetic visions in the history of humanity.

This social vision of reality is in accordance with many modern Western views. One recalls that Wolfgang Pauli stated that the psyche that observes and the matter-energy that is observed form one piece, and protested against all attempts to separate mind and matter or spirit and matter.[252] Neither is it in contradiction with Hilary Putnam's view (he calls himself a "dialogical realist") that reality itself is a dialogue between mind and universe, and that theory can never directly mirror the structure of being.[253] The need of the hour is to give greater expression to this emerging consensus that the Nagarjuna type of view of reality is still the best that humanity can have.

Such a vision can only be part of the new discipline. We can here highlight only a few of the other elements, which we now think to be of primary significance for our purposes.

Social Catharsis for Our Time

Part of that social discipline is what the present author conceives of as "preparatory righteousness." By preparatory righteousness we mean something in the Judeo-Christian tradition. At the beginning of the Christian era, the Jewish people, at least the wiser among them, believed that before the Messiah comes it would be necessary to have a community that practices social and personal righteousness in a disciplined manner which alone would be worthy of receiving the Messiah or the Teacher of Righteousness when he comes. The Qumran community, in fact, conceived itself as such a preparatory righteousness community.

The Qumran community, as far as we can see from the *Manual of Discipline* and other documents, had a two-tier system of social catharsis. On the one hand, the Qumran community as a whole, calling themselves the "Council of The Community" or the *Sodh-ha-yehad,* was a vicarious substitute for the people of Israel, practicing the righteousness the whole of Israel had failed to practice. Within that Council of the Community, there were to be another group of twelve laymen and three priests "who are perfect in all that is revealed of the whole Torah." This elect group was to "practise truth and righteousness and justice and loving devotion, and walking humbly each with his fellow in order to maintain faithfulness in the land with a steadfast intent and with a broken spirit, and to expiate iniquity through practising justice and through the anguish of the refining furnace" as the *Manual of Discipline* puts it (See 6.24 to 8.19).

There are two principles to be noted here. The catharsis of a community demands a smaller group disciplining themselves with a very strict discipline to practice righteousness, truth, and love, in order to expiate the sins of the larger community. Repentance in this perspective, the agent of catharsis, is not a mere emotion or feeling, but the disciplined practice of truth, justice, and love. The first principle to note is that repentance is the practice—of truth, righteousness, and love, rather than the shedding of tears about one's own sinfulness. The second principle affirms that the disciplined life of a small community within the larger community can vicariously bring beneficial effects to the whole community.

Mutatis mutandis, that is the kind of social catharsis we can aim at in our time. Instead of trying to "reform the structure" centrally, the small community dedicated to God enters a covenant life of steadfast discipline for the sake of the larger community and not for the small community's own salvation. This is what the present writer calls *preparatory righteousness.* It does not seek social salvation by trying to change others through persuasion or castigation; it takes the more modest and more convincing route of a small community disciplining itself, not with any self-righteous sense of providing a "model" for others to emulate, but in order to express sincerely the repentance of the larger community, in humility and without any holier-than-thou attitude towards the rest of the community. The small community does not so much judge the larger community, but rather takes upon itself a discipline of costly self-dedication, on behalf of the larger community, for it and in identification with it.

In our time, for the life of such a small disciplined community to be effective, it will have to attend to more than simply personal integrity and personal holiness. It must also seek to work with its own hands to produce what is needful for the larger community; in so setting up itself to produce goods and services in an imaginatively humane manner, it will also set up a new set of relations among the producers—a new set of the relations of production, to use Marxist terminology. The small community has a commitment to justice within itself, and even greater justice towards the larger community.

It will be a community where the reconciliation of conflicting groups through mutual openness in love within it will be practiced with great rigor, and no internal conflict would be allowed to take root. When there are conflicts with persons and groups outside, every principled concession would be made to achieve a peaceful reconciliation. The same community would have a larger vision for peace within its own nation and among other nations and regions in the world. It would have an equally strong commitment to foster a life-promoting environment on our earth. Its ways of production and distribution, as well as its way of life, would be carefully geared to provide minimum damage to the environment. It would set up examples of how to deal with environmental problems faced by the general public, but without fanfare or irritating self-commendation.

One envisions several such communities spread over the face of the earth, so that the cultural and historical particularities of each region can be taken into account in devising the way of life of the community. It will have a new structure of authority within it, more democratic, but, a democracy based not on the principle of the majority vote, but rather on the folk or tribal principle of general consensus in the community, guided by elders noted not for their capacity to enforce discipline, but rather on a record of unstinting sacrificial service to the community and of cheerful willingness to endure hardship for the sake of others.

This community could be multireligious in its composition, and part of the community's program will be to foster the higher elements in each religion and to promote respectful mutual understanding among the religions and the secular people. Its handling of the religious life of the different groups within it, as well as its devising some common forms of worship and ritual, could make a major contribution to the life of the larger society. It could pioneer in seeking ways of solving many personal, family, and group problems of people in the larger community, but without any missionary aggressiveness. The community must not become ingrown, concerned only about its own internal problems, but should always seek to be identified with the suffering of people in the larger community.

Such a community would also devise its own medical and educational systems; its way of training its own children as well as providing continuing education to its adults could set important norms for institutions outside. It should specialize in the health of the whole community, in wholistic techniques and methods of healing, in preventive medicine and positive health promotion in the community. Health and education would thus form every aspect of the life of the community—not institutionally cut off from the rest of the community.

The community would also develop new and imaginative techniques of disseminating information and promote healthy discussions about the veracity and significance of the information they get. They would thus sharpen their faculties for critically discerning information intake, uncritical acceptance of information provided by the media being a major problem of humanity today.

One could go on; but the important thing is not to have a complete and perfect preview of such a community, but simply to begin pioneering. There will be a built-in system of feedback correction in any pattern devised by the community. In fact, this capacity for constant self-criticism and self-correction without morbidity will be a hallmark of such communities.

We shall here dwell in more detail about just one aspect of the life of such a community—how the community will seek to relate itself to the transcendent.

Relating to the Transcendent

The most important trait of the transcendent is that neither concept nor language can grasp it. We shall not therefore try to define it in words or conceptualize it. Martin Buber once told an ancient Jewish story about the expulsion of Adam and Eve from Paradise, where they lived in the continuous light of the presence of the living God. As they left the Garden of perpetual light and landed on this earth of ours with its gravity and time-space, their first most moving experience was watching a normal sunset on our planet—the golden orb of the sun going down the horizon in a blaze of sinking glory. As the darkness descended they were scared to the tip of their spinal columns. They decided that it was their sin and disobedience that had brought darkness upon the whole creation. They sat down and wept all night. That was a transcendent experience, though for us today it was a normal sunset. The whole of that night was also a transcendent experience of bone-chilling darkness. And the second transcendent experience came at the end of a tear-drenched, restless, agony-filled night. Hope was almost about to die when the dawn spread its rosy hue in the eastern sky. As they watched the sun rise, again a very common thing to us today, Adam and Eve got up with great joy and hope, in that blossoming splurge of light and life. That, too, was a great transcendent experience. The first thing they did, according to the story, as the welcome day dawned, was to catch a unicorn and sacrifice it to God.

Both the sunset and the sunrise became carriers of a transcendent experience, not because of something inherent in the sunset and sunrise, but by the possibility of relating oneself through both experiences, in two different ways, to the transcendent. This is a capacity of the human soul. We do not know whether nonhumans have this capacity. I suspect they have more of it than we do: perhaps they have not lost it as much as we humans have. Birds, animals, and reptiles seem to have a special capacity to respond directly to the transcendent. The more verbally oriented the being, the less the capacity to respond directly to what lies beyond. Verbality appears to have the power to imprison us in a world of our own making, cutting us off from reality.

It seems there is no way to manipulate the transcendent either. We cannot program a set of symbolic or metaphorical experiences through which we can automatically get in touch with the transcendent, though many religious rituals seem to have been devised with that end in mind. Our very subjectivity sometimes seems to stand in the way of genuine experiences of the transcendent, though many analysts would like to write off all experiences of the transcendent as "mere subjective" experiences, as if there existed some experiences that were not subjective at all! The rationally trained person's subjective mind-set, which is itself most of the time analytical-synthetic and grasping-comprehending in its nature and approach, can more often be an obstacle rather than a help for the experience of the transcendent. One has literally to let go in order to be taken hold of.

If this is indeed the nature of the transcendent and of our relation to it, and if relation to the transcendent is a necessary foundation for an abiding and worthwhile civilization, we have a problem on our hands. It seems that it is impossible to program this relation to the transcendent in laying the foundations of a civilization.

Keeping Ourselves Open to the Transcendent

Just as our own disciplined "preparatory righteousness" prepares the way for history itself acting to bring about greater justice in society, while we cannot program the relation to the transcendent, we can do some things to hold us in better readiness to be "taken up" by the transcendent. We can only mention here some of the things we can do to prepare ourselves in this way.

Consciously ridding ourselves of our secularism and scientism seems clearly the first step. So long as we persist in the superstition that a world open to our senses and subject to our rational knowledge is the only world that exists or matters, we are obstructing the transcendent from breaking in on us. So long as we continue in the outmoded superstition that modern science is the way to all knowledge and that nothing can be known except through the scientific method, we are creating an artificial barrier between ourselves and the transcendent. If we can get oriented to the truer perceptions that the world of our experience is only one of the many dimensions of our universe, and that our scientific knowledge, while operationally useful, is extremely limited in its capacity to lead us to what really matters, we will make ourselves freer to be freed from the prison of our wrong conceptions.

It will be a great help if we can draw closer to something like the ancient Buddhist perception, now revalidated independently by modern Western thinkers like Hilary Putnam, that our world of experience is a highly conditioned perception, conditioned both by what there is and by what we are; we can hang a little looser by this world and its deceptive perceptions of what is good and worth striving for.

Deliverance from our commodity fetishism and our foolish perception that the more we have the better we are, seem to be necessary preconditions for escaping the shackles of the immanent.

Even more important is our capacity to let go of our grasp on the conceptual and the linguistic, and to let us be seized by healthy symbols and rituals through which we can let go also of our preoccupation with the individual self and the individual ego that wants to be in control and at the center of everything. Here the religions have a very creative and extremely significant role to play. They have to refurbish their ancient stock of symbols, rites, and liturgies in order to make them more accessible to the modern man, not of course to his rational mind, but to his aptitude. It is not logical rationality or rational intelligibility that should be the guiding principle of liturgical reform. That is one of the great follies of the liturgical reform movement—this naive desire to make everything in religious belief and worship simple, clear, and understandable. That helps only to keep the human person a more comfortable prisoner of his or her own rationality, safe in the pernicious delusion that he/she understands everything.

The true purpose of a good liturgical rite is to help the individual worshipper to transcend his/her ego in a simple act of trusting commitment simultaneously to the transcendent and to the community. This requires trust both in the transcendent and in the community, but also the inner perception that such commitment is in the best interests of all, including oneself. A good liturgical rite uses as much of the human body and its senses as possible, in order to prevent the rational mind from being the sole actor in the liturgy. Touch and taste, smell and hearing, as well as vision, of the extraordinary, can all be beneficially used in good worship, so that it is the worship of the whole human person and community, and not simply of the conscious individual mind and ego. That individual mind and ego have to be sidelined in order that the transcendent may truly break through to the heart of one's being and the community's being which is neither the ego nor the individual mind.

The question may well be asked: What about the secular person who owns no formal religious adherence and has no religious experience? How can the transcendent break through to his or her being? One answer is that there are many liturgical actions which are of an ostensibly 'secular' nature, but which help transcend the individual ego. The struggle for justice and integrity within and among nations, for peace inside and among nations, and for a healthy life-promoting environment can provide occasions for such group liturgical actions. Much of our political, social, and cultural actions have this liturgical nature, and so long as they are for genuine human goals transcending narrow personal or parochial interests, they do help the secular person to have an experience of the transcendent, along with people with clearly held religious convictions.

The point is to let go and let be, and to commit to the whole and experience the whole. To the religious person it is to let go and let God be, or as in the case of the Buddhist who does not accept any notion of God, to let go and let the whole take hold. Our culture is very averse to such letting go and letting be. The capacity can be developed only in the context of a genuine liturgical community act. We need training to go beyond the excessive egoism built by the Enlightenment's civilization and its acquisitive economic system; we need to practice a social discipline that includes social catharsis through the disciplined practice of what is good; we need to work out a preparatory righteousness in which small communities vicariously and unself-righteously seek to do on behalf of the whole that which they profess to be good for the whole. The world religions, which have in the past functioned as inspirers of new civilizational values, must now prepare themselves, in humble self-criticism and openness to others, to recreate their own liturgical traditions and to create new orientations in society.

Freeing Freedom

Our age is, among other things, the age of freedom and liberation. Freedom is demanded by all who feel oppressed or marginalized—women, the young, the colonized, the exploited, the blacks, the Native Americans, the aboriginals, the Dalits (others call them Harijans), ethnic minorities, bonded slaves, and so many others who held their silence because they were not allowed to speak. Emancipation, liberation, freedom from outside domination and control: these are concepts of high value in the political marketplace. Even the marriage bond is often seen as, and in too many cases is, a yoke of bondage.

And yet few concepts, apart from that of love, seem to suffer such equivocation and misinterpretation. To have a fresh understanding and practice of freedom has not yet begun to burst forth—a practice and understanding that will really make us free.

Freedom is a key word in all religions, but the meanings they give vary so much. The variation has to do primarily with the conception of what it is that people are to be freed from. The Hindu Vedantic tradition would speak of the bondage primarily as that of nescience or *avidya*, or sometimes of being caught in the meshes of an unending series of births and rebirths. And so the basic search becomes one for liberation, *mukti* or *mōkša* from nescience and rebirth.

The Pauline tradition in Christianity would see sin, death and the law as those elements to which we are in bondage, from which Christ is to bring salvation or liberation. Christ himself, in his famous Nazareth synagogue manifesto (Luke 4:18–19), quoting the Book of Isaiah (Isaiah 61:1–2), declared his mission as one of "proclaiming release to the captives and setting at liberty those who are oppressed."

The Buddhist tradition sees the fundamental bondage as that of *duhkha* or unrest, caused by *tršna* or desire, and would see *nirvāṇa* or liberation as the cutting off of desire and thereby escaping from the cycle of births and rebirths.

The modern Enlightenment tradition saw bondage as enslavement by authority and tradition, and sought emancipation from the authority of the church and the religious beliefs of the past. The inner light of reason was to emancipate humans from bondage to the darkness of superstition and ignorance; modern science was to be its privileged instrument.

But what indeed is the notion of freedom that runs through these varying conceptions? Freedom is also a central value for any new civilization. Some clarity about it would be helpful.

In the Western tradition the fountainhead seems to be the Athenian or Greek notion of *eleutheria,* and the main distinction was between the free man (*ho eleutheros*) and the slave (*ho doulos*). Freedom was no birthright of the human being, but the special privilege of the "free-born," that is, the aristocratic class. Even in Kant *Freiheit* belongs by right only to the enlightened, the *Gebildete Leute* or educated class or the gentlemen. The Latin notion of *libertas* is basically parallel to Greek *eleutheria* and maybe even etymologically related.

In the Western tradition in general, the basic meaning of the word free is: not subject to another, not dominated or restricted by another, not owing unquestioning loyalty to any one, not having a master, and only derivatively, free in mind and spirit, gentlemanly, cultured, educated, and refined.

The basic problems with the Greco-Latin notion of *eleutheria* or *libertas* were two: it was too individualistic and it was only for the fortunate few. They could conceive of a community of the free (the republic), but not of the freedom of the community. And it was always a minority that were free: the majority were always slaves.

Today we are in desperate need of a fresh interpretation of freedom, to make it more universal and less individualistic, as well as to give it some positive content.

Without marginalizing the notion of individual freedom and the notion of basic human rights based on that understanding, we need to think more of the freedom of a community to shape itself and not be molded and manipulated by others, seen and unseen. For this we must move from the emphasis on the negative aspect of freedom as the absence of external constraint, to the more positive notion of freedom as the ability to act as a community, to create the good.

The biggest enemies of freedom are not always external; they are more often internal to the person as well as to the community. A person who has not by discipline trained himself or herself to be free from internal constraints like drives, passions, hidden motives, and lack of integrity, can never be considered genuinely free. True freedom is not just a lack of external constraint or alien domination; it is the capacity to be creative of the good without being constrained to do so or not to do so. To be genuinely free is to desire and will the good, know the good and do the good, not for any other purpose than that it is the good. Such freedom is vested jointly in the person and in the community, simultaneously. Neither the person nor the community can be really free, until it has by discipline ironed out also the internal constraints within the person and the society that prevent it from desiring the good, knowing the good and doing the good. Freedom, in fact, is genuine, free, creative love that freely gives itself for others without seeking anything in return. Freedom is not doing what pleases oneself; it is creatively doing that which is good without internal or external constraint either within or without the person and the community. Freedom needs power to create; that power can be scientific-technological, social-structural, political-economic, or prayerful-meditational; but it is always disciplined power, whether it be the power of persons, groups, corporations, or communities.

In fact, freedom is the transcendent. Only the transcendent is genuinely free, unconstricted, freely willing and achieving the good. It is through the practice of genuinely creative freedom that the transcendent is best experienced, by humans as well as by others. This wider sense of freedom, the *libertas major* that St. Augustine was prepared to lay aside in favor of a more riskless *libertas minor,* or freedom only within the good, needs to be reinstated today. True freedom always includes the ability to do that which is evil or not good, but also the disciplined capacity not to use that ability.

To Conclude

The European Enlightenment has been a major factor used by history to bring humanity together into a single network that is not yet a global community. The challenge of the hour is to catalyze the transition to that global community with some common commitment to each other and to humanity (and to the created order) as a whole. This means certainly going beyond the nation as the comprehensive structure of human existence. This means also going beyond critical rationality and its taboos and restrictions. In the process, both the nation and critical rationality with its science/technology will fall into place as useful structures for functioning at certain levels, but not in any sense as a focus for absolute loyalty.

Global thinking, planning, and action will play their necessary role in the coming of the new. But the catalyst will be new pioneering communities with much internal pluralism, but still held together by a cathartic social discipline and a commitment to the whole of humanity as well as to the created order.

That commitment will be more than an act of the conscious individual mind; it will be a social act, symbolically, ritually, liturgically expressed, making it more possible for the transcendent to break through and create the new. In fact, by freedom we mean the disciplined capacity, of individuals, groups, institutions, corporations, and communities, to freely create the good, not for sale or profit, but simply because it is good. Wherever that freedom comes into being, new civilizations of quality will rise and endure—till that freedom is dissipated by lack of care or by the growth of unfreedom.

In that kind of freedom the two Enlightenments come together. The twain shall then be One, humanity in touch with the Transcendent One, indwelt and enlightened by the One, who alone is the True Light.

The light of the European Enlightenment has turned out to be far too bright for us to see what matters. The light of the Other Enlightenment, however feeble and dim it has become, seems still accessible to the culture. We need both lights, but perhaps also a fresh and freshening outburst of the light that is from above, the light of the transcendent.

For that light to burst forth, we can do little better than wait, with active hope, in expectant, creative, disciplined communities, which watchfully live and constantly repent on behalf of the whole of our human race.

Notes

Chapter 2: Religion, Culture, and the Secular: Concepts to be Clarified

1. Study of the *current* use of a word in its different meanings is, of course, necessary and useful, but a *historical* study of the development of the meaning of certain words and concepts often point to changes in the general worldview of society.

2. Means "as the king, so the religion." Some people think that the modern state came into being with the Treaty of Westphalia (1648) by which the European states agreed to settle their Protestant-Catholic wars and conflicts (e.g., the Thirty Years' War) by making the religion of the ruler the religion of the state. Our modern secular states expressly repudiate this principle by legislating the principle of "separation of church and state." Such a repudiation distinguishes the secular state from the religious (e.g., Islamic) state. It seems the word *secularization* was coined on April 8, 1646 by the French delegates at the preliminary negotiations for the Treaty of Westphalia. See *Die Religion in Geschichte und Gegenwart,* 3d ed., 6 vols. (Tuebingen: J. C. B. Mohr, 1957), 5:1280, which cites J. G. van Meiern, *Acta Pacis Westphalicae publica,* 2:15.

3. In modern English: "In one manner, religion is a . . . binding up or a binding . . . of a man's free will with certain ordinances . . . or with vows or oaths"; cited by *The Oxford English Dictionary,* 2d ed., vol. 13 (Oxford: Clarendon Press, 1989), s.v. "religion."

4. See J. F. Niermeyer, *Mediae Latinitatis Lexicon Minus,* and *Oxford Latin Dictionary* (Oxford: Clarendon Press, 1982), s.v. "religio."

5. *Oxford English Dictionary.*

6. Ibid.

7. Ibid.

8. Andrew M. Greeley, *Religion: A Secular Theory* (New York: Free Press, 1982), 162.

9. Auguste Comte, *La Philosophie Positive, par Auguste Comte, resumé par Jules Rig,* Tome Premier (Paris, 1880), 1–2.

10. A. R. Radcliffe-Brown, *Structure and Function in Primitive Society: Essays and Addresses* (Glencoe, Ill.: Free Press, 1952; reprinted 1961).

11. Mircea Eliade, ed., *Encyclopedia of Religion* vol. 12 (New York: Macmillan, 1987), s.v. "religion."

12. Formulation of the present author, from Robert Bellah, "The Sociology of Religion," in David L. Sills, ed., *The International Encyclopaedia of the Social Sciences* (New York: Macmillan and The Free Press, 1968), vol. 13, s.v. "religion."

13. Clifford Geertz, "Religion as a Cultural System," in Michael Banton, ed., *Anthropological Approaches to the Study of Religion* (London: Tavistock Publications Ltd, 1966), 4. See also C. Geertz, *The Interpretation of Cultures* (New York: Basic Books, 1973).

14. *Encyclopedia of Religion,* s.v. "secularization."

15. Clement of Rome, *Epistle to the Corinthians,* Greek text in *Sources Chretiennes* (Paris: Editions de Cerf, 1971), 167:166.

16. *Oxford Latin Dictionary,* s.v. "saecularis."

17. *Oxford English Dictionary,* s.v. "secularism."

18. For a representative selection of views, see Enrico Castelli, ed., *Hermeneutique de la Secularisation, Actes de Colloque Organise par le Centre International d'études humanistes et par l'Institut d'études Philosophiques de Rome, Rome 1976* (Aubier: Editions Montaigne, 1976).

19. Paulos Mar Gregorios, *Enlightenment: East and West* (Shimla, India: Indian Institute of Advanced Study, 1989).

20. Louis Dupré, "La Secularisation et la Crise de Notre Culture," in Enrico Castelli, *Hermeneutique.*

21. Edward B. Tylor, *Primitive Culture,* 2 vols. (1871; republished 1958), vol. 1, pt. 1.

22. A. L. Kroeber and Clyde Kluckhorn, *Culture: A Critical Review of Concepts and Definitions* (New York: Vintage, 1963), 181.

23. *New Statesman and Society,* 10 Nov. 1989, 46.

24. Jonas Frykman and Orvar Loefgren, *Culture Builders: A Historical Anthropology of Middle Class Life,* trans. Alan Crozier (New Brunswick, N.J.: Rutgers University Press, 1987). Book review in *American Historical Review,* December 1988, 1349–50.

25. George Rochberg, "News of the Culture or News of the Universe," in *The Annals of the American Academy of Political and Social Science,* November 1988, 116–26 (slightly edited).

26. G. W. F. Hegel, *Phenomenology of Spirit,* trans. A. V. Miller (London and New York: Oxford Univ. Press, 1979), #748, 453ff.

27. G. W. F. Hegel, *Lectures On the Philosophy of Religion, Together with a Work on the Proofs of the Existence of God,* trans. Rev. E. B. Speirs and J. Burdon Sanderson (London: Routledge and Kegan Paul, 1962; New York: Humanities Press, 1962), 1–2.

28. Ibid., 14–15.

29. Ibid., 15.

30. Ibid., 16.

31. Ibid., 19–20: "Die Philosophie ist in der Tat selbst Gottesdienst, ist Religion, denn sie ist dieselbe Verzichtung auf subjektive Einfaelle und Meinungen in der Beschaeftigung mit Gott. Die Philosophie ist also damit identisch mit der Religion, aber der Unterschied ist, dass sie es auf *eigentuemliche Weise* ist, unterschieden von der Weise, die man Religion als solche zu nennen pflegt." Hegel, *Vorlesungen ueber die Philosophie der Religion* (Frankfort: Suhrkamp, 1969; reprinted 1982), #1:28.

Chapter Three: What is the European Enlightenment?

32. L. Gottschalk and D. Lach, *Toward the French Revolution* (New York: Scribner's, 1973), 134.

33. L. G. Crocker, "Recent Interpretations of the French Enlightenment," in *Journal of World History* (Neuchatel, Switzerland: Editions de la Baconniere, 1964), 8:3:426–56.

34. Ira O. Wade, *The Structure and Form of the French Enlightenment,* 2 vols. (Princeton, N.J.: Princeton University Press, 1977).

35. In Eberhard Bahr, ed., *Was ist Aufklaerung? Thesen und Definitionen* (Stuttgart: Reclam, 1986), 9.

36. Ibid., 9. English translation is by the present author. Other English versions can be found in L. W. Beck, *Critique of Practical Reason* (Chicago: University of Chicago Press, 1949), 286ff., and in Beck's *Kant on History,* as well as in Hans Reiss, *Kant's Political Writings* (Cambridge: Cambridge University Press, 1970).

37. The Latin word *modernus* seems to have been coined in the seventeenth century from *modo* (now) as a parallel to the synonym *hodiernus* from *hodie* (today).

38. Bahr, *Aufklaerung,* 3–4.

39. Immanuel Kant, *Werke* 19:199.

40. Immanuel Kant, *Werke* 8:294. "Ueber den Gemeinspruch: Das mag in der Theorie richtig sein, taugt aber nicht fuer die praxis." English translation in Reiss, *Kant's Political Writings.*

41. W. Krauss, ed., *Est-il utile de tromper le peuple? Ist der Volksbetrug von Nutzen? Concours de l'Academie des Sciences et de Belles-lettres de Berlin pour l'annee 1780* (Berlin: Akademie-Verlag, 1966).

42. Julian Offray de la Mettrie, *L'homme Machine* (*Man a Machine*) (La Salle, Ill.: Open Court, 1912).

43. English translation (New York: Philosophical Library, 1827).

44. (Amsterdam: Chez M. M. Rey, 1776)

45. Heinrich Heine, "Concerning the History of Religion and Philosophy in Germany," in Heine, *Selected Works,* ed. and trans. Helen M. Mustard (New York: Random House, 1973), 276. The article was published in French in a series of three, in *Revue des deux mondes* (1834).

46. *La Civilta Cattolica* 2:122, cited in E. J. Hobsbawm, *The Age of Revolution, 1789–1848* (New York: New American Library, 1962), 258.

47. Peter Gay, *The Enlightenment: An Interpretation,* 2 vols. Volume One: *The Rise of Modern Paganism* (New York: Alfred A. Knopf, 1966); Volume Two: *The Science of Freedom* (New York: Alfred A. Knopf, 1969).

48. E. J. Hobsbawm, *Age of Revolution,* 258–59.

49. For a brief but illuminating study of Strauss's work in relation to Hegel, see Marilyn Chapin Massey's lucid introduction to David Friedrich Strauss, *In Defense of My Life of Jesus Against the Hegelians* (Hamden, Conn.: Archon Books, 1983).

50. D. F. Strauss, *Der alte und der neue Glaube* (Leipzig, 1872), republished in Eduard Zeller, ed., *Gesammelte Schriften von David Friedrich Strauss,* 12 vols. (Bonn: Fromann, 1876–78).

51. Strauss, *In Defense,* 66.

52. Jean le Rond D'Alembert, "Elements de Philosophie," in *Melanges de Literature, d'Histoire et de Philosophie,* Nouvelle edition, 6 vols. (Amsterdam, 1759), 4:3–6.

53. D'Alembert, "Elements," 3–6, cited by Ernst Cassirer, *The Philosophy of the Enlightenment* (Boston: Beacon Press, 1955), 3–4. Original version: *Die Philosophie der Aufklaerung* (Tuebingen: J. C. B. Mohr, 1932).

54. Cassirer, *Enlightenment,* 5–6.

55. Cited by Owen Chadwick, "The Italian Enlightenment," in Roy Pastor and Mikulas Teich, eds., *The Enlightenment in National Context* (Cambridge: Cambridge University Press, 1981).

56. See note 55.

57. *Dictionnaire de Spiritualité*, vol. 7, deuxieme partie (Paris: Beauchesne, 1971), s.v. "illuminismo."

58. *The Enlightenment in America* (Oxford et alibi: Oxford University Press, 1976), xvii.

59. Ibid., xiv.

60. Thomas Paine, *The Rights of Man* (London: 1966), 98–99.

Chapter Four: Europe: Adventure and Expansion

61. Denis de Rougemont, *The Meaning of Europe*, trans. Alan Braley (London: Sidgwick and Jackson, 1965).

62. Robert Graves, *The Greek Myths*, 2 vols. (London: Penguin, 1955), 1:194–97.

63. *The Bacchae* (New York: New American Library, 1982), xxii.

64. De Rougemont, *Meaning*, 38.

65. R. D. Milns, *Alexander the Great* (London: Robert Hale, 1968), 137.

66. F. C. Danvers, *The Portuguese in India* (1894; reprint, London: Frank Gass, 1966), 1:85; based on eyewitness accounts.

67. William Woodruff, *The Struggle for World Power* (London and Basingstoke: Macmillan, 1981), 1–2.

68. Joan Robinson, in Rosa Luxemburg, *The Accumulation of Capital* (New York: Monthly Review Press, 1964), 28.

69. The main sources for our knowledge of the Indo-Greek contacts of the fourth century B.C. and after are Arrian's *Anabasis VIII (Indica)*, Herodotus's *Persian Wars*, and Plutarch's *Alexander.*

70. See Milns, *Alexander the Great;* W. W. Tarn, *The Greeks in Bactria and India* (Cambridge: Cambridge University Press, 1938); and V. A. Smith, *The Early History of India* (Oxford: Oxford University Press, 1924).

71. N. A. Nikam and Richard McKeon, eds., *The Edicts of Asoka* (Chicago: University of Chicago Press, 1959).

72. John Roberts, *Revolution and Improvement: The Western World, 1775–1847* (Berkeley and Los Angeles: University of California Press, 1976), 1.

73. H. J. Habakkuk, "Population, Commerce, and Economic Ideas," in A. Goodwin, ed., *The New Cambridge Modern History* (Cambridge: Cambridge University Press, 1965), vol. 8, *The American and French Revolutions*, 25–33.

74. Ibid., 44.

75. Hobsbawm, *Revolution*, 45.

76. John Richard Green, "The Conquests of Bengal and Canada—A.D. 1757–64," in *The World's Greatest Events*, 10 vols. (1908; reprint, New York: P. F. Collier and Son, 1945), 5:210–11.

77. For a fairly recent survey of that power struggle for world domination in the eighteenth and nineteenth centuries, see William Woodruff, *Struggle for World Power.* The present author is deeply indebted to this work for many of the facts in this chapter, though not for their interpretation.

78. Antony Lentin, *Voltaire and Catherine the Great: Selected Correspondence* (Cambridge: Oriental Research Partners, 1974).

Chapter Five: Hegel: Ideas

79. Brand Blanshard, "Practical Reason: Reason and Feeling in Twentieth-Century Ethics," in Eugene Freeman, ed., *The Abdication of Philosophy: Philosophy and the Public Good* (La Salle, Ill.: Open Court, 1976).

80. J. R. G. Mure, *Hegel* (Oxford: Oxford University Press, 1965), 8.

81. Fred G. Weiss, "A Critical Survey of Hegel Scholarship in English: 1962–69," in J. J. O'Malley, et al. eds., *The Legacy of Hegel: Proceedings of the Marquette Hegel Symposium 1970* (The Hague: Martinus Nijhoff, 1973), 31.

82. J. N. Findlay, *Hegel: A Reexamination* (London: George Allen and Unwin, 1958; New York: Collier, 1962).

83. (Bloomington: Indiana University Press, 1968)

84. Franz Nauen has given us an illuminating study of the development of the minds of these three great Tuebingen theological students who became leading savants of the eighteenth-century Enlightenment, in his *Revolution, Idealism and Human Freedom: Schelling, Hoelderlin and Hegel and the Crisis of Early German Idealism*, published in 1971 in the International Archives of the History of Ideas. (The Hague: Martinus Nijhoff, 1971)

85. Benedetto Croce, *What is Living and What is Dead in the Philosophy of Hegel?* trans. Douglas Ainslee (London: Macmillan, 1915), 216–17.

86. Hans Blumenberg, *Die Legitimataet der Neuzeit* (1966), reviewed by Karl Loewith and Hans-Georg Gadamer in *Philosophische Rundschau* 15:3 (July 1968): 195–209.

87. Karl Loewith, *Von Hegel zu Nietzsche* (Stuttgart: Kohlhammer, 1964), English translation by D. E. Green, *From Hegel to Nietzsche: The Revolution in Nineteenth-Century Thought* (New York: Holt, Rinehart, and Winston, 1964).

See also Loewith's *Weltgeschichte und Heilsgeschehen: Die Theologischen Voraussetzungen der Geschichtsphilosophie* (Stuttgart: Kohlhammer, 1953), English translation, *Meaning in History: The Theological Implications of the Philosophy of History* (Chicago: University of Chicago Press, 1949).

88. Carl Schmitt, *Politische Theologie: Vier Kapitel zur Lehre von der Souveraenitaet* (Munich and Leipzig: Dunker and Humboldt, 1922), 37.

89. Mircea Eliade, *The Sacred and the Profane* (New York: Harper and Row, 1961), 117ff.

90. Rudolf Bultmann, *History and Eschatology; The Presence of Eternity* (New York: Harper and Row, 1957), 56–120, esp. pp. 62–73.

91. Karl Barth, *Protestant Thought; From Rousseau to Ritschl* (London: SCM Press, 1959; New York, Harper and Row, 1959), 268.

92. G. W. F. Hegel, *Lectures on the Philosophy of Religion* (London: Routledge and Kegan Paul, 1962; New York: Humanities Press, 1962), 1:49–50.

93. Hegel, *Lectures on Philosophy* 3:1.

94. Ibid., 7.

95. Ibid., 10.

96. Ibid., 10–11.

97. Hegel, *Lectures on Philosophy* 2:348.

98. Ibid., 349.

99. Hegel, *Lectures on Philosophy* 3:35.

100. Ibid., 110–11.

101. Hegel, *Lectures on Philosophy* 2:15ff. Hegel shows an astonishingly comprehensive (in view of the paucity of available material in Europe) knowledge of Hinduism for the beginning of the nineteenth century, when information about Indian civilization is beginning to spread in Germany. Of course, his western prejudices show through, but it is not a superficial understanding. Reinhard Leuze has studied Hegel's library and particularly his sources for the study of other religions in *Die ausserchristlichen Religionen bei Hegel* (Goettingen: Vanderhoeck and Ruprecht, 1975). Hegel studied the Chinese, Indian, Egyptian, Roman, Jewish, Persian, and Greek religions, making the best use of the very limited resources available to him at the time. According to Leuze, the books he consulted on Hinduism were mainly the *Annals of the Asiatick Society*, including a book in that series by Colebroke entitled *The Philosophy of the Hindus;* a translation of the *Bhagavad Gita* by L. V. Schroeder; *The History of the Hindostan* (London, 1768); and the Carey and Marshman translation of the *Valmiki Ramayana*, published in Serampore in 1806.

102. Miller and Findlay, *Phenomenology of Spirit*, 418.
103. Hegel, *Lectures on Philosophy* 3:107.

Chapter Six: The Dialectics of the Enlightenment

104. Schelling, *Werke* 3:299.

105. Elie Halevy, *The Growth of Philosophical Radicalism*, trans. Mary Morris (Boston: Beacon Press, 1966), 433.

106. John Stuart Mill, *On Socialism* (Buffalo: Prometheus Books, 1987).

107. Cited by Lewis S. Feur in Introduction to Mill, *On Socialism*.

108. Juergen Habermas, *Knowledge and Human Interests*, trans. Jeremy Shapiro (Boston: Beacon Press, 1971).

109. M. Horkheimer, "Traditionelle und Kritische Theorie" (1937), in *Kritische Theorie*, vol. 2 (Frankfort: S. Fischer, 1968).

110. Theodor W. Adorno, *Against Epistemology: A Metacritique*, trans. Willis Domingo (Oxford: Basil Blackwell, 1982). Original: *Zur Metacritique der Erkenntnistheorie: Studien ueber Husserl und die phaenomenologischen Antinomien* (Frankfort: Suhrkamp, 1970).

111. Edmund Husserl, *Phenomenology and the Crisis of Philosophy: Philosophy as a Rigorous Science, and Philosophy and the Crisis of European Man*, intro. by Quentin Lauer (New York: Harper, 1965).

112. For an interesting biography of Marx, see Saul K. Padover, *Karl Marx: An Intimate Biography* (New York: McGraw-Hill, 1978).

113. Hegel, *Philosophy of Right*, trans. T. M. Knox (Oxford: Clarendon Press, 1952; reprinted 1965).

Chapter Seven: Theory for Practice?

114. Juergen Habermas, *Theory and Praxis* (Boston: Beacon Press, 1973). See the appendix in Habermas, *Knowledge and Human Interests*.

115. Horkheimer, "Kritische Theorie," 162.

116. Plotinus *Ennead* 6.4.

117. Ibid., 6.2.9ff.

118. Ibid., 1.6.7.

119. Ibid., 1.6.5.

120. Ibid., 1.6.7.

Chapter Eight: Justice, Human Rights, and the State

121. *Nicomachean Ethics,* bk. 5, Loeb Classical Library (Cambridge: Harvard University Press, 1935).

122. Ibid., 2:494.

123. Judge A. T. Abdy and Bryan Walker, Introduction to *The Rules of Ulpian (A Digest of Roman Law),* in M. M. Miller, ed., *The Classics: Greek and Latin* (New York: Vincent Parke and Company, 1909), 343ff.

124. Cicero, *De Re Publica* 3.22.33, trans. C. W. Keyes, Loeb Classical Library (Cambridge: Harvard University Press, 1928), 211.

125. Rom. 2:14–15.

126. Ibid., 13:1–2.

127. Titus 3:1.

128. 1 Peter 2:13–14.

129. See my *Enlightenment,* 63–68.

130. *Summa Theologica, prima secunda,* quaestiones 90–108.

131. John Rawls, *The Concept of Justice* (Cambridge: Harvard University Press, 1971).

132. (Cambridge: Cambridge University Press, 1982)

133. Sandel, *Liberalism,* 1.

134. Ibid.

135. J. S. Mill, *Utilitarianism,* in *The Utilitarians* (Garden City: Doubleday, 1973), 465, cited in Sandel, *Liberalism,* 2.

136. The University of Wisconsin Press (Madison, 1987) in association with Basil Blackwell (Oxford, 1987). On modernity there have recently been a good number of writings, besides Hans Blumenberg's *Die Legitimitaet der Neuzeit.* Among the most noteworthy are the articles by C. Castoriadis in journals such as *Telos* and *Thesis Eleven;* Juergen Habermas, "Modernity versus Post-modernity"; "The Entwinement of Myth and Modernity," in *New German Critique* 26 (1982); and Agnes Heller, *The Power of Shame* (1985) and *A Theory of History* (1982).

137. Rundel, *Origins of Modernity,* 1–2.

138. (The Hague: Martinus Nijhoff, 1971)

139. Hans Saner, *Kant's Political Thought: Its Origins and Development,* trans. E. B. Ashton (Chicago: University of Chicago Press, 1973), 7. Original: *Kants Weg vom Krieg zum Frieden,* vol. 1: *Wiederstreit und Einheit: Wege zu Kants*

politischen Denken (Muenchen: R. Piper and Company Verlag, 1967). In English excerpts of Kant's dissertation can be found in *Kant's Inaugural Dissertation and Early Writings on Space,* trans. John Handyside (Chicago: Open Court, 1929).

140. Ibid. 1:483.

141. Ibid., 7–8.

142. The difference has been worked out in detail in Erich Adickes, *Kant als Naturforscher* (Berlin, 1924), 1:163ff.

143. See Emil Arnoldt, *Gesammelte Schriften* (Berlin, 1909), 5:338–40, cited by Saner, *Kant's Political Thought,* 318.

144. English translation in L. W. Beck et al. eds., *Kant on History, Liberal Arts* 162 (1963).

145. Kant, *Allgemeine Naturgeschichte und Theorie des Himmels, etc.,* in *Werke* (Berlin: Akademie Edition, 1900), 1:319. See also Saner, *Kant's Political Thought,* 12.

146. See Kant, *Opus Postumum,* in *Werke* 21:138.

147. *Anthropologie in pragmatischen Hinsicht, Werke* 7:330.

148. *Critique of Judgment, Werke* 5:263.

149. *Bemerkungen zu den Beobachtungen ueber das Gefuehl des Schoenen und Erhabenen, Werke* 20:102ff.

150. *Reflexion zur Rechtsphilosophie, Werke* 19:611.

151. *Die Metaphysik der Sitten (The Metaphysics of Morals), Werke* 6:354.

152. English translation by John Ladd, Part 1: *The Metaphysical Elements of Justice,* in *Liberal Arts* 72 (1965).

153. English translation by Mary Gregor, *The Doctrine of Virtue* (New York: Harper and Row, 1964; Philadelphia: University of Philadelphia Press, 1972).

154. Kant, *Anthropology From a Pragmatic Point of View,* trans. Mary Gregor (The Hague: Martinus Nijhoff, 1974), 191, cited by Rundel, *Origins of Modernity,* 21.

155. Rundel, *Origins of Modernity,* 31.

156. *Ueber den Gemeinspruch: Das mag in der Theorie richtig sein, taugt aber nicht fuer die Praxis, Werke* 8:294; English translation by J. F. Bernard, *Critique of Judgment* (New York: Hafner, 1951).

157. John Rawls, "A Well-ordered Society," in Peter Laslett and James Fishkin, eds., *Philosophy, Politics and Society* (Oxford: B. Blackwell, 1979), cited

by Michael J. Sandel, *Liberalism and the Limits of Justice* (Cambridge: Cambridge University Press, 1982).

158. Rawls, *Concept of Justice*, 3.

159. Ibid., 579.

160. (Minneapolis: Augsburg, 1986)

161. (Minneapolis: Augsburg, 1987), 156ff.

162. Karen Lebacqz, *Justice in an Unjust World; Foundations for a Christian Approach to Justice* (Minneapolis, Minn.: Augsburg Publishing House, 1987), 156–57.

163. (New York: Basic Books, 1974). Lebacqz devotes her third chapter in *Six Theories of Justice* to Nozick's work. For another view of Nozick, see Alan Brown, *Modern Political Philosophy; Theories of the Just Society* (Harmondsworth, Middlesex: Penguin Books, 1986), which was published at about the same time as Lebacqz's *Six Theories.* Brown, on the other hand, lists five theories of justice: Utilitarianism, Rawlsianism, Nozickism, Marxism, and Neo-Aristotelianism.

164. (Washington, D.C.: N. C. C. B., 1985)

165. Reinhold Niebuhr, *Moral Man in Immoral Society* (New York: Scribner's, 1932).

166. (Maryknoll New York: Orbis Books, 1974).

167. *Grundlinen der Philosophie des Rechts oder Naturrecht und Staatswissenschaft im Grundrisse* (Frankfort: Suhrkamp, 1970; reprinted 1982). English translation by T. M. Knox, *Hegel's Philosophy of Right* (Oxford: Clarendon Press, 1952; 1965).

168. *Briefe* 2:189.

169. *Rechtsphilosophie* #4, English translation by present author.

170. Karl Marx, *Critique of Hegel's 'Philosophy of Right'*, (Cambridge: Cambridge University Press, 1970), vii.

171. Karl Marx, *A Contribution to the Critique of Hegel's 'Philosophy of Right'*, English translation, published as Introduction in Marx, *Critique.*

172. Hobsbawm, *Revolution*, 139.

173. Marx, *Critique*, 7.

174. Hegel, *Philosophy of Right*, par. 279; Marx, *Critique*, 28.

175. Marx, *Critique*, 29.

176. Ibid.

Chapter Nine: Science, Technology, and the Enlightenment

177. Paulos Mar Gregorios, *Science for Sane Societies* (New York: Paragon, 1987).

178. Sir Karl Popper, *Objective Knowledge: An Evolutionary Approach* (Oxford: Clarendon Press, 1972). Here Popper claims that he is eradicating traditional epistemology and replacing it by "an objective theory of essentially conjectural knowledge." In his *Conjectures and Refutations* he works the idea out further.

179. Popper, *Objective Knowledge*, 81.

180. Ibid., 191.

181. Ibid., 258.

182. Ibid., 261.

183. Alfred Tarski, "Die Wahrheitsbegriff in den formalistischen Sprachen," in *Studia Philosophica* (1935), 1:261ff. English translation in Alfred Tarski, *Logic, Semantic, Meta-mathematics* (Oxford: Clarendon Press, 1956). Paper 8, 152–278, cited by Popper, *Objective Knowledge*, 314ff.

184. For a detailed treatment of scientific explanation, see Wesley C. Salmon et al., *Statistical Explanation and Statistical Relevance* (Pittsburgh: University of Pittsburgh Press, 1971), as well as the whole of the June 1977 issue of *Philosophy of Science* 44:2. See also C. G. Hempel, *Aspects of Scientific Explanation* (New York: Free Press, 1965), 402–03.

185. Imre Lakatos, "Falsification and the Methodology of Scientific Research Programmes," in Imre Lakatos and A. Musgrave, eds., *Criticism and the Growth of Knowledge* (Cambridge: Cambridge University Press, 1970). Proceedings of the International Colloquium on the Philosophy of Science, London, 1965, vol. 4.

186. L. Laudan, *Progress and Its Problems* (Berkeley: University of California Press, 1977), cited by Joseph Rouse, *Knowledge and Power: Towards a Political Philosophy of Science* (Ithaca and London: Cornell University Press, 1987), 1–2.

187. Richard Rorty, *Philosophy and the Mirror of Nature* (Princeton: Princeton University Press, 1979), and also his *Consequences of Pragmatism* (Minneapolis: University of Minnesota Press, 1982).

188. Richard Bernstein, *Beyond Objectivism and Relativism* (Philadelphia: University of Philadelphia Press, 1983).

189. Nancy Cartwright, *How the Laws of Physics Lie* (Oxford: Oxford University Press, 1983).

190. See note 186.

191. Rorty, *Mirror of Nature*, 330–31.

192. Bernstein, *Beyond Objectivism*, 172.

193. Thomas A. McCarthy, *The Critical Theory of Jürgen Habermas* (Cambridge: MIT Press, 1978).

194. Martin Heidegger, *Unterwegs zum Sprache* (1959), English translation by Peter Hertz, *On the Way to Language* (New York: Harper and Row, 1971). See also Heidegger's *"Was Heisst Denken?"* (Tuebingen: Niemeyer, 1954), translated in English as *What is Called Thinking?*

195. See, for example, his "Die Neuzeit des Weltbildes," in Martin Heidegger, *The Question Concerning Technology and Other Essays*, trans. William Lovitt (New York: Harper and Row, 1977), 115ff. See also his lecture on "Wissenschaft und Besinnung" in *Vortraege und Aufsaetze* (Pfullingen: Neske, 1954), which contains many of the articles cited above.

196. See note 195.

197. Heidegger, *Question Concerning Technology*, 13.

198. Ibid., 21.

199. Ibid., 24.

200. Ibid., 26.

201. Ibid., 27.

202. Harold Alderman, "Heidegger's Critique of Science and Technology," in Michael Murray, ed., *Heidegger and Modern Philosophy* (New Haven and London: Yale University Press, 1978), 46, based on Heidegger's *Holzwege*, 70 and 236, and his *Question Concerning Technology*, 296–308.

Chapter Ten: Reason's Unreason

203. E. Schroedinger, *What is Life?* (London: Cambridge University Press, 1969), 133.

204. Bernstein, *Beyond Objectivism*, 172.

205. For a brief but illuminating discussion of the problems involved, see Richard F. Kitchener, ed., *The World View of Contemporary Physics: Does it Need a New Metaphysics?* (Albany: State University of New York Press, 1988).

206. Cited by Otto Poeggeler, "Being as Appropriation," in Michael Murray, ed., *Heidegger and Modern Philosophy.*

207. Edward C. Whitmont, *The Symbolic Quest: Basic Concepts of Analytical Psychology* (Princeton: Princeton University Press, 1969; 1978), 27–28.

208. Rajnath, *Deconstruction: A Critique* (New York: Macmillan, 1989). Rajnath is Professor of English at the University of Allahabad in India.

209. J. Hillis Miller, "Stevens' Rock and Criticism as Cure II," in *Georgia Review* 30 (Summer 1976): 345; and "Nature and the Linguistic Moment," in Knoeplmacher and Tennyson, eds., *Nature and the Victorian Imagination*

(Berkeley: University of California Press, 1977), 440. Both texts cited by Vincent B. Leitch, "The Lateral Dance: The Deconstructive Criticism of J. Hillis Miller," in Rajnath, *Deconstruction*, 257.

210. Theodor W. Adorno, *Against Epistemology.*

211. Husserl, *Logische Untersuchungen* 1:205–07, cited by Adorno, *Against Epistemology*, 75.

212. Hans-Georg Gadamer, *Truth and Method* (London: Sheed and Ward, 1975 Revd. ed. N.Y. 1988); original: *Wahrheit und Methode* (Tubingen: Mohr, 1965).

213. *Gitābhāshya* 12.3; see also 13.24.

214. I suggest the following: Robert Keith Wallace, *The Neurophysiology of the Enlightenment* (Fairfield, Iowa: Maharishi International University Press, 1986; 1989), which has an impressive bibliography at the end; John White, ed., *Frontiers of Consciousness: The Meeting Ground Between Inner and Outer Reality* (New York: Julian Press, 1874; reprinted 1985); Deepak Chopra, *Quantum Healing: Exploring the Frontiers of Mind/Body Medicine* (New York: Bantam Books, 1989); and Larry Dossey, *Recovering the Soul: A Scientific and Spiritual Search* (New York: Bantam Books, 1989).

215. P. Lahti, K. V. Laurikainen, and J. Viiri, eds., *Symposium of the Foundations of Modern Physics 1987; Discussion Sections, Report Series*, FTL-L45 (Finland: University of Turku, 1988), 49.

216. C. G. Jung and W. Pauli, *Naturerklaerung und Psyche* (Zurich: Rascher Verlag, 1952). See also K. V. Laurikainen, *Beyond the Atom: The Philosophical Thought of Wolfgang Pauli* (Heidelberg: Springer-Verlag, 1988); F. David Peat, *Synchronicity: The Bridge Between Matter and Mind* (New York: Bantam Books, 1987).

217. Frank Wilczek and Betsy Devine, *Longing for Harmonies: Themes and Variations from Modern Physics* (London: W. W. Norton, 1988), 120.

218. Stephen W. Hawking, *A Brief History of Time: From the Big Bang to Black Holes* (New York: Bantam Books, 1988), Introduction by Carl Sagan, ix.

219. John Philoponos, *De Aeternitate Mundi Contra Proclum* (London: Duckworth, 1985), 529, cited by Richard Sorabji, *Time, Creation and the Continuum: Theories in Antiquity and the Early Middle Ages* (London: Duckworth, 1983), 215.

220. See note 219.

221. P. M. Gregorios, *Cosmic Man: The Divine Presence* (New York: Paragon Press, 1988).

222. *Vyasabhashya on Yoga Sutra of Patanjali* 3.52.

223. S. K. Sen, "Time in Sankhya-Yoga," in *Indian Philosophical Quarterly* 8 (September 1968): 412.

224. Rupert Sheldrake, *A New Science of Life: The Hypothesis of Formative Causation* (London: Blond and Briggs, 1981; 1985), and *The Presence of the Past* (London: Fontana, 1989).

225. Sheldrake, *Presence of the Past*, iii.

226. Rom. 8:19–23.

Chapter Eleven: Turning to the Other Enlightenment

227. Eusebius, *Praeparatio Evangelica* 11:3:28; for fragments of Aristoxenes, see F. Wehrli, *Die Schule des Aristoteles, Text und Kommentar* (1945), Part 2, *Aristoxenes.*

228. Eliade, *Encyclopaedia*, 6:99a ff.

229. A. C. Lloyd, "The Later Neoplatonists," in A. H. Armstrong, ed., *The Cambridge History of Early and Medieval Philosophy* (Cambridge: Cambridge University Press, 1967), 305.

230. Ivan M. Linforth, *The Arts of Orpheus* (Berkeley and Los Angeles: University of California Press, 1941), 289; see also A. R. Burn, *The Lyric Age of Greece* (London: Edward Arnold, 1960), 366ff.

231. Plato *Phaedo* 65E–66A.

232. R. T. Wallis, *Neoplatonism* (London: Duckworth, 1972), 160.

233. Plato *Symposium* 212B, English translation by W. Hamilton (Hammondsworth: Penguin, 1951; 1967), 94–95.

234. Aristotle *Metaphysics*, bk. 3, 4:30, 1078b.

235. Ibid.

236. *Phaedo* 115.

237. *Republic* 498–99 (bk 6).

238. *Meno* 99–100.

239. Wallis, *Neoplatonism*, 160.

240. On the Anabaptists and Thomas Muentzer, see Eric W. Gritsch, *Reformer Without a Church* (Philadelphia: Fortress Press, 1967); Steven E. Ozment, *Mysticism and Dissent* (New Haven: Yale University Press, 1973); Hans J. Hillerbrand, *A Fellowship of Discontent* (New York: Harper and Row, 1967); and George H. Williams, ed., *Spiritual and Anabaptist Writers*, in *Library of Christian Classics*, vol. 25 (Philadelphia: Westminster Press, 1957).

241. Text in Hans J. Hillerbrand, "Thomas Munzer's Last Tract Against Luther," in *Mennonite Quarterly Review* 38 (1964): 20–36.

242. On Wycliffe, see Herbert E. Winn, *Wyclif: Select English Writings* (Oxford: Oxford University Press, 1929); and John Stacey, *John Wyclif and Reform* (Philadelphia: Westminster Press, 1964).

243. On the Quakers, see Howard Brinton, *Friends for Three Hundred Years* (New York: Harper, 1952); and Melvin B. Endy, Jr., *William Penn and Early Quakerism* (Princeton: Princeton University Press, 1973).

Chapter Twelve: The Twain Shall Be One

244. Fred Polak, *The Image of the Future* (New York: Oceana Publications, 1961), 1:53, 55.

245. Richard Rorty, *Essays on Heidegger and Others, Philosophical Papers Volume 2* (Cambridge: Cambridge University Press, 1991), 70ff.

246. Milan Kundera, *The Art of the Novel*, trans. Linda Asher (New York: Grove Press, 1986).

247. Rorty, *Essays*, 75.

248. Ibid., 9ff.

249. Jayanta Bhatta, *Nyāya-Mañjari (The Compendium of Indian Speculative Logic)*, trans. J. V. Bhattacharya (Delhi: Motilal Banarsidass, 1978), 1:295.

250. Donald Davidson, *Inquiries into Truth and Interpretation* (Oxford: Clarendon Press, 1984), 246ff.

251. Rorty, *Essays*, 13.

252. See K. V. Laurikainen, *Beyond the Atom*.

253. Hilary Putnam, *Reason, Truth and History* (Cambridge: Cambridge University Press, 1981). Richard Rorty criticizes Putnam for being too ethnocentric and wanting to draw limits to the proliferation of views that go beyond the western consensus. Putnam's consensus view is a "community view," though that community is limited by him to the western thinkers or their followers and imitators. Rorty wants more pluralism and therefore more uncontrolled proliferation of diverse worldviews. See Richard Rorty, "Solidarity or Objectivity," in John Rajchman and Cornel West, eds., *Post-Analytic Philosophy* (New York: Columbia University Press, 1985). A sheer pluralism like that seldom provides an adequate basis for concerted community action. Rorty cannot disagree.

Index